THE PEOPLE

The People

JULES MICHELET

Translated with an introduction by
John P. McKay

UNIVERSITY OF ILLINOIS PRESS
Urbana   Chicago   London

To the memory of my grandfather
A. A. JEFFREY

Contents

Note on the Translation   ix

Translator's Introduction   xiii

The People

Preface: To Edgar Quinet   3

PART ONE. OF BONDAGE AND HATE

    I. The Bondage of the Peasant   25

    II. The Bondage of the Factory Worker   40

    III. The Bondage of the Artisan Worker   53

    IV. The Bondage of the Manufacturer   62

    V. The Bondage of the Shopkeeper   69

    VI. The Bondage of the Official   75

    VII. The Bondage of the Rich and the Bourgeoisie   82

    VIII. Review of the First Part: Introduction to the Second   92

PART TWO. OF FREEDOM THROUGH LOVE: NATURE

    I. The Instinct of the People: A Neglected Question   103

    II. The Instinct of the People: Weakened but
Still Powerful   108

    III. Do the People Gain Much by Sacrificing Their Instinct?
Bastard Classes   115

    IV. The Simple Ones: The Child, the Interpreter
of the People   119

  V. Is the Natural Instinct of the Child Perverse?   125

 VI. Digression: The Instinct of Animals:
     A Plea in Their Favor   130

VII. The Instinct of the Simple and the Instinct of Genius:
     The Man of Genius Is Preeminently the Simple, the
     Child, and the People   138

VIII. The Birth of Genius: A Model for the Birth of Society   143

 IX. Review of the Second Part: Introduction to the Third   149

PART THREE. OF FREEDOM THROUGH LOVE: OUR NATIVE LAND

   I. Friendship   157

  II. Of Love and Marriage   165

 III. Of Association   170

  IV. Our Native Land. Are Nationalities about
      to Disappear?   178

   V. France   185

  VI. The Superiority of France, as Both Dogma and Legend.
      France Is a Religion   190

 VII. Faith in the Revolution. This Faith Has Withered
      and Has Not Been Transmitted by Education   194

VIII. No Education without Faith   200

  IX. God in Our Native Land. The Young Country
      of the Future: The Country of Sacrifice   203

Index   211

Note on the Translation

An instant success — Michelet wrote his aunts that shortly after publication *Le peuple* sold one thousand copies in a single day in Paris alone — the work was immediately translated into English, and not once but twice. The English edition was translated by Charles Cocks and published by Longman, Brown, Green and Longmans of London in 1846. Cocks taught English in Paris, knew Michelet personally, and could claim to have translated *The People* with "the author's special approbation." There was also an American edition in 1846, translated by G. H. Smith for D. Appleton and Company, New York, and G. S. Appleton, Philadelphia. Like Cocks, Smith translated a number of Michelet's works, including his *History of France* and *History of the Roman Republic,* with or without the author's special approbation. Both editions are now rare and almost totally inaccessible; to my knowledge neither has ever been reprinted in Great Britain or the United States. I secured copies of both translations, which are now in the library of the University of Illinois at Urbana-Champaign.

Both editions are inadequate and badly out-of-date, although each has its virtues. Cocks displays a dogged literal quality that sometimes helps to unravel particularly elliptical sentences, and then shows how the final version should not sound. Smith has a more imaginative style and prefers a much freer translation. The result is an alternating pattern of felicitous phrases catching Michelet's sense if not his words, and strange, ill-begotten aberrations that reflect neither.

Both versions do, however, suggest how the work sounded in English at the time it was written. In my version I tried to keep something of this Victorian flavor whenever it did not result in awkwardness or confusion. At the same time, my basic goal has been to render Michelet as clear and direct as possible, so that the reader will be caught immediately and directly by his heartfelt message. Naturally I tried to catch the beauty and variety of his nervous, delicate style, but clarity has been the first consideration.

As far as the editing is concerned, I have omitted most of Michelet's reference footnotes, though only a few of the explanatory ones. The reference footnotes are to works that most readers would not consult and could not even if they wished. The specialist can easily find these additional references in any French edition of the work. (He will most profitably turn to the excellent critical edition by Lucien Refort, in the series of publications of the Société des Textes Français Modernes, published by Librairie Marcel Didier [Paris, 1946]. This critical edition used the 1846 edition, as I did, and was quite useful and frequently consulted.)

If it seemed best to limit the impedimenta to Michelet's message in this way, so I tried to keep my own explanatory notes (marked by asterisks) to a minimum. I have added a qualifying adjective or phrase directly to the text when possible in order to illuminate an unfamiliar person or event without placing an unnecessary roadblock at the bottom of the page.

As must always be the case, it is a great pleasure to acknowledge those who have extended their aid and friendship. Professor David Landes, now of Harvard University, first mentioned *Le peuple* to me when I was a graduate student at the University of California, Berkeley. He subsequently encouraged me in my idea of a new translation and generously made a number of warmly appreciated comments relating to the introduction. Professors Keith Hitchins, Robert McColley, and Ellery Schalk also read parts of the work and gave me the benefit of their suggestions. Dr. John Johnson read the entire manuscript, and his editorial expertise certainly improved the final product. Among my many French friends and acquaintances who helped in some

way, I owe a special debt to M. and Mme René Vadrot of Paris.
I also wish to thank the John Simon Guggenheim Memorial
Foundation and the University of Illinois. A small portion of a
Guggenheim Fellowship, granted for another project, was used to
complete the manuscript, while the University Subvention Fund
subsidized the typing of the final draft. To my family and my
parents must go more than the usual thanks. My wife, Jo Ann,
not only typed the entire manuscript but became an invaluable
partner in the entire enterprise.

Translator's Introduction

"And I shall continue, gentlemen. To the end of my life I will go on pouring out my heart. I will never fail you."[1] Thus did Jules Michelet answer the approximately fifteen hundred students who had come to express sympathy and support for their popular professor in the face of his suspension from the College of France in early January 1848. Engaged in strident attacks on the church and the Jesuits since 1843 and now warning of impending upheavals, Michelet had fallen victim to the fears of the bourgeois monarchy of Louis Philippe on the very eve of the Revolution of 1848.

Strange words for a history professor, some will say, even if he is appointed to the chair of history and moral philosophy. Certainly conventional wisdom maintains that the professional historian is basically a scientist and craftsman who must be able to handle difficult material and keep his passions and prejudices under control in the conscientious pursuit of objective truth. Michelet, however, succeeded in going beyond conventional practitioners of his trade. He was a cool and skillful observer, a scholar who knew the realities of dusty, difficult documents slumbering in the archives, and could surmount them. At the same time, he was a sensitive man of great depth and compassion. This meant he could bring the dead bones of the documents wonderfully alive by sympathizing and empathizing with the people and times they represented. He was also increasingly able to define his broad compassion into specific commitments, commitments reflecting

[1] *L'étudiant,* ed. Ernest Lavisse (Paris: Calmann Levy, 1899), p. 94.

his own development as well as the march of humanity. In short, Michelet combined the careful investigation of the historian, and the exacting precision of the archivist, with the sensitivity of the poet and the vision of the prophet. The harmony he found in these diverse qualities is a lasting achievement of the human spirit.

No wonder Jules Michelet is often regarded as France's greatest historian. Many close students of his entire work feel, and I agree, that *The People,* which is not precisely a book of history, is perhaps his finest single volume. Three of many reasons for this judgment stand out. First, *The People* compresses the work and development of a lifetime — what Michelet had done and what he would do — into one masterful performance. Second, this book provides us today with a wealth of insight into the whole range of major historical questions relating to the France and Europe of his time, to that France and Europe in the throes of a wrenching transformation born of economic and political revolution. Finally, Michelet speaks to our condition, to our predicaments. Here is an anguished man struggling with social and psychological problems that can still poison and divide societies, like, alas, our own today. Even if we do not accept Michelet's solutions, he still has much to say and much to teach.

Who, then, was this man who sought to understand the crisis of his age and provide an answer? All those who have found themselves drawn to Michelet and have tried to unravel the enigma of his creation have soon recognized the pivotal role of the historian's own life and experiences. Michelet himself once wrote, "No one has influenced me since my birth. I was born basically alone."[2] Of course Michelet was a man of his times, and he reflected most of the fundamental intellectual movements of the first half of the nineteenth century. Indeed, one of the great values of *The People* is to present a sort of intellectual panorama of the dominant currents of thought in the period. Romanticism, nationalism, republicanism, the revolutionary ideal, the faith in

[2] As quoted by Gabriel Monod, *Jules Michelet: Études sur sa vie et ses œuvres* (Paris: Hachette and Co., 1905), p. 102.

progress, the cult of genius — all these and other generalizations of the scholar's shorthand take form and meaning there.

Michelet was quite right, however, in implying that the formal presentation of such ideas had little influence on how he developed himself. With the exception of the early eighteenth-century thinker Giovanni Vico, into whom he probably read what he was ready to read, Michelet drew mainly upon his own intellectual resources, his personal experiences, and his study of history. He really developed himself, like some of those autodidacts from the French working class in this period, as opposed to being formed and fashioned by the leading thinkers of his day. This ability to develop himself and find his own truths helps explain why Michelet had so many admirers and so few disciples, much less a "school" to follow him. In the last analysis, Michelet stands alone.

Michelet's childhood provided the bedrock of experience upon which he drew throughout his life. This childhood is beautifully presented in the dedicatory preface of *The People*. There Michelet recounts with pride the love that bound his family together in the face of dismal poverty. We see his early days as printer in the family shop, coupled with little formal education and almost complete freedom, as the small, pale boy grew "like a blade of grass without sun between two cobblestones of Paris."[3] There is also the outline of the desperate gamble on education that led to subsequent escape from poverty in the conquest of practically every academic honor.

For a time the shy, awkward, lagging youth of fifteen — the perfect butt of his insensitive classmates from the comfortable bourgeoisie — had a terrible struggle, and he was forced to repeat the first year of the college he entered in 1813. Then he sped forward. Two first prizes in 1816, baccalaureate in 1817, doctor of letters from the Sorbonne in 1819, third in the recently established *agrégation des lettres* in 1821, and lycée professor in the same year at the age of twenty-three: here was a brilliant academic career in the making. And Michelet lived up to his promise.

[3] *The People,* present edition, p. 14.

He was more brilliant as a professor than as a student, as we shall see in a moment.

So whatever his origins might be, Michelet's career was a handsome success. He appears as a perfect example of the rapid upward social mobility of exceptional individuals who succeeded in fleeing from their class and their poverty, that bittersweet victory of the nineteenth century. His career is doubly instructive, since such mobility was more often attained through achievement first in the educational system and then in the liberal professions or the bureaucracy — as opposed to industry and commerce — than is usually believed. Thus Michelet is sometimes presented, directly or through insinuation, as a sort of *nouveau riche,* a man who clearly entered the bourgeoisie by profession, income, and circle of social contacts. Yet Michelet always claimed to be a man of the people, a simple man who remained with them in spite of his successes, as he tells us in *The People.* Were those claims of solidarity with the masses — the simple, the poor, the workers, the outcasts — only flamboyant rhetoric at best, and sheer cant at worst?

The question is certainly a natural one. The cult of the people seems often least pure among its most pious apostles. One thinks, for example, of the American liberal establishment — not to mention the new radical establishment — which has its share of well-paid, self-appointed, self-proclaimed servants of the poor and the oppressed who lead conventional middle-class lives, are contemptuous of ordinary people as they actually appear in everyday life, and debase their ideological commitment into self-righteous mutual aid societies. And the European liberal intelligentsia has had greater experience at this game. A properly displayed profession of socialism was already the normal pattern among French intellectuals and literati before 1848, no matter how rich or bourgeois they actually were.

This is the amazing part: on the whole, Michelet lived the life he preached. His private diaries, his work, his personal life, his character, and his vision all suggest that Michelet's heart and spirit rested with those he championed. He remained the man of ordinary men, and he emerges as a great authentic voice in the ascension of the masses in our time. *Remained* is probably the wrong word; it is too passive. No, Michelet kept developing himself as a man of and a spokesman for the people. He strengthened, revived, and re-created his early ties to the people throughout his lifetime with conscious acts of will and humanity.

It was not always easy. As Michelet confesses, "The difficulty is not to rise but rather, in rising, to remain one's self."[4] But on the whole he succeeded. For me, at least, Michelet's final contribution is as much his life as his work, as he himself described it and hoped it would be. "The mark [the genius] will leave is not the work of his genius alone, but that life of simplicity, childhood, goodness, and holiness to which all ages will come to seek a sort of moral regeneration. This or that discovery of his will become perhaps less useful in the progress of the human race; but his life, which in his lifetime seemed his weak side and in which envy found its satisfaction, will remain the treasure of the world and the eternal festival of the heart."[5]

Simplicity, regularity, and devotion are the hallmarks of Michelet's family life. The man who believed so strongly in instinct seems to have sought instinctively the close, warm, unified, and controlled family circle of his youth. Accordingly, there is in his personal life little trace of the distraught romantic artist that Michelet's style and times might suggest. Nor is there any evidence of the old aristocracy's moral and sexual licentiousness, which the French upper middle class is supposed to have imitated and perpetuated after it seized political and economic dominance during the French Revolution. This all too well advertised code of conduct, which has done so much to give the world a mistaken (or at least incomplete) view of French manners, was abhorrent to Michelet.

After an unrequited youthful infatuation, Michelet slipped naturally into the kind of family and married life he often idealized. In 1818, at the age of twenty, he began a regular and monogamous relationship with Pauline Rousseau, a kind, modestly

---

[4] *Ibid.,* p. 18.
[5] *Ibid.,* p. 141.

educated, and slightly unattractive young woman who lived in Michelet's pension. This relationship continued for six years, while the young student was attaining the honors and credentials of the young professor, and while Pauline continued to earn her living as a day nurse and housekeeper. In his third year of teaching, in 1824, Michelet married his mistress, who was then pregnant.

Marriage and family meant order and economy for the somewhat self-centered scholar.[6] They were also indispensable to the development of his creative impulse. Michelet reiterated this personal truth throughout his life and work, as in *Love* (1858), a hymn to the vitality of evolving monogamous passion — the only kind of love Michelet even considers. "A good wife and a good trade: if you have that, young man, you are free" — free for the concentration of vital forces that supposes above all else the fixity of the home. And concentrate he did.

Everyone is struck by Michelet's tremendous output and capacity for work. This passion for work has sometimes been criticized as a kind of unnatural and unhealthy compensation for unspecified hidden torments. Yet unless one assumes that all great sustained efforts are the product of some basic failure to adapt to the pleasures and varieties of the world, one cannot help but be struck by the regular harmonious quality of his effort.

He was like the best of the ordinary workingmen he celebrated as having succeeded in combining freedom and discipline. The almost frantic pace of the 1830s should therefore be seen against the background of omnivorous reading, true intellectual curiosity, and profound reflection in the 1820s. Such freedom led him to the almost unknown social thinker Vico through a reference in a footnote; his discipline led him to learn another language, Italian, in order to read and ponder Vico's basic work, which he then translated with excitement and admiration in 1827. These abilities

---

[6] See Michelet's calculated rationalization of his marriage in a letter quoted by Paul Viallaneix, *La voie royale: Essai sur l'idée du peuple dans l'œuvre de Michelet* (Paris: Librairie Delagrave, 1959), p. 14. I found Professor Viallaneix's long work extremely useful. It is rich in analysis and documentation and contains a comprehensive bibliography. This book, unfortunately already out of print, should be reissued.

also produced his *Précis of Modern History* the same year and his *Introduction to Universal History* in 1831. No wonder Michelet is sometimes called one of the last of the Renaissance men. He sought to encompass all knowledge and consistently refused division and narrow specialization.

Rewarded in 1827 with an important promotion to the École Normale Supérieure because of his books and teaching, Michelet completed his two-volume *History of the Roman Republic* in 1831. Then he hesitated a moment: should he plunge deeper into antiquity, or go on to the Middle Ages and the history of France?

Certainly the Gothic revival of romanticism, which struck a chord in Michelet's sensitive nature, was partly the reason for his choosing the latter. Perhaps more important was his appointment as director of the historical section of the National Archives almost immediately after the Revolution of 1830. There in the heart of Paris he found himself amid a wealth of charters and documents of every kind, materials that had gone largely unnoticed by earlier historians and that constituted a tremendous challenge and opportunity for the real history of his country. Michelet then began one of those concerted efforts, one of those creative bursts, that every scholar has occasionally experienced and alternately rejoiced and anguished in. Yet for Michelet the burst lasted a dozen years and resulted in a complete history of the Middle Ages, the first six volumes of his *History of France*.

By five or six in the morning Michelet was in his study hard at work, and he continued until one or two in the afternoon. In those extremely productive years of the 1830s he practically established a workshop where all members had a task. His beloved and aging father went to the libraries to check out books needed in the day's effort; the two or three research assistants would read and note; Pauline ran the house, cooked for all, and cared for the two children. And the master craftsman organized and wrote for hours at a time, pausing now and then to look out his window and contemplate the country he saw behind his beloved Paris. Hard work, but as Paul Viallaneix has remarked, work that faithfully followed the pattern and tempo of the artisan crafts and those early years in the print shop.

As an honest craftsman, Michelet also knew when to stop. From four to six each day the door was open, and all students and visitors were welcome. Gabriel Monod, Michelet's student and future biographer, has left a picture of the calm and sociable Michelet in those moments of pleasure and relaxation.

> He was always immaculate. I can still see him erectly seated in his chair, with his spotless waistcoat . . . holding a white handkerchief in his hand, which was delicate, nervous and cared for like that of a woman, and his head covered with long, white silky hair. The hours sped by quickly listening to him! He spoke with such great depth and such great fantasy, such great joyous serenity and sympathetic goodness, and with wit without malice and poetry without declamation! His conversation had wings. . . . He was an incomparable conversationalist, and you felt in him, even though he was not trying to give such an impression, that inexplicable bit of divinity that makes the man of genius. What gave grace to that genius was that he combined modesty with it. He knew how to listen and let himself be contradicted. He asked for your opinion . . . and often presented his ideas with reserve, questioned others, and would find out what they thought.[7]

Many historians, though not Michelet himself, believe that Michelet's history of the Middle Ages is his most solid, useful, and lasting accomplishment. They single out his conscientious scholarship with its penetration of the original sources, which is combined with an uncanny ability to enter into the spirit and essence of the people and times he was portraying. Certainly one finds in the early Michelet one of the earliest and most brilliant examples of the historian who is able to empathize with very different views and persons. For example, when some people criticized his lectures in 1835 as being partial to Luther, he answered that they could have said as much for his treatment of those heroes of the Counter-Reformation, Saint Teresa of Avila and Saint Ignatius of Loyola. "It is, however, an indispensable condition for the historian to enter into all doctrines, to understand all forces, and to be passionately involved in every state of mind."[8] Perhaps the

---

[7] Gabriel Monod, *Jules Michelet* (Paris: Sandoz and Fischbacher, 1875), pp. 94-95.

[8] As quoted by Monod, *Jules Michelet* (1875), p. 30.

most famous example of the early Michelet is his treatment of the national revival under Joan of Arc.[9]

The last years of his work on the Middle Ages brought trying moments and new challenges. In 1837 Michelet left the École Normale to teach at the College of France. His classes were suddenly much different. Instead of a small, select elite working carefully, he now faced a large excitable crowd that was more interested in eloquent language and bold synthesis than precise analysis. Since Michelet took his teaching seriously and tried hard to reach his students, this change unquestionably aided the formation of the mature Michelet, who was prophet and poet as well as observer and historian.

Similarly, Pauline's death in 1839 marked a crisis in Michelet's life and forced him to enter a period of intense self-examination. Michelet felt he was in part responsible, for while he had been consuming his energies in prodigious accomplishment, Pauline had been relegated to being cook and "my *sensual me*," to use Michelet's own words.[10] For the rest of his life he sought the warmth and regularity of his life with Pauline, but that life uplifted by a true meeting of hearts and minds.

His brief and somewhat obscure relationship with Madame Dumesnil shortly after Pauline's death was one such attempt. Madame Dumesnil's son was an enthusiastic listener of Michelet's lectures at the College of France, and he began coming regularly to Michelet's house and eventually married his daughter. Madame Dumesnil also came to live in Michelet's house for a short time, and although the relationship apparently remained platonic, the evenings when the two families gathered to talk around the fire were a great solace. This friendship formed precisely the meeting of hearts he desired. Madame Dumesnil's death in 1842 understandably left the historian deeply saddened once again.

[9] This has often been printed separately from his *History of France*. There is a good modern translation by Albert Guérard (Ann Arbor: University of Michigan Press, 1957).

[10] See the entry in his journal for 24 July 1839, the day of Pauline's death. Michelet's journals, which allow us to follow his most intimate thoughts, have been masterfully edited by Paul Viallaneix in two large volumes, published in 1959 and 1962 by Gallimard.

A bit prosaically, Michelet sought to reestablish the simple home. He took one maid in 1843 and then another in 1845 as his mistress, indeed the mistress of his quiet household. These young girls without education or culture kept Michelet in contact with the most intimate dimension of the life of common folk. There is no doubt that these loving experiences, which existed simultaneously with the writing of *The People,* contributed to his understanding of those women of the people who "are by no means coarse . . . and who . . . listen to men above them with a confidence they did not have before."[11]

As Michelet kept revitalizing his ties to the people through these relationships, his numerous inquisitive travels, and his rapport with his students, he also did so through his work. One of the novelties and strengths of his study of the Middle Ages was that again and again he sought to see how the people were actually living and developing through the fog of insatiable feudal ambition and endless war. And as he sought and saw the growth of the people in the Middle Ages, he grew more and more excited to show the achievement of the people come of age.

Increasingly the Middle Ages seemed important only as part of the long, difficult preparation for the French Revolution, that moment of maturity when the French people began the true emancipation of mankind. That great dawn of human history was now to be told by the committed historian, the son of the people who would concentrate his feelings on the side of the people and guard against his earlier, generous, but impartial and therefore superficial sympathy for all. At this time (1845) he wrote *The People* — between his six volumes of empathetic history of the Middle Ages and the first of seven partisan volumes on the French Revolution.[12] Coming at this great turning point and reflecting the qualities of both his early and mature work, *The People* sums up Michelet's intellectual evolution.

The historian of the rise of the people found in his second wife,

---

[11] *The People,* present edition, p. 168.

[12] Part of this second cycle is currently available in Jules Michelet, *History of the French Revolution,* trans. Charles Cocks, ed. Gordon Wright (Chicago: University of Chicago Press, 1967).

Athénaïs Mialaret, a constant companion until his death in 1874. She represented another step in the development of Michelet the moralist and spokesman for unwavering love and family devotion. An intellectually inclined woman, Athénaïs became an enterprising and effective co-worker. And if those strange pains in her stomach and perhaps a deep-rooted sexual anxiety made her a mediocre lover who responded with difficulty to the advances of her still-vigorous husband, there was that compensation Michelet so often spoke of. Or perhaps he himself fashioned that compensation through a generous effort to understand and sympathize with his wife, which led him to idealize and almost idolize love and the female principle, as may be seen in such later works as *Love* (1858) and *Women* (1860). He saw her love and unselfish devotion in the years of his fall and recovery. He explained away her shortcomings, saw her goodness, and loved her more.

Michelet had returned in triumph to the College of France during the revolutionary surge of March 1848, but he then refused to accept the consequences of the Napoleonic coup d'état in 1851. Fired from his teaching position in 1851, he refused to take a loyalty oath to the regime in 1852 and lost his post as director of the historical section of the National Archives. The result was greatly reduced economic circumstances, now bordering on real poverty for himself and his new wife. Easily and with almost a sense of emancipation, Michelet took up the frugal life of the honest workman, continued to write and work, and remained true to his convictions. His extremely popular nature books of the mid-1850s reestablished a certain financial independence, but Michelet continued to live modestly until his death in 1874.

In short, we may agree with this generation's most thorough and perceptive student of Michelet: the legend of Michelet's plebeian essence is to be taken seriously.[13] He was not corrupted by success, and he never lost contact with the masses and the life they led. His life and his spirit harmonized with his message. Yet this in itself might well be of no interest, or even revolting. A Marquis de Sade or a Hitler might also live in harmony with his

[13] Viallaneix, *La voie royale*, p. 56.

inner truth and produce only a monstrosity. And for a long time old elites have wondered or feared that the rise of the people is the coming of the barbarians, and that, sadly, more is being lost than gained. There is no sense in staying close to common men unless they have something to teach.

The great value of Michelet's life and message is precisely that many of his personal truths, which grew out of living with and contemplating ordinary people, are themselves basic human truths. And these truths, which are of a historical, societal, and personal nature, are a call to greatness and humanity worthy of the divine spark we all share. This is, at least, my reading of the man and the work, as I wish to suggest in a few highly selective comments on the riches each reader will uncover in *The People*.

I first came across *The People* as the unjustly neglected classic study of French society in the first part of the nineteenth century. *The People* is indeed that, and the insight from this point of view alone is enough to warrant consideration. Almost half of the book is a portrait of the social change and social dislocation peasants, workers, factory owners, officials, and all other groups of France experienced in the difficult transformation from agrarian to industrial society. This portrait of France is certainly unsurpassed, and it is also representative of general European problems in this time of rapid social and economic change.

Particularly noteworthy is Michelet's feeling for how the condition of each group is evolving over time. One is not a great historian, or even a serious student of history for that matter, without bringing to current problems an understanding that will often elude his contemporaries. Clearly *The People* is excellent testimony to Michelet's dictum that "he who limits himself to the present will not understand the present."[14]

In addition to this general understanding of the complexity and dynamic character of the social process, Michelet has a flair for penetrating details and sympathetic description in very human terms. His examination of the effects of industrialization on the

[14] *The People,* present edition, p. 9.

new factory workers, for example, could almost stand as a compassionate, honest, somewhat "pessimistic" summary of the most discerning scholarly discussions and studies on the subject. Thus he emphasizes the factory worker's psychological problems — boredom, dependence, dehumanization — in his new circumstances, while recognizing the attempt to show any alleged decline in living standards from earlier times as the quicksand it is. Michelet understood the hard life of preindustrial labor better than many other historians have, and certainly well enough to avoid idealizing that condition. Another example is his analysis of established capitalists who are unimaginative and timid, in contrast with the "new" men constantly rising from below, particularly in the textile industry. Here is a suggestive commentary on the problem of the French business class and the paradox of an apparently immobile upper middle class and a rate of economic growth that was quite rapid in the 1830s and 1840s. The treatment of other groups is often equally enlightening.

While some of Michelet's insights will no doubt escape readers who are unfamiliar with such questions, no one will miss the main thrust of his analysis. As the parts suffer, so is the whole dangerously ill. France, according to Michelet, is on the verge of tearing herself apart, as modernization and industrialization exacerbate the political and ideological dissensions of the restoration era. Michelet felt a tremendous concern and terrible anguish before this prospect of social disintegration and civil war, and perhaps recurring civil war. Nor was Michelet exaggerating the danger. France did engage in bloody class war in June 1848; she repeated the tragedy in the Commune of 1871; she did wander for almost fifty years before reconstituting some fundamental unity. Michelet knew what he was talking about.

Here is a second contribution of *The People*. A contemporary reader will feel on many a page a flash of recognition. Michelet understood the general problem of social division and hatred as well as the particular one. Those hates and dissensions of the fragmented society that Michelet speaks of with such anguish are problems that plague us today. We, too, fear that some of the basic bonds holding us together are weakening. When Michelet speaks of politicians who exploit our fears and drive us further apart, of critics who cannot or will not see our good qualities, of the lack of knowledge and understanding of separated groups, or of how each class tries to isolate its children in the educational process as soon as possible, one is forced to examine his own country and conscience.

Is there not a certain ambiguity, however, about the nature of the social problem and the division between classes as presented by Michelet? This question deserves special attention, for it has perplexed and mystified not only France but the world as well.

On one hand, Michelet says that the division in society is between the bourgeoisie and the people: "Ancient France was divided into three classes; new France has only two — the people and the bourgeoisie."[15] Here is an early formulation of the socialist position, which in its dominant Marxian variety would emerge as the doctrine of irreconcilable class struggle, the struggle between the haves and the have-nots, the struggle between the bourgeoisie and the ever-enlarging proletariat. Here is the essence of that latter-day Manicheism that would divide society between two opposing principles, one good and one bad.

On the other hand, Michelet is quite critical of the early socialists. He consistently speaks of the people in such a way as to include almost the entire society. Only the aristocracy and the clergy are constantly ignored as in no way forming part of the people. The bourgeoisie is referred to as the people corrupted, but by no means as implacable class enemies. The tragedy would be precisely to create such class hatred and strict division. Everyone is capable of being part of the people and therefore uniting the society in this way. There is only a difference of degree, only a difference in the extent to which the potential values and qualities of the people are actually realized in individuals.

This ambiguity on the nature of class relations is one of the work's strengths. As I noted, Michelet shared in the romanticism of his age, and this no doubt contributed to his sometimes unre-

[15] *Ibid.*, p. 83, n. 1.

strained lyricism. But he was a historian first and a romantic poet second. As he put it with his usual incisiveness, "I would not live by my pen. I wanted a real craft."[16]

Therefore when Michelet's concern and commitment compelled him to focus on the dynamics of society in an attempt to chart a course that would avoid disaster, he spoke from his heart, but he still proceeded like a scrupulous historian who respects and presents those hard-to-fit facts uncovered by keen observation. He did not romanticize or fictionalize or, still worse, merely theorize. Rather, he looked at the data before him and tried to interpret them honestly. To do so, he used not only statistics and personal experience, but above all the investigation of the "living documents" — those countless discussions with people from all ranks of society. It is this precise observation, the product of the historian's craft, that does so much to make this the classic portrait of French society.

So he presented puzzling contradictions born of careful investigation rather than the strictly logical formulas of rigorous theorizing. The problems of private property and the ownership of what Marx would shortly call the means of production — a source of irreconcilable division? On one hand, there was the reality of the new factory production of the industrial revolution; on the other, the fact of widespread peasant ownership and the attachment to peasant property. The low wages and difficult conditions of mechanized industry — a source of division? Yes, but what of the reality of the higher standards of living as the machine-produced textiles were diffused, and the corresponding moral progress of all?

In short, here are the contradictions — the improvements and the hardships — of the early stages of industrialism, when the lines of thought and analysis were quite fluid and had not yet hardened into dogma. Ultimately this is tribute to the truth and importance of Michelet's insights. Working class or working classes, middle class or middle classes, many divided groups or two unifying enemies on different sides of the barrier? Michelet recognized condi-

[16] *Ibid.,* p. 17.

tions in 1845 that supported both positions. Only then could the honest man conclude that on balance the barriers were many but reducible, not unique and insurmountable.

No doubt Michelet's own experience was important here. As he said, he was a man who had many classes within himself and lacked that complete unity he would have wished. He was candid enough to admit that to remain simple and among the people required a continuous effort. But just as he contained different classes and contradictions, so did society. And in both cases a generous heart and an act of will could impose a harmony. This may be seen in the dedicatory preface, which was written not first but last. There one sees a serenity and a certainty concerning his own position among the people that many an earlier page lacks. In writing *The People* and in reexamining himself, Michelet had developed himself and strengthened his humanity and ties to the masses. Others could do the same.

In the second and third parts of the book, Michelet seeks the cause of France's social dislocation and division, and pleads for the cure of common bonds in the love of one's country. This is his answer to the earthquake of industrialization and modernization. The reader must be careful not to skip over these sections. I remember in my own case how certain ideas of the increasingly didactic and moralistic Michelet left me rather cold on my first reading, particularly those in certain sections of Part Two. Later investigation showed that others who have enthusiastically praised Michelet's analysis of the people's ills have questioned sharply the cures he prescribed.[17]

The reasons for such a feeling are not hard to find. We live in an age where shallow cynicism all too often passes for wisdom, and where pure idealism is often pure fanaticism. Thus Michelet's faith in instinct and the innate goodness of the masses, his call to Love as the solution for the problems he had so acutely described, and the attacks on the church and traditional religion in the baroque pseudo-Christian language of the mid-nineteenth century may at first appear as little more than worn-out prejudices of an-

[17] See, for example, Edmund Wilson, *To the Finland Station* (New York: Doubleday Anchor Books, 1953), pp. 27-30.

other time. As for Michelet's nationalism in general, and his deifi-
cation of France in particular, that is a credo many will be quick
to label retrograde and atavistic.

Yet upon further reflection, it seems to me that in spite of un-
questionable shortcomings and excesses, Michelet the prophetic
moralist is as profound as Michelet the social analyst. It is all too
easy to read Michelet's message as pious pronouncements of what
things should be — impractical Sunday school maxims divorced
from the harsh realities of our mundane existence. It is easy, but
it is superficial and inadequate. Much of Michelet's message is not
simply preaching about what should be — within the family, between those who love, among the members of a nation, and so
on — but contains an inspired vision of some of these ultimate
realities and most basic human truths. "Listen, my young friends,"
he is saying. "Here are the grains I have winnowed. They are the
fruits of my life; may they be seeds of knowledge and fulfillment
for yours."

Michelet's discussion of the family and the loving ties that hold
it together is no vain abstraction, for example. It reflects the
double reality of the tight, intimate circle he created and re-
created all his life, which was absolutely essential for his happiness and equilibrium. He is also telling us that this is the natural
and instinctive pattern. Of course patterns and styles of familial
and conjugal relationships are themselves subject to historical
change. Some women may now uncover inequality where Michelet saw cooperation and a reasonable division of labor. Yet they
will want to consider to what extent they still seek a similar fulfillment, though by means of a more equitable partnership.

Similarly, Michelet's conception of creativity and development
is based on his own experiences, which observation led him to
generalize. The discussions on the nature of genius, and the union
of simplicity and mental development that genius nurtures, make
sense when one understands that Michelet is speaking of himself
and his own enormously creative process. This helps explain the
power of his insights on education — insights not into what education should be in some ideal world but simply into what it is
when it works — and the picture of the destructive consequences

of an education that is based on the ceaseless negativism of the purely critical intellect. Michelet had seen firsthand that endless negative criticism leads to a terrible destruction: the destruction not only of the fabric of society, which is horrible enough, but also of the "educated" youth himself, who loses contact with his society and destroys himself.

It follows for Michelet that education must be positive. (Did Michelet in his heart regret what he termed "those purely negative polemics" against the clergy that he had just written — *The Jesuits* in 1843 and *The Priest* in 1845?) It must lift up and not push down. This could be done by teaching Frenchmen love of France and devotion to her. With such treatment Frenchmen would find an antidote to unchecked social dislocation and psychological tension. For them and for other peoples as well, the unity of the all-embracing nation would refashion a sense of community and interdependence to replace old values being eaten away by the acids of individualism, competition, and industrialization. Here is a positive program that rises above hand-wringing and pious lamentations and leads to a new social unity.

Many today will question whether the road to the good society passes primarily by way of the nation-state, as others will wonder if personal happiness is so closely tied to the family. Americans in particular may be quick to see nationalism more as a curse than a blessing, a foreign affliction they have generally escaped. Part of the reason for this may be that throughout most of our history we never faced a real external threat of our own dimensions. Therefore we were never forced to establish systematically a "we-they" spirit. Yet nationalism is certainly one of the world's strongest ongoing forces. No doubt one of the reasons is that, as Michelet says, it corresponds to deep and profound realities that will not be wished away. Another is that nationalism is a more positive and constructive force than we often believe.

Of the many things Michelet has to teach us here, notice first the generous character of his conception of the nation. Of course there is the much-abused rival, the English, against whom in part the French defined themselves historically. There is also a certain chauvinism and florid rhetorical militarism that may be explained by the relative isolation of France, especially of French liberals, in Metternich's Europe. Yet basically there is early nationalism at its best, and in the form in which it is most beneficially revived and diffused. Every people, like every citizen, has a natural right to exist in freedom and to develop its character and genius. The independence and freedom of other nations, as for other citizens within a nation, does not lessen the freedom of the first nation, but promotes the unity of the world through diversity on the common theme.

In Michelet's pages one sees how love of nation can be a force for human progress. Even the "infant" peoples are entitled to a collective personality and their own destiny. Here is certainly one of the first and most prophetic views of nationalism as the liberating force that would break the old empires and is still shaking the new ones. When this vision of the liberating force of nationalism is coupled with that of the rise of the common people, then Michelet, the soaring poetic prophet, appears once again as a great and profound realist as well.

THE PEOPLE

Preface:
To
Edgar Quinet*

This book is more than a book; it is myself, and that is why it belongs to you.

Yes, it is myself, and I dare say it is you as well, my friend. You were right in observing that our thoughts are ever in unison, whether we share them or not. We live with the same heart. A beautiful harmony which may surprise some. But what could be more natural? All our various works have sprung from the same living root: the feeling of France and the idea of the fatherland.

Accept, then, this book on the People, because it is you — because it is myself! We represent as much as any perhaps — you by your military and I by my industrial origin — the two modern aspects of the People and their recent advancement.

I have made this book out of myself, out of my life, and out of my heart. It is the product of my experience rather than of my studies. I have derived it from my observation and my conversations with friends and neighbors; I have picked it up along the highways, for fortune loves to favor the man who is always following the same line of thought. I have found it above all in the

---

* Quinet was a colleague at the College of France and a friend of twenty years. The two scholars were particularly close at this time. They were highly critical of the conservative influence of the Jesuits in France, and both had been strongly attacked as preaching anti-Christian doctrines to their students.

recollections of my youth. To know the life of the people and their toils and sufferings, I had only to question my memory.

For I too, my friend, have worked with my hands. I am entitled to the true name of modern man — that of *workman* — in more than one sense. Before I wrote books, I quite literally composed them; I arranged letters before I grouped ideas; and I have known the sadness of the workshop and the fatigue of long hours.

Those were sad times! In those last years of the Empire, all seemed to perish for me at the same time — my family, my fortune, and my country. No doubt I owe what is best in me to those trials; what little value I possess as a man and as a historian is due to them. From these hardships, and the tender remembrance of precious souls that I have known in the most humble conditions, I have kept especially a profound feeling for the people and the full knowledge of the treasure that is in them — *the virtue of sacrifice*.

No one should be surprised that after knowing the past condition of that people as well as anyone, and after sharing their life myself, I feel a burning desire that the truth be spoken about them. When the progress of my *History of France* led me to study the questions of the day and I cast my eyes upon the books where they are discussed, I must confess that I was surprised to find almost all of them contradicting my recollections. So I closed my books and went among the people again as much as I could; the solitary writer plunged again into the crowd and listened to the noise and noted the words. It was indeed the same people; only the outward appearances had changed, and my memory had not tricked me. So I went about consulting men, listening to their account of their own condition, and gathering from their lips what is not always found in the most brilliant writers — words of common sense.

I began this inquiry at Lyons about ten years ago. I have continued it in other towns, studying urban problems with practical men of the most positive minds, as well as the true situation of the rural areas, which is so neglected by our economists. It is hard to believe what a mass of new information I have thus acquired, and which is not in any book. Next to the conversation of men of

genius and of the most outstanding scholars, that of the people
is certainly the most instructive. If you cannot talk with Béranger,
Lamennais, or Lamartine, go into the fields and chat with a peasant. What is to be learned from the middle class? As for the
salons, I never left them without finding my heart shrunken and
chilled.

My wide-ranging studies of history had revealed facts of the
greatest interest about which historians are silent — the different
phases and the changes in the pattern of small landholding before
the Revolution, for example. In the same way, my on-the-spot investigation taught me many things that are not in the statistics.
I will mention one which some will find trivial perhaps, but which
I consider important and worthy of every attention.

This is the immense increase in cotton textiles of all types acquired by poor families since about 1842, even though wages have
fallen, or at least fallen in real value because of increased prices.
This fact, important in itself as an advance in cleanliness (which
is connected with so many other virtues), is all the more so since
it develops a growing stability in the household and the family.
Above all it increases the influence of the woman, who earns little
herself and can make this purchase only by using part of her husband's wages. The woman represents economy, order, and providence in these households. Every increase in her influence is progress in morality.[1]

This instance is not without its use in showing how insufficient
is all the documentation gathered from our statistical publications
and the other works on economy. They are unable — even if they

---

[1] This prodigious acquisition of cotton textiles, to which all the manufacturers can testify, also implies some acquisition of other goods and
household furniture. We must not be surprised if the savings banks receive less from the worker than from the household servant. The latter
buys no furniture and little clothing, for he finds ways to have his
masters clothe him. People ought not to estimate, as they do, the progress
of savings by that of the savings bank, or believe that whatever is not
put there is spent in the bars. It seems that the family — I speak especially of the wife — has desired above all else to make clean, attractive,
and agreeable the little home which supersedes the bistro. This also accounts for the taste for flowers, which has reached classes bordering on
poverty.

are correct — to make us understand the people. They give partial and artificial findings which have been taken from a particular angle and which are easily misinterpreted.

Writers and artists who follow a process directly opposed to these abstract methods ought to be able to carry the feeling of life to their study of the people. Indeed some of the most eminent among them have tackled this grand subject, and their talent did not fail them; their success has been immense. Europe, so long so unimaginative, avidly receives the products of our literature. The English scarcely write anything nowadays except articles for reviews; as for books in German, who reads them except the Germans?

It would be worthwhile examining whether these French books which have so much popularity and authority in Europe truly represent France, or whether they have not exhibited certain exceptional and very unfavorable aspects of character. And these pictures, where people seldom see anything but our vices and our defects, have they not done our country an immense disservice among foreign nations? The talent, the honesty of the authors, and the well-known liberality of their principles gave overwhelming weight to their words. The world has accepted their books as a terrible judgment of France upon herself.

France has this against herself: she shows herself naked to the nations. In one way or another all the others remain clothed and dressed. Germany, and even England with all her parliamentary commissions and all her publicity, are little known by comparison. They cannot see themselves for lack of centralization.

What is first seen on a naked figure is its defects. They strike the eye at once. What would be the result if an obliging hand placed on our blemishes a magnifying glass which made them appear colossal, and reflected such a pitiless light upon them that the most natural accidents of the skin should leap out at the horror-struck eye?

That is precisely what has happened to France. Her undeniable faults, which are adequately explained by her unbounded activity and the impact of interests and ideas, have grown under the hand of these powerful writers and have become terrible monstrosities. And now Europe looks upon her as a monster herself!

Nothing has served the politics of the so-called *alliance of respectable classes* better than this. Every aristocracy — English, Russian, or German — has only to point out one thing as testimony against France: the portraits she draws of herself with the hand of her great writers, most of whom are friends of the people and partisans of progress. "Are not the people thus described the terror of the world? Have we enough armies and fortresses to pen them up and watch them, until we have a chance to crush them?"

Some classic and immortal novels revealing the domestic tragedies of the wealthy classes have firmly established in the mind of Europe that domestic ties no longer exist in France. Others, works of great talent and wild fantasy, have represented the ordinary life of our cities as nothing but a point where the police track down habitual criminals and escaped convicts. A painter of manners, admirable for his genius for details, delights in depicting a loathsome village ale-house, a tavern for rogues and thieves. And beneath this hideous sketch he has the nerve to write a word which is the name of the greater part of the inhabitants of France.*

Europe reads eagerly and with admiration. She recognizes this or that petty detail, and from some minute incident which seems true, she easily infers the truth of the whole.

No people could stand such a test. This singular mania for slandering ourselves, for exposing our wounds and actually seeking our own disgrace, would be fatal in the long run. I know that many denounce the present to hasten a better future. They exaggerate the evils to let us enjoy more fully the bliss their theories are preparing for us. But watch out, watch out! That is a dangerous game. Europe is not interested in these clever tricks. If we say we are despicable, she will believe us.[2] Italy was still a real

---

* Michelet is successively referring to George Sand, Eugène Sue (particularly *The Mysteries of Paris*), and Honoré de Balzac. Balzac's *The Peasants*, written in 1844 with the intention of debunking the idea of the nobility of the people in general and the peasants in particular, infuriated Michelet as a slanderous work "against the People and democracy."

[2] These days philosophers, political economists, and politicians all seem to unite in lessening the idea of France in the mind of the people. This

power in the sixteenth century. The land of Michelangelo and
Christopher Columbus did not lack energy. But when she had
proclaimed herself miserable and infamous by the voice of Machiavelli, the world took her at her word and marched on her.

We are not Italy, thank God; and the day the world might con-
spire to come and take a close view of France would be hailed by
our soldiers as the finest in their lives.

Let it suffice for nations to know well that this people does
not at all resemble these so-called portraits. It is not that our
great painters have always been incorrect, but they have generally
delighted in exceptional details or accidents in each species; only
a minority has sought the worst side of everything. The broad fea-
tures of their subject appeared to them too well known, too trivial
and vulgar. They wanted effects, and they have often searched
for them off the beaten path. Born of agitation and tumult, they
have painted with a passionate and stormy strength, and occasionally with a touch true as well as sensitive and strong. What
they generally lacked was the sense of the grand harmony.

The Romantics believed that art is found especially in the ugly.

---

is extremely dangerous! Remember that this nation is above all others a
true society, in the highest sense of the term. Remove it from its social
idea and it becomes very weak. The people have been told for fifty years
by all governments that the France of the Revolution, which was their
glory and faith, was a disorder, an absurdity, and a pure negation. On
the other hand, the Revolution, which had obliterated old France, told
the people that nothing of their past deserved to be remembered. Ancient
France has disappeared from their memory, and the new one has grown
pale. It was no fault of the politicians if the people did not become a
tabula rasa, and forget themselves.

How can they be other than weak at this moment? They do not know
themselves; everything is done to make them lose the feeling of that
grand unity which was their life. Their soul is being taken away from
them. Their soul was the feeling of France, France as the grand brotherhood of living men and as a glorious association with all Frenchmen of
the past. The nation contains these forebears, carries them, and faintly
feels them moving, but it cannot recognize them. They are not told what
that great deep voice is which murmurs within them like the distant bass
of an organ in a cathedral.

Men of reflection and study, authors and writers — we all have a holy
and sacred duty toward the people! It is to lay aside our sorry paradoxes
and our witticisms, which have aided the politicians in concealing France
from the people, in obscuring their idea of her, and in making them
despise their native land.

They thought that art finds its most powerful effects in moral ugliness. Fickle love seemed more poetic to them than family ties, theft more than labor, or the galleys more than the workshop. If they had gone down into the profound realities of life today through their own personal sufferings, they would have seen that the family, the work, and the humblest life of the people have themselves a sacred poetry. To feel and show this is not a mechanical affair; there is no need to accumulate theatrical devices here. It requires only that we have eyes formed for that gentle light, eyes to look into the dark, into the petty and the humble; and the heart helps, too, to see into those corners of the home and those shadows of Rembrandt.

Whenever our great writers have looked there, they have been admirable. But generally they have turned their eyes toward the fantastic, the violent, the whimsical, the unusual. Nor have they deigned to warn us that they were sketching the exception. Their readers, and especially their foreign readers, thought they were describing the rule. So they said, "That is the way those people are."

And I — who have sprung from them, who have lived and toiled and suffered with them, who more than any other has earned the right to say that I know them — I am coming forward now against all these views to establish the personality of the people.

I have not taken this personality from the surface, in its picturesque or dramatic aspects. I have not seen it from the outside, but experienced it from within. And in this very experience I have understood more than one deep quality of the people which they have but do not understand. Why? Because I was able to trace it in its historical development and see it come from the depths of time. He who limits himself to the present will not understand the present. He who is satisfied with seeing the exterior and painting the form will not even be able to see it. To see that personality accurately and translate it faithfully, he must know what it covers. There is no painting without anatomy.

It is not in this little book that I can teach such a science. It is enough for me to give a few essential observations on the state of our manners and a few general results, while setting aside all details bearing on method, preparation, and formation.

One word must be said here, however. The chief and most prominent trait, which has always struck me the most forcefully throughout my long study of the people, is that among the disorders of destitution and the vices of misery, I have found a richness of feeling and a goodness of heart which are very rare among the wealthy classes. Moreover, everyone has been able to observe this. At the time of the cholera epidemics, who adopted the orphan children? The poor.

The faculty of devotion and sacrifice is, I must confess, my standard for classifying mankind. He who possesses this quality in the highest degree is the nearest to heroism. Intellectual superiority, which results partly from education, can never be balanced against this sovereign faculty.

To this there is a standard reply. "The people are generally short-sighted. They follow an instinct of goodness, the blind impulse of a good heart, because they do not foresee all that it may cost them." Even if this observation were just, it certainly does not do away with the unremitting devotion and the ceaseless sacrifices one may see so often in those hard-working families. There devotion is not even exhausted in the immolation of one life, but often continues from one to another for several generations.

I have here many excellent stories which I might relate. But that would hardly be proper. Yet I am strongly tempted to tell you one story, my dear friend — that of my own family. You do not know it yet, for we discuss philosophical or political matters more often than personal questions. I yield to this temptation. It is for me a rare opportunity to acknowledge the persevering and heroic sacrifices that my family made for me, and to thank my relatives, modest people who sometimes hid their superior gifts in obscurity and wished to live only in me.

The two families from which I am descended, one from Picardy and one from the Ardennes, were originally peasants who added a little industry to their agricultural pursuits. Since these families were very large — twelve children in one, nineteen in the other — many of my father's and mother's brothers and sisters did not marry, in order that they might better contribute to the education of some of the boys whom they sent to college. This is the first sacrifice to note.

Particularly in my mother's family, the sisters, all remarkable for their economy, seriousness, and austerity, made themselves the humble servants of their brothers and remained in the village in order to pay their way. Several, however, though uneducated and living in that wilderness on the border of the forests, were richly endowed with natural abilities. I have heard one of them quite advanced in years relate the old stories of the border as well as did Walter Scott. What was common to them all was great clearness of mind and soundness of judgment. There were plenty of priests among their cousins and relations, priests of various sorts, both worldly and fanatical, but they had no power over them. Our judicious and austere maidens never let them take the slightest hold on them. They would readily relate how one of our granduncles (named Michaud, or perhaps Paillart?) had been burned at the stake for having written a certain book.

My father's father, a choirmaster at Laon, gathered up his little savings after the Reign of Terror and came to Paris, where my father was employed at the printing office for paper money. Instead of buying land as so many others did at that time, he entrusted all he had to my father, his eldest son, who put it all into a printing shop quite exposed to the risks of the Revolution. To facilitate the arrangement, a brother and a sister of my father did not marry, though my father did. He married one of those sober girls from the Ardennes whom I have just mentioned. I was born in 1798, in the choir of a church of nuns, which was then occupied by our printing shop: occupied but not desecrated, for what is the Press in modern times but the holy ark?

This printing shop prospered at first, fed by the debates of our assemblies, the news of our armies, and the exciting life of the times. About 1800 it was struck by the general suppression of newspapers. My father was allowed to print only an ecclesiastical journal; and after this undertaking had been begun at considerable expense, the sanction was suddenly withdrawn in favor of a priest whom Napoleon thought safe, but who soon betrayed him.

We know how this great man was punished by the priests for believing the consecration of Rome to be better than that of France. He saw more clearly in 1810. But on whom did this anger fall? On the Press. In two years he hurled sixteen decrees against it. My father, already half ruined by him for the profit of the priests, was now entirely ruined in expiation of their faults.

One morning we received a visit from a gentleman who was more polite than most of the imperial agents and who informed us that His Majesty, the Emperor, had reduced the number of printers to sixty. The largest ones were preserved; *the smaller ones were closed,* but with a fine indemnity — at the rate of five sous for each franc. We were among these smaller ones. There was nothing before us but to resign ourselves and starve to death. But we were in debt. The Emperor gave us no reprieve from the Jews, as he had done for Alsace.* We had but one resource; it was to print for our creditors a few works that belonged to my father. We no longer had any hired help, and we did all the work ourselves. My father was occupied with tasks outside the shop and could not assist us; my sick mother became a binder, and cut and folded; I, a child, composed the type. My grandfather, very old and feeble, took upon himself the hard work of the press, and worked the machine with his trembling hands.

These books which we printed, and which sold pretty well, contrasted completely by their triviality with those tragic years of immense destruction. They were only petty jokes, little games, amusements for evening parties, charades, and acrostics. There was nothing there to nourish the soul of the young compositor.

* Michelet does not mention that the contract on which this arrangement was based was subsequently broken in the courts by the usurer Vatard. This resulted in all the family's goods being seized and his father being imprisoned for several months. The anguish of this ghastly personal experience, as opposed to any racial nonsense, is undoubtedly the basic cause of Michelet's frequently expressed anti-Semitism. This prejudice, which contrasts with Michelet's generosity and humanity, is certainly unworthy of the man, but it is not inexplicable.

But precisely the dryness and the emptiness of these miserable productions left me all the more freedom. Never, I think, did I travel more in my imagination than while I stood rooted before my work. And the more my personal romances fired my mind, the faster my hands went and the quicker the letters fell into place. Then I realized that manual work which requires neither extreme care nor great strength is by no means incompatible with imagination. I have heard many distinguished women say they could think and speak effectively only when doing their needlework.

I was twelve years old. I knew nothing yet but four words of Latin, which I had picked up from an old bookseller, formerly the village teacher, who doted on grammar. A man of the old mold, he was an ardent revolutionary who had nevertheless saved at the risk of his life those *émigrés* he detested. At his death he left me all he had in the world — a manuscript of a very remarkable but incomplete grammar, which he had worked on for thirty or forty years.

Quite alone and very free, left entirely to myself by the excessive indulgence of my parents, I was all imagination. I had read a few books that had fallen into my hands: a book on mythology, a work by Boileau, and a few pages of *The Imitation of Christ*.

In the great and continuous difficulties of my family, with my mother ill and my father so busy away from home, I had not yet received any religious education. And then in those pages I suddenly saw at the close of this sad world a deliverance from death, another life and hope! Religion thus received, without human interference, now became very strong within me. It was something of my own, a free and living thing, so well tied up with my life that it found support in everything, strengthening itself at each step of the way with a multitude of tender and holy things from art and poetry, which people erroneously believe are foreign to it.

How shall I describe the dreamy delight into which I was cast by the first words of *The Imitation*! I was not reading, I was listening — as though that gentle and paternal voice were addressed to me. I still see that large room, cold and unfurnished;

it seemed to me illuminated with a mysterious radiance. I could not follow the book very far, since I understood nothing of Christ, but I felt God!

The next strongest impression of my childhood is of the museum of French monuments, which has so unfortunately been torn down. It was there and nowhere else that I first received a vivid impression of history. I filled those tombs with my imagination; I felt the dead through the marble; and it was not without a little terror that I visited the low vaults, where Dagobert, Chilperic, and Fredogonda were sleeping.

The scene of my labors, our workshop, was almost as somber. For some time this was a cellar facing on the main street, although we were on the ground floor of the small street in back. For companions I had my grandfather when he occasionally came to see us, but I always had a certain industrious spider that worked by me, and most certainly more seriously than I.

Among very severe hardships, which were far heavier than what ordinary workers have to bear, I had some real compensations: the kindness of my parents, and their faith in my future prospects, which was truly incredible when we remember how backward I was. Except for the hours of work, I had complete independence, which I never abused. I was an apprentice, but without being brought into contact with coarse-minded people whose brutality would perhaps have crushed that precious flower of liberty within me. In the morning before work I went to see the old grammarian, who gave me five or six lines to do. From this experience I learned that the quantity of work has much less to do with education than people believe. Children can learn only a little every day. They are like a vase with a narrow neck: whether you try to pour in a little or a lot, you will never get much in at a time.

In spite of my lack of any musical talent, which was the despair of my grandfather, I was very sensitive to the majestic harmony of Latin; that grand and sonorous Italian melody warmed me like a ray of southern sunshine. I had been born like a blade of grass without sun between two cobblestones of Paris. This warmth from another climate had such beneficial effects upon me that before I knew anything about the meter and rhythm of the ancient languages, I had already sought and found in my exercises some rustic Roman melodies, like the prose epics of the Middle Ages. A child, provided he is left free, follows precisely the path taken by infant peoples.

Except for the sufferings of poverty, which were very great for me in winter, the time of manual labor, Latin, and friendship is very sweet to remember. (I had at one moment a friend, and I will speak of him in this book.) Rich in youth, imagination, and perhaps already even love, I did not envy anyone anything. It is my conviction that man would never know envy by himself — he must be taught it.

Then everything grew more difficult. My mother became worse, and so did France — Moscow! 1813! The indemnity was exhausted. In our extreme poverty a friend of my father's offered to get me a job in the imperial printing office. What a temptation for my parents! Others would not have hesitated. But faith had always been strong in our family: first faith in my father, for whom all had sacrificed; then faith in me. I was to repair everything, save everything.

If my parents had followed reason, made me a worker and saved themselves, would I then have been lost? No, I see among the workers men of much merit, men who are quite the equals of men of letters in intelligence and are their superiors in character. But what difficulties would I have encountered! What a struggle against the lack of every advantage! And against the press of time! My impoverished father and my sick mother decided that I should study no matter what might happen.

Our situation weighed heavily upon us. Knowing neither verse nor Greek, I entered directly into secondary education at Charlemagne College. My embarrassment may be imagined, as I had no tutor to assist me. My mother, so firm until then, wept and despaired. My father set about writing Latin verses — he who had never made any before.

The best thing for me in that terrible passage from solitude to the crowd and from night to day was undoubtedly Professor Andrieu d'Alba, a kind-hearted, pious man. The worst was my

classmates. I stood among them like an owl in broad daylight —
quite frightened. They found me ridiculous, and I think now they
were right. At the time I thought their laughter was due to my
dress and poverty. I began to notice one thing — that I was poor.

I thought that all rich men were wicked, and I saw very few
who were not richer than myself. I fell into a misanthropic humor
rare among children. In the most deserted quarter of Paris, the
Marais, I sought the most deserted streets. Yet amid this excessive
antipathy for the human species, this good point remained: I
felt no envy.

My greatest delight, which restored my heart, was to read two
or three times a canto of Virgil or a book of Horace on Thursday
or Sunday. Gradually I memorized them, though I have never
been able to learn a single lesson by heart.

I remember well — in the midst of that thoroughgoing misery,
of those privations in the present and those fears for the future,
with the enemy at the gates (1814!) and my own enemies ridiculing me every day — a certain day and a certain Thursday
morning when I sat thinking about myself. Without a fire and
with the snow lying deep, not knowing whether I would find my
bread at night, everything seemed finished for me — and then I
had within me a pure stoic feeling, but without any trace of
religious hope; and with my hand numb from the cold I struck
my oak table (which I still have), and felt a powerful, virile joy
of youth and promise.

Tell me, my dear friend, what should I fear today? I, who
have suffered death so many times in myself and in my studies?
And what should I want? God has given me through history the
means of participating in everything.

Life has only one claim on me, that which I felt last February
12, about thirty years after that Thursday morning. It was a
similar day, equally covered with snow, and I found myself seated
at the same table. But one thought tore my heart. "You are warm,
the others are cold; that is not just. Oh! who will relieve me from
this cruel inequality?" Then looking at my hand, the one that
since 1813 still shows the marks of the cold, I consoled myself
by saying, "If you had gone to work with the people, you would

not be working for them now. Go ahead: if you give your country its history, I will pardon you for being happy."

Let me return to those early years. My faith was not absurd; it was based on my will. I believed in the future because I was making it myself. My studies ended soon and well.[3] I had the good fortune to escape the two influences which were ruining young men: that of doctrinaire thought, so majestic and sterile, and that of making lackluster literature, which the reviving book business welcomed no matter how bad.

I would not live by my pen. I wanted a real craft. I took the one my studies had prepared me for — teaching. I thought even then, like Rousseau, that literature ought to be something reserved, the grand luxury of life and the inner blossom of the soul. How happy I used to be on those mornings after I had given my lessons to return to my neighborhood near Père Lachaise Cemetery, there to read at my leisure all day long such poets as Homer, Sophocles, or Theocritus, and occasionally the historians. One of my old companions and dearest friends, Mr. Poret, was reading the same books, and we used to talk about them on our long walks in the forest of Vincennes.

This carefree life lasted a full ten years, and during that time I never imagined I would ever write. I taught languages, philosophy, and history all at the same time. In 1821 I succeeded in the competition for the doctorate at the Sorbonne, and took a teaching position in a college. In 1827, two works appearing at the same time — my *Vico* and my *Précis of Modern History* — gained me a professorship in the teachers' college, the École Normale.[4]

Teaching was of great advantage to me. The terrible trial of college had altered my character and had made me reserved and closed, shy and distrustful. Marrying young and living in almost

[3] I owed much to the encouragement of my illustrious professors, Messrs. Villemain and Leclerc. I shall always remember how once after the reading of a lesson that had pleased him, Professor Villemain left his chair, and with a charming sensitiveness came and sat down on the bench beside me.

[4] I left it with regret in 1837, when the eclectic influence prevailed there. In 1838 the Institute and the College of France both elected me for their candidate, and I obtained the chair I now occupy.

complete solitude, I desired less and less the society of men. That which I found with my students at the École Normale and elsewhere opened my heart again and let it swell. Those young people, who were amiable and confiding and who believed in me, reconciled me to mankind. I was touched and often sad to see them succeed each other so rapidly. Hardly had I become attached to them than they were gone. They are all dispersed now, and several (so young!) are dead. Few have forgotten me. For my part, whether they be living or dead, I will never forget them.

Without knowing it, they rendered me an immense service. If I had as a historian any special merit to put me on a level with my illustrious predecessors, I would owe it to teaching, which for me was friendship. Those great historians have been brilliant, judicious, and profound. As for myself, I loved more.

I also suffered more. The trials of my childhood are always with me; I never lost the feeling of toil and a hard, laborious life. I am still one of the people.

I said that I grew up like a blade of grass between two cobblestones; but that blade has retained its vigor as well as have those of the Alps. My desert in the heart of Paris, the independence of my study and my teaching (always free and always the same), has developed me without changing me. They who rise almost always lose in doing so, because they alter themselves. They become mongrels, bastards; they lose the originality of their own class without gaining that of another. The difficulty is not to rise but rather, in rising, to remain one's self.

Today the rise and progress of the people are often compared to the invasion of the Barbarians. I like the word, and I accept the term. Barbarians! That is to say, full of new, vital, and regenerating vigor. Barbarians! That is to say, travelers marching toward the future Rome, going on slowly no doubt, each generation advancing a little and then halting in death, but others continue forward all the same.

We have, we Barbarians, a natural advantage. If the upper classes have culture, we have much more vital heat. They cannot work hard; nor have they intensity or eagerness or conscientiousness in their work. Their elegant writers, real spoiled children of the world, seem to glide among the clouds; or proudly eccentric, they do not deign to regard the earth. How could they fertilize it? That earth must drink the sweat of man and be impregnated with his heat and living virtue.

Our Barbarians lavish all this upon her, and she loves them. Their love is boundless and sometimes too great, for they may devote themselves to details with the delightful awkwardness of Albert Dürer, or with the excessive polish of Jean Jacques Rousseau, who does not conceal his art enough, and by this minute detail they compromise the whole. We must not blame them too much. It is the excess of the will, the superabundance of love, and occasionally the luxuriance of their sap and vigor. When this sap is misdirected or blocked, it wrongs itself; it wants to give everything at once — leaves, fruit, and flowers; it bends and twists the branches.

These defects of many great workers are often found in my books, which lack their good qualities. No matter! They who come forward imbued with the sap of the people bring, nonetheless, a new degree of life and rejuvenation, or at the very least a great effort. They generally fix their aim higher and farther than others, consulting their heart rather than their strength. Let that be my contribution for the future: not to have attained but to have marked the aim of history, to have given it a name that no one had conceived. Thierry called it *narration,* and Guizot *analysis.* I have named it *resurrection,* and this name will last.

Who would be more severe than myself if I were to criticize my own works! The public has treated me all too kindly. Do you think that I do not see how very imperfect this present volume is? "Why then, do you publish it?" some will ask. "You must surely have some great interest at stake!"

An interest? Yes, several, as you shall see. I will lose many ties of friendship by it. And I emerge from a tranquil life that conforms completely to my tastes. I must postpone my great book, the monument of my life.

"To enter public life then?" Never. I know myself. I have neither the health nor the talent to manage men.

"Well then, why ... ?" If you really insist on knowing, I will tell you.

I speak because no one would speak in my place. Not that there is not a crowd of men more capable of doing so, but all have soured, and all hate. As for me, I have always loved. Perhaps I also knew better the antecedents of France; I lived in her grand eternal life and not in her present condition. I was more alive in sympathies and more dead in interests; I came to the questions of the day with the disinterest of the dead.

Besides, I was suffering far more than any other from the deplorable divorce that some are trying to produce among men and among different classes — I who combine them all within me.

The situation of France is so grave that there was no place for hesitation. I do not exaggerate the power of a book, but the question is one of duty and not of ability.

Well! I see France sinking hour by hour, swallowed up like Atlantis. While we are here quarreling, our country is disappearing.

Who does not see that from east to west a shadow of death is weighing upon Europe, and that every day there is less sun: Italy has perished, Ireland has perished, Poland has perished, and Germany wishes to follow! Oh, Germany! Germany!

If France were dying a natural death and if her hour had come, I could perhaps resign myself; like a passenger on a sinking ship, I would close my eyes and commend myself to God. But her situation is nothing like that, and that is why I am indignant. The idea of our ruin is absurd, ridiculous; it comes only from ourselves. Who has a literature? Who still sways the mind of Europe? We do, weak as we are. Who has an army? We alone.

England and Russia, two feeble, bloated giants, impose an illusion on Europe. Great empires and weak peoples! Let France be united for an instant, and she is as strong as the world.

The first thing is that we should get our bearings again before the crisis, and not have to alter our line, our maneuvers, and our system in the presence of the enemy as in 1792 and 1815.[5]

---

[5] I have never seen in history a peace of thirty years. The bankers, who have never foreseen any revolution (not even that of July 1830, which many of them were preparing), reply that nothing will stir in Europe. The first reason they give is that *peace is profitable for the world.* Yes indeed, for the world, but very little for us. Others are running, and

The second is that we should trust in France, and not at all in Europe.

Here everyone goes to seek friends elsewhere: the politician goes to London, the philosopher to Berlin, and the communist says, "Our brothers, the Chartists!"[6] The peasant alone has preserved the tradition of salvation; to him a Prussian is still a Prussian, an Englishman still an Englishman. His common sense has been right in spite of all you humanitarians! The other day your friend Prussia and your friend England drank the toast of "Waterloo!" to France.

Children, children, I say unto you: Climb up on a high mountain and look to the four winds; you will see nothing but enemies.

Try, then, to understand one another. As for that perpetual peace which some promise you — while the arsenals are smoking and the black smoke of feverish activity rises over Cronstadt and Portsmouth! — let us try to begin that peace among ourselves. No doubt we are divided, but Europe believes us to be more divided than we are. That is what makes her bold. The harsh things we have to say, let us say them; let us pour out our hearts and hide none of the evils, but then let us find the remedies.

One people! one country! one France! Never, never, I beg you, must we become two nations! Without unity, we perish. How is it that you fail to see this?

Frenchmen of every condition, of every class, and of every party, remember one thing: you have on earth only one sure friend — France! For the ever-enduring coalition of aristocracies, you will always be guilty of one crime — to have wished fifty years ago

we are walking; we shall soon be the last ones. In the second place, they say, "War can begin only with a loan; and we will not grant it." But what if they begin with a treasure, as Russia is now making one; or what if the war pays for the war, as in the time of Napoleon? And there are other possibilities.

[6] Pick at random the most liberal German or Englishman, and then talk to him of liberty. He will answer, "Liberty." And then just try to see what he means by it. You will then see that this word has as many meanings as there are nations, that the German and English democrats are aristocrats at heart, that the barrier of nationalities which you thought had been swept away remains almost intact. All these people whom you believe so near are five hundred miles from you.

to deliver the world. They have not pardoned that, and they never will. You are their constant fear. Among yourselves you may be distinguished by different party names, but as Frenchmen, you are all equally condemned. Be assured that for Europe, France will never have but a single, inexpiable name, which is her true and eternal fame — the Revolution!

24 January 1846

PART ONE

&

Of Bondage and Hate

CHAPTER I

∾

The Bondage of the Peasant

If we wish to know the innermost thought and passion of the French peasant, it is very easy. Walk, any Sunday, into the country and follow him. There he is, a bit in front of us. It is two o'clock; his wife is at vespers; and he is in his Sunday best. Take my word for it, he is off to see his mistress.

What mistress?

His land.

I am not saying that he goes straight to her. No, he is free today, free to go or not as he pleases. And does he not see her enough every day of the week? So he turns away for a while, and tends to another matter. And yet he goes all the same.

True, he was passing very near, and that gave him the opportunity. He looks over at her, but it seems he will keep his distance. What would he do now? And yet he approaches.

In any event, he probably will not work. He has on his Sunday clothes, with a clean blouse and a white shirt. But nothing stops him from pulling a few weeds or throwing aside that stone. That stump is still there, but he does not have his pickax. That must wait until tomorrow.

Then he stops, folds his arms, and looks seriously and thoughtfully. He looks a long, long time, and seems to forget himself. Finally, if he believes someone is watching or if he sees someone passing, he slowly moves away. Then after thirty steps he stops, turns, and casts upon his land one last look, a deep and brooding look. But for the keen observer, that look is full of passion, full of heart, and full of devotion.

If this is not love, then by what sign shall we know it in this world? It is love; do not laugh at it. The land demands it this way if it is to produce. Otherwise this poor land of France, with few cattle and no manure, would give nothing. It yields because it is loved.

The land of France belongs to the fifteen or twenty million peasants who farm it; the land of England belongs to an aristocracy of thirty-two thousand individuals who have others farm it for them.[1]

The English do not have our roots in the soil, and they emigrate to wherever they see material advantage. They speak of their country; we speak of our *patrie,* our fatherland.[2] With us, man and the land are joined together, and neither will forsake the other. There is between them a rightful marriage for life and for death; the Frenchman has wedded France.

France is a land of justice. In doubtful cases she has generally ruled that the land belongs to him who tills it. England, on the contrary, has ruled in favor of the lord and driven off the peasant.[3] She is now farmed only by hired laborers.

[1] And of these thirty-two thousand, twelve thousand are mortmain corporations. If one replies to this that in England almost three million persons share the landed property, this is because they are including in the term the land around houses — little patches of ground, yards, parks and gardens, and whatever — and not just the land itself. This is especially true in the manufacturing districts.

[2] Our Anglo-Frenchmen say *le pays* — the country — in order to avoid saying *la patrie* — the fatherland. [Translator's note: *Patrie* is a difficult word to translate, and it occupies an important place in this work. I have translated it in various ways — as fatherland, native land, or even country, but not as nation.]

[3] This is one of the spiritual aspects of our Revolution: man and man's work seemed to it of inestimable value and were not to be put on the scale with the purse. Man outweighed the land. Even in districts that are not feudal but organized upon the principle of the Celtic clans, the English jurists have applied the feudal law with the greatest rigor, and decided that the lord was not only the political suzerain but the proprietor as well. Thus the Duchess of Sutherland had a county of Scotland larger than the department of the Upper Rhine adjudged to her, and then from 1811 to 1820 she drove off of it three thousand families who had occupied it ever since Scotland had existed. The duchess had a trifling indemnity offered them, which many did not accept.

What a serious moral difference! Whether one's property is large or small, it lifts the heart. The man who would not have respected himself on his own account does so because of his property. This feeling strengthens the just pride that an incomparable military tradition gives our people. Pick at random from the crowd an ordinary day-laborer who owns one-twentieth of an acre, and you will not find the spirit of a hired man and a mercenary. He is a landowner and a soldier (as he was before and would be to-morrow) ; his father was part of *la grande armée*.

Small landholdings are nothing new in France. People have erroneously imagined that they were recently established in a single great crisis, and that they are a result of the Revolution. This is a great mistake: the Revolution found this movement far advanced and sprang from it itself. In 1785 that excellent observer Arthur Young was astonished and frightened to see our land *so divided*. In 1738 the Abbé de Saint-Pierre observed that "almost all day laborers have a garden or a piece of land or a vineyard." In 1697 Boisguilbert deplored the fact that under Louis XIV the small proprietors were forced to sell a great part of the holdings they had acquired in the sixteenth and seventeenth centuries.

This great story, so little known, has one particular feature: in the very worst times, in those periods of universal poverty when even the rich are poor and are forced to sell, the poor man finds himself able to buy. With no other buyers coming forth, the peasant in rags steps up with his piece of gold and buys a bit of land. What a strange mystery! This man must have a hidden treasure. And indeed he has one — his constant labor, his temperance, and his thrift. As a patrimony God seems to have given this indestructible race the talent to work and to fight, to go without eating if necessary, and to live on hope and brave good cheer.

Those periods of disaster, when the peasant was able to buy land cheaply, have always been followed by a sudden burst of prosperity which people could never explain. About 1500, for example, when a France exhausted by Louis XI seemed to be completing her ruin in Italy, the departing nobility was forced to sell. The land passing into new hands suddenly flourished again, and men worked and built. In the style of monarchical history, this fine moment has been called the time of *good Louis XII.*

It lasts such a short time, unfortunately. Scarcely is the land restored to good condition than the tax collector pounces on it. Next the wars of religion seem to level everything to the ground — a time of horrible troubles and dreadful famines, when mothers devoured their children! Who would believe that the country could rise again after that? Well, hardly were the wars over than from those ravaged fields and burned and blackened cottages came the savings of the peasant. He bought land, and in ten years France had a new face. In twenty or thirty years the wealth of the kingdom doubled and tripled. This moment, again baptized with a royal name, is called *good Henry IV* and *great Richelieu.*

What a wonderful movement! What man would not gladly play his part? Why then must it always stop, and why must so much effort be almost lost after a few rewards? When we hear the sayings "the poor man saves" and "the peasant buys" — simple phrases that are said so quickly — do we really know what labors, sacrifices, and deadly privations they contain? We ourselves sweat when we observe in detail the ups and downs, the successes and reversals, in this stubborn struggle and when we see the invincible effort with which this miserable man has seized, lost, and retaken the land of France. He is like the poor shipwrecked sailor who touches a rugged shore and holds on as each receding wave continuously drags him toward the sea, and who clutches again, mangles himself, and still clings to the rock with bleeding hands.

This movement, I am forced to say, slowed or even stopped about 1650. The nobles who had sold found a way to buy back at a low price. While our Italian ministers — a Mazarin, an Emeri — were doubling the taxes, the nobles who crowded the court easily obtained exemption from taxation, so the doubled burden fell upon the weak and the poor. They were forced to sell or give away the land so recently theirs, and to become again hirelings, tenants, sharecroppers, and day laborers. By what unbelievable efforts were they able to hold or regain the land through all the wars and bankruptcies of the grand king and the regency, that land which was in their hands in the eighteenth century as we just saw? It is truly inexplicable.

I beg and beseech those who make and enforce our laws to study in detail the fatal reaction of Mazarin and Louis XIV in those pages full of indignation and sorrow on this subject by that great citizen Pesant de Boisguilbert. May that history serve as a warning at a moment when various forces are eagerly striving to check the main work of France — the acquisition of the land by the laborer.

Our judges, especially, need to understand this matter and strengthen their consciences, for they are attacked by tricks and fraud. The large landowners have been aroused from their natural apathy by the lawyers and have recently opened countless unjust lawsuits. The communes and small landholders must now contend with lawyers specializing in old records who all work together to falsify history in order to cheat justice. They know that judges rarely have time to examine their fabrications. They know that those they attack almost never have proper deeds and titles. The communes in particular have either kept them carelessly or never had any. This is because their rights are very old and are from a period when people trusted in tradition.

In frontier districts especially, the rights of poor peasants are much more sacred, since without them no one would have settled such dangerous country.[4] The land would have been deserted, and there would have been neither people nor cultivation. And it is only today, in a time of peace and security, that you come and challenge the right to the land of those without whom the land would not have existed! You ask for their deeds of title. They are buried; they are the bones of their ancestors who guarded your frontier and who still hold the sacred line.

There is more than one province in France where the cultivator has a right to the land that is certainly superior to any other — that of having made it. I am not speaking metaphorically.

---

[4] Add to this the fact that in the Middle Ages, when the territory was divided into many provinces, the *frontier was everywhere*. Even somewhat later the English frontier was in the center of France: in Poitou until the thirteenth century, in Limousin until the fourteenth, and so on.

Look at those parched rocks and arid hills of the south; where, I ask you, would the land be without man? Property there is the creation of the proprietor. It lies in the indefatigable arm which hammers the flint to dust all day long and mixes it with a little earth. It lies in the strong back of the wine-grower, who is always pushing farther up the hill his field that is always eroding away. It lies in the docility and patient passion of the wife and child who pull the plough along with a donkey. It is a sad sight, and Nature herself sympathizes. The little vine holds on between the rocks. That sober and courageous tree, the chestnut, strikes root in pure flint; it seems to live on air and to thrive on fasting, just like its master.[5]

Yes, man makes the land. And it is the same even in richer regions. Let us never forget this if we wish to understand how much and how passionately he loves it. Remember how for centuries generation after generation have given it the sweat of the living and the bones of the dead, as well as their savings and sustenance. This land, where man has so long laid down the best part of man — his sap and his substance, his energy and his virtue — this land is a human land; he feels and he loves it like a human being.

He loves it; and to have it he consents to anything, even to losing sight of it. He emigrates, going far abroad if he must, and is

---

[5] I felt all this on a trip from Nîmes to Puy in May 1844. I was passing through the Ardèche, that barren country where man has created everything. Nature had made it frightful, but thanks to man it is now charming, at least in May. Even then it is always rather austere, though it possesses a moral charm that much more touching. There nobody will say that the lord has given the land to the serf, for there was none to give. Thus how my heart was wounded to see still standing on the heights those dreadful dark towers which so long levied tribute on people so poor, so deserving, and owing nothing to anyone but themselves. For me the real monuments were the humble houses of stone and flint in the valley where the peasants live. Those houses have a very somber, even sad, aspect with their poor little thirsty gardens; but the arcades which support these houses, the large flights of steps, and the spacious landings under the arcades give them much character. It was the time of harvest and the time for making silk. The poor country even seemed rich. Beneath the somber arcade of every house was a maiden winding skeins while tapping the pedal of the winder with her foot, and she smiled with her pretty white teeth as she spun her gold.

sustained by this thought and remembrance. What do you think that poor errand boy from Savoy is dreaming of as he sits on your doorstep? He dreams of the little field of rye and the poor pasture he will buy when he returns to the mountains. It will take ten years, but no matter! To have land in seven years the Alsatian sells his life and goes to die in Africa. To have a few feet of vine-yard the woman of Burgundy takes her breast from the mouth of her child, puts there instead a stranger's child, and weans her own too young. And the father says: "You will live or you will die, my son; but if you live, you will have land!"

Is this not a hard, almost blasphemous thing to say? Think carefully before you decide. "You will have land" really means, "You will not be a mercenary, hired for today and dismissed to-morrow; you will not be a serf for your daily bread; you will be free!" Free! Oh, what a glorious word, a word which contains all human dignity — for there can be no virtue without freedom.

Poets have often spoken of the attractions of water and its dangerous fascinations that have lured the foolhardy fisherman. More dangerous still, if possible, is the attraction of land. Large or small, it is strange and fascinating because its is always incom-plete, always in need of *rounding out*. Only a little is lacking — only this section, this corner, this ... Here is the temptation: to round out the holding, to buy, to borrow. "Hoard up your money if you can, but do not borrow," says Reason. But that is so slow. "Then borrow!" says Passion.

The landlord is a timid man and does not like lending. Al-though the peasant shows him a free and unencumbered holding, our laws are such that he fears a wife or a ward may spring from the soil with special rights which will destroy the value of his mortgage. Thus he dares not lend. Who will lend? The local usurer or the local notary, who holds all the peasant's legal docu-ments and knows his condition better than the peasant does him-self, who is certain he runs no risk, and who — out of friendship of course — will lend or find someone to lend at seven, eight, or even ten percent!

Will he accept this fatal money? Rarely does his wife believe he should. His forefathers, our old French peasants, certainly would not have done so. A humble and patient race, they relied only on personal savings, on a sou they took from their food, or on the small coin which was occasionally saved on return from market and which that very night went to rest with its comrades at the bottom of a pot buried in the cellar, as is still the custom today.

The peasant of today is no longer that man. He has higher aspirations; he has been a soldier. The great things he has done in this century have accustomed him to believe easily in the impossible. The acquisition of land is a battle for him; he goes to it as to the charge, and he will not retreat. It is his battle of Austerlitz: he will win it; of course there will be a desperate struggle, but he has seen plenty of these under the Old Commander.

If he fought with great courage when there was nothing to gain but bullets, do you think he will go meekly into his struggle with the land? Follow him: before daybreak you will find him at work with his children and his wife, who just gave birth and drags herself over the wet ground. At noon, when the rocks crack from the heat and the planter rests his black man, this voluntary black does not stop . . . Look at his food and compare it with that of the urban worker; the latter eats better every day than the peasant on Sunday.

This heroic man thought that by the power of his will he could do anything, even slow down time. But here it is quite different than in war, and time will not be slowed. It weighs heavily, and the struggle drags on between usury, which time increases, and man's strength, which it weakens. The land brings him two, usury demands eight. Thus usury fights against him like four men against one. Each year's interest carries away four years' labor.

Are you now surprised that this Frenchman, this merry singer of yesterday, no longer laughs? Are you surprised if, when you meet him on the land that devours him, you find him dark and gloomy? You pass and greet him warmly, but he will not look at you and pulls his hat down. Do not ask him the way; if he answers, he may very well send you in the wrong direction.

Thus the peasant isolates himself and becomes more and more bitter. His heart is too tight to be opened to any feeling of goodwill. He hates the rich, he hates his neighbor, he hates the world. As alone on his miserable property as on a desert island, he becomes a savage. His unsociability, born of his feeling of misery, makes that misery irremediable: it prevents him from getting along with the other peasants, who ought to be his natural helpmates and friends; he would sooner die than take one step toward them. On the other hand, the townsman has no desire to approach this fierce-looking man; he is almost afraid of him. "The peasant is mean, hateful, and capable of anything ... It is not safe to be his neighbor."

So the wealthier classes become more and more distant; they pass some time in the country, but they do not live there. Their home is in town. They leave the field wide open for the village banker — the notary — who becomes the secret confessor of all and who preys on all. "I will no longer have any dealings with these country folk," says the substantial landholder. "The notary will arrange everything; I will leave it to him. He will account to me, but he can give and divide the leases as he sees fit." And in many areas the notary becomes the only leaseholder, the only intermediary between the rich landowner and the tiller of the soil. This is a great misfortune for the peasant. To escape the bondage of these large landowners, who were generally willing to wait and be put off with words for a long time, the peasant has taken for his master this local man of law and money, who knows only when a bill is due.

As for the large landowner, his ill will toward the peasant is almost always excused and justified by the pious individuals who surround his wife. The materialism of the peasant is the common text for their laments: "Impious, material age!" they cry. "Those people love only the land! That is the sum of their religion! They worship only the manure of their fields!" Miserable Pharisees, if this land were merely land, they would not purchase it at such inflated prices; it would not drag them into this frenzy and delusion. You, who are supposedly spiritual and not at all materialistic, no one would ever catch you doing this; you calculate to the last franc what each field yields in corn or wine. Yet the peasant adds the riches of his imagination; this time he is the fanciful one, he is the poet. In this filthy, poor, and obscure land he distinctly sees the gold of freedom gleaming. Freedom, for the man who knows the unavoidable vices of the slave, is the possibility of virtue. A family that rises from day laborers to property owners respects itself, rises in its own esteem, and changes completely. It reaps from its land a harvest of virtues: the father's sobriety, the mother's thrift, the son's brave toil, the daughter's chastity, and all those other fruits of freedom. Are these, I ask you, material possessions? Can you pay too much for such treasures?[6]

Men of the past who call yourselves men of faith, if you are really such, admit that this was a faith, the faith that in our own days defended the freedom of the world against the world itself through the arms of this people. Please do not always go running on about chivalry. This was a chivalry, and the proudest one — the chivalry of our peasant soldiers. It is said that the Revolution suppressed the nobility, but in fact it did just the opposite: it made nobles of thirty-four million Frenchmen. When one of the nobility who emigrated during the Revolution was boasting of the glory of his ancestors, a peasant who had won on the field of battle replied, "I myself am an ancestor!"

This people is noble by reason of those great deeds. It is Europe that has remained plebeian. But we must take serious measures to defend this nobility, for it is in mortal danger. If the peasant becomes the serf of the usurer, he will not only be miserable but will lose heart. Do you think that the sad debtor, anxious and trembling, ever afraid to meet his creditor and always sulking about, preserves much courage? And what kind of race would rise in such conditions, terrorized by the Jews and whose emotions would come from arrest, seizure, and expropriation?

The laws must be changed, for the law must reflect this lofty moral and political necessity.

[6] The peasant is still not through. After the priests come the artists to slander him, particularly the neo-Catholic artists, that impotent race of weeping mourners for the Middle Ages who know only how to weep and copy. To weep for stones, that is, because for all they care, men may starve to death. They forget that the merit of these stones is to remind us of man and to bear his imprint. For such people the peasant is nothing but a demolisher; every old wall he tears down and every stone his plough turns aside is an incomparable ruin.

If you were Germans or Italians, I would say, "Consult the jurists; you have only to observe the rules of public equity." But you are France. You are not only a nation but also a principle, a great political principle that must be preserved at any cost. If that principle is to live, you must live. You live for the salvation of the world!

In the second rank in Europe by your industry, you are in the first by that vast and profound legion of peasant-soldier land-owners, the strongest foundation that any nation has had since the Roman Empire. Because of this, France impresses the world and is ready to come to its aid. The world regards this with fear and hope. What is it in reality? It is the army of the future — ready for the day the Barbarians appear.

One fact reassures our enemies. This great, silent France which underlies everything has been dominated for a long time by a petty, noisy, and bustling France. No government since the Revolution has concerned itself with the problem of agriculture. Industry, the younger sister of agriculture, has put the elder out of mind. The Restoration favored landed property, but only the great landed property. Even Napoleon, so dear to the peasant whom he understood so well, began by abolishing the income tax, which had fallen on the capitalist and had thus relieved the land. He swept away the mortgage laws that the Revolution had used to place money within the reach of agricultural laborers.

Today the capitalist and the industrialist rule by themselves. Agriculture accounts for more than half of our tax receipts but receives less than one percent of our expenditure! Economic theory treats agriculture almost as poorly as the government does; it is concerned mainly with industry and industrialists. Several economists speak of the *laborer* when they are speaking of the *worker,* thereby forgetting a mere twenty-four million agricultural laborers.

And yet, on the whole, the peasant is not only the most numerous part of the nation but also the strongest, the healthiest, and the best if we honestly weigh all the physical and moral aspects.[7]

---

[7] The urban population makes up one-fifth of the nation, but it accounts for two-fifths of the criminals.

With the decline of the beliefs that formerly sustained him, abandoned to his own resources between the old faith he has lost and the modern light he has not been given, he still has for support the national feeling, the great military tradition, and something of the honor of the soldier. He is self-centered and no doubt grasping in business; but who can blame him, when we know what he suffers? So take him as he is, with his faults, and compare him in his ordinary life with shopkeepers who cheat all day long and with the noisy crowd from the factory.

Man of the land and living completely in it, he seems formed in its image. Like it, he is greedy: the land never says "Enough!" He is as stubborn as the land is firm and demanding; he is patient like it and equally indestructible. Everything passes away, but he endures. Would you call this having faults? Ah! if he had not had them, France would have ceased to exist long ago.

Do you want to judge our peasants? Then look at them on their return from military service! You see these fearsome soldiers — the best in the world, scarcely home from Africa and the war of lions — set quietly to work between their mother and sister, resume their father's life of thrift and self-denial, and now wage war only against themselves. You watch them seeking by the most honorable means and without violence or complaint to accomplish the holy work of France: the marriage of man and the land.

All France would help those who are carrying on this work if she had a true sense of her mission. By what fatality must she stop short today in this task? If present conditions continue, the peasant will cease to buy and will be forced to sell, as in the middle of the seventeenth century, and will become once more a wage laborer.[8] Two hundred years lost! That would be the downfall not of a class but of the fatherland.

Each year the peasants pay more than 500 million francs to the state and a billion to the usurers! Is that all? No, the indirect tax is perhaps as heavy; that is, the tax which industry places on

[8] Hippolyte Passy assures us that from 1815 to 1835, the number of landowners, compared with the rest of the population, has diminished two and a half percent.

the peasants through tariffs, and which keeps out foreign goods and also limits the export of our agricultural products.

These extremely hard-working men are the worst fed. They eat no meat, for our cattle breeders (who are really industrialists) prevent the agriculturalist from eating any, *in the interest of agriculture*.[9] The poorest workman eats white bread, but he who grows the wheat eats only black. They make the wine, and the townsman drinks it. The whole world drinks joy from the cup of France, with the exception of the French vine-grower.[10]

The industry of our towns has recently received considerable aid, the burden of which falls once again upon the land — at the very moment when small rural industry and the humble work of the spinster are being killed off by the flax machine.

The peasant, who in this way is losing his domestic industries one by one (flax today, perhaps silk tomorrow), has great difficulty holding onto his land. It slips away from him and carries with it all the fruits of his years of labor, saving, and sacrifice. His life itself is expropriated. If anything is left, speculators relieve him of it. He listens with the credulity born of despair to all the fables they spin: Algiers produces sugar and coffee; every

[9] Our cattle breeders also sell him his only cow and his working oxen at very high prices. The breeders defend themselves by saying that there are no farmers without manure, and no manure without cattle. They are right, but they still act against themselves. Changing nothing and improving nothing (except for luxury products and the triumphs of vanity), and maintaining high prices for inferior articles, they prevent all the poorer areas of the country from buying the small cattle that suit them and thereby from obtaining the necessary manure. Thus man and the land are unable to replenish their strength, and they perish from exhaustion.

[10] The calculation of Paul Louis Courier comes to mind here. He calculated that on the average an acre of vineyard returned 150 francs to the vine grower and 1,300 francs to the treasury. This was an exaggeration. But we must compensate for the fact that this acre is now much more indebted than in 1820. Yet there is no occupation which demands more of the laborer or in which he more deserves his wages. Pass through Burgundy in the spring or the autumn; for forty miles you travel over country that is dug up, turned over, planted, and replanted with vine props two times a year. What labor! And all in order that this produce, which has cost so much, may be adulterated and dishonored at Bercy and Rouen. That infamous art calumniates nature and this excellent beverage: the wine is as badly treated as the vine grower.

man in America earns ten francs a day; one must cross the sea, but so what? The Alsatian believes them when he is told that the ocean is scarcely broader than the Rhine.[11]

Before he falls so low and quits France, every resource will be tried. The son will sell himself as a recruit. The daughter will become a servant. The little child will enter the nearest factory. The wife will go as a wet nurse to the bourgeois's house, or take to her own home the infant of a petty shopkeeper or even a worker.[12]

---

[11] This is what an Alsatian said to a friend of mine (September 1845). Our Alsatians who emigrate thus sell the little they have as they leave; the Jew is there ready to buy. The Germans try to carry their goods away with them; they travel in wagons, like the barbarians who emigrated into the Roman Empire. I remember how once in Swabia on a very hot, dusty day I met one of these emigrating wagons, full of chests, furniture, and effects all heaped together. A small wagon attached behind the large one carried a two-year-old child with a sweet and pretty face. The child went along crying, under the care of a little sister who walked beside but was not able to calm it. After some women had blamed the parents for leaving their infant behind, the father sent his wife back to get it. Both those people seemed dejected, almost senseless, and prematurely dead, through misery perhaps, or regret. Would they ever be able to reach their destination? It was hardly likely. And could that infant's frail carriage last through so long a journey? I dared not ask myself. Only one member of that family seemed alive and able to survive. It was a boy about fourteen, who at that very moment was putting on the brake for going downhill. That boy with black hair, and a serious but impassioned countenance, seemed full of moral strength and ardor; at least I thought so. He already felt himself the head of a family, their provider, and charged with their safety. The real mother was the sister, who took the part of one. The infant, weeping in his cradle, also had his part and not the least important one: he was the unity of the family, the bond between the brother and sister, and their common foster child. In his little wicker wagon he was transporting the domestic hearth and the fatherland: wherever he lived, if he lived, Swabia would still be found, even in an unknown world. Alas! How much will these children have to do and suffer! In looking at the eldest and his beautiful, serious countenance, I blessed him from the bottom of my heart, and gave him as much as was in my power.

[12] No painter of manners, novelist, political economist, or socialist has deigned to speak about the wet nurse, as far as I know. However, there is a sad story that is not sufficiently known! People do not know how much these poor women are exploited and abused, first by the vehicles which transport them (often barely out of their confinement), and afterward by the employment offices which place them. Taken as nurses on

The worker who has a job is the object of the peasant's envy. The man who calls the manufacturer a bourgeois is himself a bourgeois for the man of the country. The latter sees him on Sunday promenading like a gentleman. Attached to the land, the peasant believes that the man who carries his trade with him, and who works without worrying about the weather or even the cold and snow, is as free as a bird. He does not know and does not wish to see the bondage of the man in industry. He assumes what the worker's life is like from the young traveling artisan he meets on the roads making his tour of France: the artisan who gains enough for his food and lodging at every stop, and who then picks up his long walking-stick and knapsack again and goes toward the next town singing his songs.

the spot, they must send their own child away, and consequently it often dies. They have no contract with the family that hires them, and they may be dismissed at the first caprice of the mother or doctor. If the change of air and place should dry up their milk, they are discharged without any compensation. If they stay there, they pick up the habits of the easy life, and they suffer enormously when they are forced to return to their life of poverty. A good number become servants in order to stay in the town. They never rejoin their husbands, and the family is broken.

CHAPTER II

᪐

The Bondage of the Factory Worker

"How sparkling the city is! And how sad and poor the country is!" That is what you hear the peasants say when they come to town on holidays. They do not know that if the country is *poor,* the city with all its brilliance is perhaps more *miserable.* Few people even bother to make this distinction.[1]

On Sunday you may watch two crowds moving in opposite directions through the city gates: the worker toward the country, the peasant toward the town. Between these two movements, which appear so similar, there is a great difference. The peasant is not on a mere outing; he admires everything in the town, wants everything, and would stay there if he could.

Let him look closely first. Once a man leaves the country, he seldom returns. Those who come as servants and share in most of their master's pleasures do not worry about returning to their life of abstinence. Should those who become factory workers wish to return to the country, they could not. They are quickly unnerved in the city and become unfit for rough labor or the sudden variations of hot and cold: the open air would kill them.

But if the city attracts so strongly, it seems that it should not be blamed too much for this; the city also repels the peasant whenever he comes, with its special taxes and very high prices for simple necessities. Besieged by these crowds, it tries in this way to drive off its assailants. But nothing stops them; no terms are too

---

[1] This distinction was clearly made by the esteemed and now regretted Mr. Buret in his work *De la misère* (1840). In this work he accepted perhaps too uncritically the exaggerations of the English parliamentary inquiries.

hard. They will come for whatever is available: as servants, workers, machine watchers, and machines themselves. One thinks of those peoples of ancient Italy who in their frantic desire to enter Rome sold themselves as slaves in order to become freedmen and citizens at a later date.

The peasant does not let himself be frightened by the complaints of the worker, or by the terrible pictures the worker draws of his situation. He who earns one or two francs a day does not understand how you can be miserable with wages of three, four, or five francs. "But what of the fluctuations in work and unemployment?" Well, what of it? He saved out of his small earnings; how much more easily will he save now for a rainy day out of such a large salary.

Even if better wages are not considered, life is easier in town. There people generally work under cover; this alone — having a roof over one's head — seems a great improvement. Without speaking of the heat, the cold of our climate is a punishment even for those who seem the most accustomed to it. For my part, I have spent many winters without a fire without being less sensitive to the cold. When the frost passed, I felt a happiness to which few enjoyments are comparable. Spring was a delight. The changes of seasons, of so little interest to the rich, form the base of the poor man's life and are his real events.

By moving to town the peasant also gains as far as food is concerned; if not more wholesome, it is at least more tasty. It is not uncommon to see him grow fat in his first months of city life. In return for this his complexion changes, and not for the better. He has lost a most vital and even nourishing something in his migration, something which alone explains how rural laborers remain strong even on an inadequate diet. He has lost that pure free air, which is constantly refreshed and renewed by the scent of growing things. I do not believe that the air in town is as unhealthy as people say it is; but it is that bad in the miserable dwellings where each night many poor workmen are crowded together among prostitutes and thieves.

The peasant never anticipated this. Nor did he take into account that in earning more money in the city, he was losing his treasure — his sobriety, his thrift, his greed if we must call a spade a spade. It is easy to save while far from temptations to spend, when saving is the only available pleasure. But how difficult it is, and what resolution and self-control it takes, to hold your money and to keep your pocket buttoned when everything entices you to spend! And remember that the savings bank holds an invisible wealth and does not begin to give those emotions the peasant feels in burying and digging up his treasure with so much pleasure, mystery, and fear. Still less has it the charm of a handsome piece of land which he can always see, which he constantly turns over, and which he is always seeking to enlarge.

The worker has need of great virtue in order to save. If he is a simple, good-natured fellow who goes along with the crowd, everything goes quickly in a thousand different ways — cabarets, cafés, and so on. If he is hard-working and honest, he marries at some happy, prosperous moment when work is plentiful: at first the wife earns a little, but when she has children, nothing; the husband who was well off when he was single does not know how to meet his fixed and overwhelming everyday expenses.

In the past, in addition to the tolls at the town gates, there was another obstacle which barred the peasant from the towns and prevented him from becoming a worker. This barrier was the difficulty of entering into any trade, due to the length of apprenticeship and the spirit of exclusiveness in guilds and corporations. Families in the craft industries took few apprentices, and those, for the most part, were their own children, whom they exchanged among themselves. But now new occupations have been created which require scarcely any apprenticeship and welcome any man. The real worker in these trades is the machine, and the man does not need much strength or skill; he is there only to watch and aid that iron workman.

This unfortunate class of people enslaved to machinery comprises four hundred thousand souls, or a little more.[2] This is

[2] It is true that writers who give a higher figure include workers who are occupied in factories which employ machinery but are not enslaved to machines. These men are and always will be an exception. As for the extension of *machinism* (to designate this system by a word), is it to be feared? Will machinery invade everything? Will France become another

about one-fifteenth of our workmen. All those who have no skill come and offer themselves at the factories to serve machines. The more they come, the lower are their wages, and the more miserable they grow. On the other hand, goods produced cheaply in this way fall within reach of the poor, so that the misery of the machine-worker of the factory diminishes somewhat the misery of the artisan and peasant, who are probably seventy times more numerous.

This is what we saw in 1842. The cotton mills were at the last gasp, choking to death. The warehouses were stuffed, and there were no sales. The terrified manufacturer dared neither work nor stop working with those devouring machines. Yet usury is not laid off, so he worked half-time, and the glut grew worse.

England in this respect? To these grave questions I unhesitatingly answer no. We must not anticipate the extension of this system on the basis of the years of the great European war, when it was encouraged by monstrous gains unknown to ordinary trade. Eminently suited to lower the price of objects that are to descend to all classes, machinism has met an immense demand — that of the lower classes. In a time of rapid ascension, the lower classes wanted immediately to have comfortable things and even make a brilliant appearance; but they remained satisfied with a brilliance that was mediocre, even vulgar, and as we say, completely mass produced. For although manufacturers have risen through admirable efforts to very fine and unexpected results, their products, manufactured in great quantity by uniform means, are immediately stamped with a monotonous character. The progress of taste sometimes makes this monotony quite boring. Many an irregular handmade work comes to charm the eye and mind more than those faultless manufactured masterpieces, whose absence of life sadly reminds us of the metal that was their father and the steam that was their mother.

We should also remember that no man now wishes to belong to *such and such a class,* but to be *such and such a man* — he wants to be himself. Consequently he will care less for the products fabricated *by classes* without any individuality that speaks to his own. The world is advancing in this direction; each person seeks, in better understanding the general, to characterize his own *individuality* as well. It is very likely that, all things being equal, people will prefer in place of uniform products of machinery those constantly varied products which bear the imprint of human personality, and which spring from a man and change like man himself. There lies the real future of industrial France, much more than in mass production, where she remains inferior. In any event, the two systems of industry help each other. The more cheaply basic needs are satisfied by machinery, the more will taste rise above the products of machinism and seek the products of an entirely personal art.

Prices fell, but in vain; they went on falling until cotton cloth stood as six sous. Then something completely unexpected occurred. The words *six sous* aroused the people. Millions of purchasers — poor people who never bought anything — began to stir. Then we saw what an immense and powerful consumer the people is when it is engaged. The warehouses were emptied in a moment. The machines began to work furiously again, and chimneys began to smoke. That was a revolution in France, little noted but a great revolution nonetheless. It was a revolution in cleanliness and embellishment of the homes of the poor; underwear, bedding, table linen, and window curtains were now used by whole classes who had not used them since the beginning of the world.

The point should be fairly clear without further examples. Machine production, which seems an entirely aristocratic power because of the centralization of capital it requires, is actually a very powerful force for democratic progress because of the low cost and general use of its products. It brings within the reach of the poor a world of useful objects, even luxurious and artistic objects, which they could never reach before. Wool, thank God, has descended to the people everywhere and warms them; silk is beginning to adorn them. But the great and fundamental revolution has been in cotton prints.* It has required the combined efforts of science and art to force rebellious and ungrateful cotton fabrics to undergo every day so many brilliant transformations and to spread them everywhere within the reach of the poor. Every woman used to wear a blue or black dress that she kept for ten years without washing, for fear it might tear to pieces. But now her husband, a poor worker, covers her with a robe of flowers for the price of a day's labor. All the women of the people who display an iris of a thousand colors on our promenades were formerly in mourning.

* The cotton industry, first revolutionized in Great Britain in the classic Industrial Revolution, was indeed developing rapidly in this period. French industry as a whole was following a similar if less striking evolution. Recent quantitative studies suggest the rather surprising conclusion that total French industrial production was increasing as rapidly in the 1830s and 1840s as in any similar period between 1700 and 1945.

These changes, thought to have no importance, have immense significance. They are not simple material improvements, but progress for the people in those external appearances which men use to judge one another. It is, so to speak, *visible equality*. In this way the people rise to new ideas which they did not reach before; fashion and taste are an initiation into art for them. In addition, and still more important, better dress changes a man; he wants to be worthy of it, and he tries to align his moral behavior with it.

It requires no less than this progress and obvious advance of the masses to make us accept the hard condition with which we must purchase it: having in the midst of a population of men a miserable, stunted tribe of machine-men who live but half a life; who produce marvelous things, but who do not reproduce themselves; who beget only for death; and who perpetuate themselves only by incessantly absorbing other groups which they swallow up forever.

To have created creators in machines, powerful workmen who invariably pursue the work set before them, is certainly a great temptation for pride. But what humiliation to see man fallen so low before the machine! The head turns and the heart tightens when for the first time we visit those fairy halls where polished iron and dazzling copper seem to move and think by themselves, while pale and feeble man is only the humble servant of those steel giants. "Look," a manufacturer said to me, "look at that ingenious and powerful machine take filthy rags, pass them through the most complicated transformation without ever making a mistake, and turn them into fabric as fine as the most beautiful silk of Verona!" I admired in sadness. It was impossible for me not to see at the same time the pitiful faces of those men, those faded young girls, and those deformed or swollen children.

Many sensitive people silence their compassion, in order not to suffer from it, by quickly concluding that this population appears so wretched only because it is bad, tainted, and inherently corrupt. They judge it generally at the moment when it is the most shocking to see, as it appears leaving the factory after the final bell suddenly throws it into the street. This exit is always noisy.

The men speak very loudly, and you would think they were quarreling; the girls scream to one another with shrill and hoarse voices; the children fight, throw rocks, and are violent in their behavior. It is not a pretty sight: the passerby turns away; the lady is afraid, believes a riot is starting, and takes another street.

We must not turn away. We must enter the factory while it is working, and then we will understand how the silence and captivity during long hours demand noise, cries, and movement as they leave if they are to reestablish their vital equilibrium. That is especially true for the great spinning and weaving mills — true hells of boredom. *Ever, ever, ever,* is the unvarying word thundering in your ears from the automatic equipment which shakes even the floor. One can never get used to it. At the end of twenty years it is like the first day: the boredom, the shock, and the nausea are the same. Does the heart beat in that crowd? Very little, for it is as if its action were suspended; during those long hours it seems that another heart, common to all, has taken its place — a metallic heart, indifferent and without pity — and that this great deafening, rumbling noise is only its regular beating.

The solitary task of the handloom weaver was far less painful. Why? Because he could dream. The machinery will permit no daydreams, no absence of mind. Would you for a moment lessen the tempo in order to quicken it later on? You cannot. Hardly is the indefatigable fly frame with its hundred spindles thrown back before it returns to you. The handloom weaver works quickly or slowly even as he breathes quickly or slowly; he acts as he lives, and the work fits the man. In the factory the man must fit the work; the being of flesh and blood, whose energy varies with the hours of the day, must adapt to the unchanging pattern of this thing of steel.

It usually happens that with manual labor which follows our initiative, our innermost thought becomes identified with the work and puts it in its proper place, and the inert instrument we move is far from being an obstacle to intellectual activity but actually becomes its aid and companion. The mystic weavers of the Middle Ages were famous under the name of *Lollards* because while they worked they actually *lulled,* that is, sang and hummed in low tones some nursery rhyme. The rhythm of the shuttle, pushed forth and pulled back at equal intervals, patterned itself to the rhythm of the heart, and by evening it often happened that in addition to the cloth, a hymn or a ballad had been woven.

What a change, then, for him who is forced to quit domestic work and enter the factory! To quit his own poor home, leaving the worm-eaten furniture of the family with so many old cherished objects, is hard, but it is still harder to give up the free possession of his soul. Those vast factory halls, so white, so new, and flooded with light, hurt the eye accustomed to the shadows of a dark dwelling. There is no obscurity into which the mind may plunge there, no dark corner where the imagination may build its dream, no illusion possible in such a glare of light constantly and cruelly warning him of reality.

We should not be surprised if our handloom weavers of Rouen and our French handloom weavers of London have resisted the factory with all their courage and stoic patience, preferring to go hungry and die, but to die at home. We have seen them struggling for a long time with the weak arm of man, and an arm emaciated by hunger, against the brilliant, pitiless productivity of those terrible steam-driven Briareuses of industry that work day and night with a thousand arms at once. With every improvement of the machine, the unfortunate human rival added to his labor and subtracted from his food. Our colony of weavers in London has thus gradually died out. Poor people! so honest, so resigned, and so innocent in their lives. They were never tempted by poverty and hunger into crime! In their miserable Spitalfield they skillfully cultivated their flowers, and the Londoner liked to visit them.

I spoke just now of the Flemish weavers of the Middle Ages, the so-called Lollards and Beghards. The Church, which often persecuted them as heretics, reproached these dreamers with but one thing, *love:* an exalted and refined love for the invisible lover God, and sometimes also vulgar love in the forms it assumes in the crowded centers of industry. Yet even the vulgar was mystic as well, for it taught as its doctrine a community which was more than fraternal and which was to establish a sensual paradise here on earth.

This tendency toward sensuality remains the same among the workers of today, though they lack the poetic dreaming to soar above it. An English puritan, who has recently drawn a delightful picture of the happiness the factory worker enjoys, does confess that *the flesh grows very warm there* and rebels. This is not due simply to the indiscriminate mingling of the sexes, to the heat, and so on. There is a moral cause. It is precisely because the factory is a world of iron, where man feels everywhere only the hardness and the icy chill of metal, that he draws so much the closer to woman in his moments of liberty. The factory is the reign of fate and necessity. The only living thing is the severity of the foreman, who punishes often and never rewards. There a man feels so little a man that as soon as he leaves the factory, he must greedily seek the most intense excitement for the human senses, one which concentrates the sentiment of boundless liberty in the brief moment of a beautiful dream. This excitement is intoxication, especially the intoxication of love.

Unfortunately the boredom and monotony these captives feel the need to escape make them incapable of faithfulness and fond of change in that free part of their life. Love always changing its object is no longer love: it is only debauchery. The remedy is worse than the disease; unnerved by the slavery of work, they become still more so by the abuse of liberty.

Physical weakness and mental impotence. The feeling of impotence is one of the great miseries of this condition. This man, who is so weak in face of the machine and who must follow its every motion, is dependent on the factory owner, and even more on the thousand unknown forces which may suddenly create unemployment and take away his bread. The old handloom weavers, who were not the serfs of machinery like these workers, humbly admitted this impotence and even taught it as their theology: "God can do all, man nothing." The true name of this class is the one Italy first gave in the Middle Ages: *the Humble.*[3]

[3] On several occasions I have sketched the history of industry in my lectures and books. (See especially my *History of France,* vol. V.) In

Our workers do not resign themselves so easily. Sprung from warlike races, they are constantly struggling to rise again: they wish to remain men. They seek as much as possible a false energy in wine. Does it take much to get drunk? Take a look at the cabaret itself if you can get over your disgust. You will see that a man in an ordinary state, and drinking unadulterated wine, could drink much more without any problem. But for the man who drinks wine every day, who comes there unnerved and fainting from the atmosphere of the factory and drinks under the name of wine a vile alcoholic mixture, drunkenness is inevitable.

Extreme physical dependence, the claims of simple animal instinct which lead once more to dependence, and mental impotence and the void of the mind — these are the real causes of their vices. Too many people notice only outward causes, as, for example, the fact that the sexes are thrown together in a tight crowd — as if human nature is so evil that it becomes entirely corrupt when people come together. Our philanthropists have this fine idea, so they work to isolate men and wall them up if they can; they think they can preserve or cure man only by building him tombs.

That crowd is not evil in itself. Its disorders spring in large measure from its condition, from its subjection to the mechanical order which is itself a disorder and a death for living bodies and which thereby provokes a violent return to life in the few moments of freedom. If fatality ever existed, it is surely this. How heavily, how almost invincibly, does this fate weigh upon the women and children! The woman is pitied less, but perhaps she

order to understand it, however, it would be necessary to go further back, and not commence with the time of those great and powerful corporations which dominated the medieval city. We must first look at the workman, who was of humble origin and despised from the beginning. In those days the original inhabitant of the town, the proprietor of the suburb, and even the tradesman, who had his hall, church bell, and courts, were unanimous in despising the workman, the *blue-nail,* as they called him. Then the burgher barely let him live outside the town in the shadow of the walls between two enclosures. Then it was forbidden to do him justice if he could not pay taxes; and they fixed, in a fantastically arbitrary manner, the prices at which he might sell his goods — one for the rich, one for the poor, and so on.

should be pitied more. She is in double bondage: she is a slave to work, but she earns so little with her hands that the poor creature must also earn with her youth and the pleasure she gives. When old, what becomes of her? Nature has ordained that woman cannot live unless she leans on man for support.

At the height of the great duel between England and France, when the English manufacturers went to Prime Minister Pitt and told him that the high wages of the workers made it impossible for them to pay their taxes, he pronounced a fearful sentence: "Take the children!" That sentence weighs heavily upon England, like a curse. Since that time the race has declined. This people, previously so athletic, is unnerved and weakened. What has become of that rosy hue and bloom which was so admirable in the English youth? Withered and wasted. They believed Mr. Pitt — *they took the children.*

Let us profit from this lesson. The future is at stake: the law ought to have more foresight than the father; in the absence of his mother, the child ought to find a mother in his native land. She will open the school for him as a place of refuge, as a shelter and a sanctuary against the factory.

The mental void, the absence of every intellectual interest, is, as we have said, one of the principal causes of the debasement of the factory worker. His is a work which requires neither strength nor skill and never asks for thought! Nothing, nothing, and always nothing! No moral force could withstand that! The school ought to give to the young mind what such dull work never will —some lofty, generous idea that may return and sustain it in those long blank days and long boring hours.

In the present state of things the schools are organized to create boredom, and they only add fatigue to fatigue. Night schools are generally a farce. Imagine the poor little children who left home before daylight and are now returning, tired and sweaty, to their homes two or three miles from Mulhouse, or those with lantern in hand who are slopping and stumbling through the night along the muddy lanes of Déville; and now call on them to begin their studies and go to school!

Whatever the miseries of the peasant may be, when they are

compared with those now under consideration there is a terrible difference which does not have merely an accidental influence on the individual, but generally a profound impact on the race itself. It may be summed up in a word: in the country the child is happy.

Almost naked, barefoot, with a morsel of brown bread, he tends a cow or the geese, lives in the air, and plays. The agricultural tasks given gradually serve only to strengthen him. The precious years during which man builds his body and his strength for all his life he thus spends in great freedom and the comfort of the home. Go now, you are strong; whatever you do or suffer, you can cope with life.

At a later period the peasant will be miserable, and perhaps dependent; but he has at the outset gained some twelve to fifteen years of freedom. This alone makes an immense difference in his total happiness.

The factory worker carries all his life a heavy burden — the burden of his childhood that weakened him early and very often corrupted him. He is inferior to the peasant in physical strength, and inferior in the regularity of his morals. But for all that, the factory worker has something which redeems him: he is more sociable and more gentle. The most miserable among them, in their most dire necessity, have abstained from every act of violence; they have waited with patient resignation though dying of hunger.

The author of the best inquiry of the day, a steady and cool observer who will not be suspected of any overexcitement, gives this important testimony in favor of this class of men: "I have found among our factory workers but one virtue which they possess to a higher degree than the happier classes. *They have a natural disposition to aid and assist each other in every kind of difficulty.*"[4]

---

[4] Villermé, *Tableau de l'état physique et moral des ouvriers des manufactures de coton* (1840). We have seen in November 1839, when unemployment was widespread and the manufacturers could keep only the most senior workers, how these workers demanded that the work and wages be shared so that nobody would be dismissed. Many of them who

I do not know whether this is the only superiority they possess, but how great it is! That they should be the least fortunate, and yet the most charitable! That they should preserve themselves from that hardheartedness so natural to misery! That in this outward bondage they still preserve a heart free from hatred — *that they love more!* Ah! that is a noble triumph and one that doubtless exalts the man whom we believed so degraded in the sight of God!

---

are reproached with concubinage would marry if they had the necessary money and papers. As for the assertion of those who pretend that factory workers earn enough if they make wise use of their wages, let us here offer the judicious judgment of Villermé. He concludes that for them to earn enough, four conditions are necessary: they must be well; they must always be employed; each family must have two children at most; and they must be free from every vice. Here are four conditions that are seldom found. [Translator's note: Villermé's study is the classic treatment of the condition of the French factory worker in the early stages of industrialization. Michelet made full and excellent use of it, as he did of Agricol Perdiguier's useful *Livre du compagnonnage* in his study of the artisan.]

CHAPTER III

~

The Bondage of the Artisan Worker

The child who leaves the factory and the service of the machine to be apprenticed to a master certainly rises in the industrial scale; more is required of his hands and of his mind. His life will no longer be the accessory to a lifeless movement; he will act himself and be truly a workman.

Here is greater intelligence, but also greater suffering! The machine was regulated, and the master is not.[1] It was impassive, without caprice, anger, or brutality. Moreover it left the child free at certain hours; at night, at least, he might rest. But the apprentice of the craftsman or small manufacturer belongs to his master day and night: his work is limited only by the orders coming in. In addition to his work, he has all the miseries of the servant, and must endure not only the master's whims but all those of the family. All the vexations of the husband and wife are likely to fall upon his shoulders. A bankruptcy occurs, and the apprentice is beaten; the master comes home drunk, and the apprentice is beaten; there is little work, there is much work ... he is beaten all the same.

These are the ancient working conditions of the handicraft industry, which was nothing but bondage. In the contract of apprenticeship the master becomes a father, but only to apply the words of Solomon, "Spare not the rod." As early as the thirteenth century, public authority intervened to moderate this paternity.

[1] Léon Faucher has pointed out this difference very well. Among his works, see *Études sur l'Angleterre*, where this excellent economist proves himself a great writer and reveals that in addition to the hell of the factories, there is another that was not suspected — the hell of apprenticeship.

The master was not the apprentice's only source of severity and violence; in trades where there was a hierarchy, the blows fell harder as the apprentice moved higher. Certain terms of the journeyman guilds still testify to this severity. The *compagnon,* or journeyman, is the *wolf;* he is tormented by the *ape,* that is, the master who hunts the *fox,* the young candidate for journeyman, who pays it back with interest to the *rabbit,* the poor apprentice.

The apprentice used to pay for the privilege of being ill treated and beaten for ten years; he paid at every step they let him take in his struggle toward full membership. At length, when he had worn out the rope as apprentice and the walking stick as journeyman, he was judged by a corporation which was not interested in increasing its members and which might send him back, rejected without appeal.

Today the gates are open. Apprenticeship is shorter if not easier. Apprentices are taken all too readily. The miserable little profit made upon them (which goes to the master, the father, or the guild itself) is a continual temptation to admit new ones and thus create more workmen than needed.

The artisan of former times, who was admitted with difficulty into a small group enjoying a sort of monopoly, suffered none of the cares of our workers today. He earned much less, but he was seldom without work.[2] A gay and active companion, he was a great traveler. He stopped wherever he found work. His master

---

[2] We have already spoken of the wages of factory workers. If we were to study wages in general, we would find that this much debated question comes to this: *Wages have risen,* some say, and they are right, because they start from 1789 or even earlier. *Wages have not risen,* say others, and they are also right, because they start from 1824. Since that time, factory workers earn less, and the other workers have only an illusory increase. The value of money has changed, and the man who earns what he did then really receives one-third less. He who earned and continues to earn three francs receives little more than the value of two francs. Also remember that necessities have grown more numerous along with ideas, so a man suffers in not having a thousand things that he was indifferent to before. True, wages are very high in France in comparison to Switzerland and Germany, but here the various needs of life are much more keenly felt. The average wage in Paris, stated by both L. Faucher and L. Blanc as three francs fifty per day, is sufficient for a single man,

generally lodged him, and sometimes fed him with wholesome light food. In the evening after he had eaten his dry bread, he went up to his garret under the tiles and slept contented.

How many changes have taken place in his condition, for both good and bad! There is material improvement, but there is also an ever-changing uneasy condition and the dark uncertainty of the future — a thousand new elements of mental suffering! These changes may be summed up in a word: *He has become a man.*

To be a man, in the true sense, is first and above all to have a wife. The workman, generally single in former times, is often married today. And married or not, he generally finds a woman in his house when he returns. A home, a fireside, a wife — ah, life has been transformed!

A wife, a family, and children soon enough! Expense! And what if there is no work? Misery!

It is very touching to see all these hard-working men hurrying homeward in the evening with long strides. See this man after his long day's labor, often two miles from home after a miserable breakfast and a lonely dinner, who has been standing for fifteen hours — see how those legs move home. He flies to his nest! To be a man one hour a day is certainly not asking too much.

And what a sacred sight! He is carrying the bread home, and once there he rests himself. He is no longer anything, but gives himself up to his wife like a child. Nourished by him, she now nourishes and warms him. They both care for the child, who does nothing, who is free, and who is their master. That the last should be first — here indeed is the city of God!

but inadequate for the father of a family. I will give here the average wages which several authors have tried to fix for France since the time of Louis XIV; but I do not know whether it is possible to establish an index from such different elements.

1698 (Vauban)	1.20	francs
1733 (Saint-Pierre)	1.60	”
1788 (Arthur Young)	1.90	”
1819 (Chaptal)	2.50	”
1832 (Morogue)	3.00	”
1840 (Villermé)	4.00	”

This is for labor in towns. Wages have increased very little in rural areas.

The rich man never tastes this great pleasure, this supreme blessing of man, which is to feed his family every day with the best of his life — his work. The poor man alone is a father; every day he creates anew, and reproduces his family.

This grand mystery is better understood by the wife than by all the wise men of the world. She is happy in owing everything to the man. This alone gives a unique charm to the poor household. Nothing is foreign or unimportant there; everything bears the stamp of a loving hand and the seal of the heart. The man often knows little of the sacrifices she makes in order that on his return he may find his dwelling modestly yet gracefully decorated. Great is the wife's desire for furniture, clothes, and linen.

This last article is new; the *linen closet,* the pride of the countrywoman, was unknown to the wife of the town workman before the revolution in industry. Cleanliness, purity, modesty — those feminine graces have made the home an enchanted place: the bed has been surrounded with curtains; the child's cradle, dazzling with whiteness, has become a paradise; and all was cut out and sewed in a few evenings ... Finally she puts a flower in the window ... What a surprise! The returning husband no longer knows his own home!

This taste for flowers, which has spread (there are now several markets for them here in Paris), and these small expenses to decorate the home, are they not deplorable when a man never knows whether he will be working the next day? No, do not call this *expenditure,* but rather *economy.* It is a great one if these innocent attractions of the wife make the house charming to the husband and can keep him there. Let us decorate, I beg of you, both the house and the wife! A few yards of printed cotton make her another woman, and she becomes young and winsome again. "Oh, please stay here with me." It is Saturday night; she gently puts her arms around his neck, and saves for her children the bread he was about to squander.[3]

Sunday comes and the wife has conquered. The husband,

[3] Bread! The landlord! These two thoughts are always in the wife's mind. What skill, virtue, and strength of mind are needed to save up the rent! Who will ever know and appreciate this achievement?

shaved and changed, allows her to help him into a good warm coat. That is soon done. But what is a long serious business is the child. They want him all dressed up for this day. Then they set out; the child walks on before under his mother's eye; let him take special care not to spoil her masterpiece, his Sunday best.

Look at these people carefully and rest assured that no matter how high you go you will never find anything morally superior. This woman is virtue itself, with the particular charm of unaffected reason and tact that enable her to govern strength without being aware of it. This man is the strong, the patient, and the courageous, who bears for society the heaviest load of human life. A true *companion of duty* (according to the noble title of the craft guild!), he has stood strong and firm like a soldier at his post. The more dangerous his trade, the more sure is his moral conduct. A famous architect, who rose from the people and knew them well, once told a friend of mine, "The most honest men I have known were of this class. They know as they leave in the morning that they may not return in the evening, and they are always ready to stand before God."

Such a trade, no matter how noble it may be, is not what a mother wants for her son. Her son has great promise; he will go far. The priests and teaching fathers speak highly of him and caress him a great deal. His drawings and holiday decorations already adorn the school walls and are hung between Napoleon and the Sacred Heart. He will certainly be sent to the free school to study drawing and design. The father asks why. His mother replies that drawing will always be useful to him in his trade — a reply with a double meaning, we must confess, under which she hides a far different ambition. Why should this child, so fine and gifted, not be a painter or a sculptor as well as anyone else? She steals a few sous from her purse for crayons and that very expensive paper. Her son will soon show his works and carry off all the prizes. The grand name of Rome is already thundering in her dreams!

Thus the mother's ambition all too often succeeds in making a poor, miserable artist out of someone who would have earned

a better living as a workman. The arts are scarcely remunera-
tive. Even in peacetime all those in easy circumstances, especially
women, become artists themselves instead of purchasing works of
art. Let a war or a revolution come and art is absolute starvation.

Often the aspiring young artist, full of ardor and inspiration, is
stopped short. His father dies and he must help his family, so he
becomes a worker. Great is his mother's grief and great are her
lamentations, and they take the heart out of the young man.

All his life he will curse his fate: he will work here, but his
soul will be elsewhere. What a cruel prospect ... And yet nothing
will stop him. Do not come to give him advice; you would not
be welcome. It is too late; he must overcome every obstacle. You
will always see him reading and meditating; he reads at mealtime,
in the evening, and far into the night. On Sunday he stays shut
up in his room lost in thought. It is hard to imagine how great is
the hunger for reading for those in that state of mind. I once
knew a textile worker, whose work was the most irreconcilable of
all with study amid the whirl and vibrations of twenty power
looms, who put a book at the corner of his loom and read a line
each time the carriage receded and left him a second.

How long the day is when it passes thus! How tormenting are
the last hours! For him who waits for the bell and curses its slowness, the odious workroom seems quite fantastic at the end of day;
the demons of impatience are cruelly playing in the gathering
shadows. "O liberty! O light! Will you leave me here forever?"

I pity his family when he comes home, if he has one. A man
locked in this struggle and wholly intent on personal improvement
considers everything else of little value. The capacity for love
diminishes in this somber life. He loves his family less, for it is in
the way; he separates himself even from his native land, blaming
it for the injustice of his fate.

The father of our studious workman, though cruder, duller,
and inferior in many respects, had more than one advantage over
his son. The national feeling was more powerful within him; he
thought less about mankind and more about France. The great
French family and his own dear little family constituted his
world, and he put his heart there. But alas! what has become

of that charming harmonious household that we used to admire?

Learning by itself does not harden or chill the heart. If it has this effect in the present case, it is because it is cruelly deformed when it reaches the mind. It does not show itself in its true, natural, and perfect light, but obliquely and partially like those scattered and false rays penetrating into a cellar. Learning makes one hateful and envious not by what it teaches but by what it withholds. For example, he who does not know the complicated means by which wealth is created will naturally believe it is not created and does not grow but only changes hands. He will believe that one becomes rich only by robbing his fellow men. Every acquisition will seem to him a theft, and he will hate all who possess . . . But why hate? For the possessions of this world? Yet the world itself would be worthless were it not for love.

Whatever the inevitable error of inadequate study may be, we must respect the student. What is more touching and more serious than to see the man who until now learned by chance *wanting* to study — pursuing knowledge with a passionate will through so many obstacles?

It is this *voluntary* drive for learning which places the worker not only above the peasant in this respect but also above the classes thought to be superior. In fact those classes have books, leisure, everything, and are wooed by learning, but once they are freed from compulsory education, they abandon study and no longer care about the pursuit of truth. I see many such men who have passed with honors through our finest schools, men still young in years but already old at heart, forget the learning they struggled for, without even having the whirlwind of the passions for an excuse, and drift in boredom — sleeping, smoking, and dreaming.

I know that obstacles are great incentives. The worker loves books because he has so few. Sometimes he has only one, but if it is good, he will learn so much the better. A single book used over and over, pondered and assimilated, is often more fruitful than a vast mass of undigested reading. I lived for years on a volume of Virgil and found myself well off. An odd volume of

Racine, purchased by chance at a stall on the quay, created the poet of Toulon.*

They who are inwardly rich always have sufficient resources. They enlarge what they have, develop it by thought, and carry it to infinity. Instead of envying this world of clay, they make one for themselves that is gold and light. They say to this world, "Keep your poverty which you call riches; I am richer myself."

The greater part of the poetry written by workers in recent times is stamped with a peculiar character of meekness and melancholy which often reminds me of their predecessors, the workmen of the Middle Ages. If some of them are bitter and violent, they are the minority. This lofty inspiration would have transported these true poets still higher if they had not followed the aristocratic models with too much deference.

They are only beginning. Why are you in a hurry to say they will never reach the highest ranks? You set out with the false idea that time and culture do everything; you count for nothing the inner development the soul attains by its own strength even in the midst of manual labor — a spontaneous growth which thrives on obstacles. Men of books, you must learn that this man without books and of little culture has a compensation, a substitute for them: he is a master of sorrows.

Whether he succeeds or fails in his quest, I see no other way. He will follow his own road, the road to meditation and suffering. "He sought the light" (says my Virgil), "caught a glimpse of it, and groaned!" And though always groaning, he will always seek it. Who that has once had a glimpse of it could ever renounce it?

"Light! more light!" Such were the last words of Goethe. This prayer of expiring genius is the general cry of nature and echoes from world to world. What that mighty man, one of the eldest

* This refers to the "worker-poet" Charles Poncy of Toulon (1821-91). Encouraged by George Sand, Poncy was part of the general movement of certain intelligent and self-taught workers toward poetry and scholarship between 1835 and 1848. These rather amazing autodidacts, who were mainly from the artisan class, were actively patronized by the greats of the French literary world of the day. This rapprochement supported the humanitarian and idealistic currents of pre-1848 social thought, as Michelet reflects here.

born of God, then said, His most humble children — the lowest creatures in animal life, the mollusks — say also in the depths of the sea. They will not live anyplace where light does not reach. The flower wants light, turns toward it, and decays without it. Our companions in toil, our animals, rejoice or grieve like ourselves according to whether it comes or goes. My grandson, two months old, weeps as day draws to a close.

This summer while walking in my garden I saw a bird on a branch who sang to the setting sun; he was perched facing the light and was clearly delighted. And so was I to see him; our sad caged birds had never given me the idea of this intelligent and powerful creature, so small and yet so impassioned. I thrilled with joy at his song. He drew back his head and threw out his breast; never was a singer, never was a poet, in such natural ecstasy. Yet it was not love (the mating season had passed) : it was evidently the charm of day and the loveliness of sunset that filled him with joy.

Barbarous the learning and cruel the pride that so degrade animal nature and separate man so widely from his inferior brethren!

I said to him through my tears, "Poor child of light, who reflects it in his song, how right you are to sing to it! Night, full of threats and perils for you, is very close to death. Who knows whether you will even see day again?" Then passing mentally from his destiny to that of all the beings so slowly rising from the depths of creation toward the day, I said with Goethe and the little bird, "Light, O Lord! More light!"

∾

CHAPTER IV

The Bondage of the Manufacturer

I read in the little book of the Rouen weaver that I have already quoted, "Our manufacturers were *all workers originally.*" And again: "Most of our manufacturers today [1836] were hard-working and thrifty workers in the early years of the Restoration." This is quite general, I believe, and not peculiar to the industry of Rouen. Several building contractors have told me that they *had all been workers,* and had come to Paris as masons, carpenters, and so on.

If workingmen have been able to rise in the vast and complicated business of great factories, it will be more easily believed that they have become masters in those branches of industry which require much less capital, such as petty manufactures, crafts, and retail trade. Licensed tradesmen, who scarcely increased during the Empire, have multiplied twofold during the thirty years that have passed since 1815. About six hundred thousand men have become manufacturers or tradesmen. Now in our country whoever can manage to get by stays as he is, and will not run the risk of entering industry. Thus we may say with confidence that half a million workingmen have become masters, and obtained what they believed to be independence.

This movement was especially rapid in the first ten years — from 1815 to 1825. Those brave men of war wheeled suddenly to the right toward industry, charged forward as in an assault, and carried easily every position. Their confidence was so great that they even imparted some of it to the capitalists. Men of such spirit would carry with them even the most cautious and hesitant. It was easy to believe that they were about to relive in industry the whole series of our victories and give us revenge there for our recent defeats.

There is no denying that these parvenu workmen who founded our manufacturing enterprises had excellent qualities: spirit, boldness, initiative, and often a sure eye for business. Many of them have made their fortunes; let us hope their sons will not ruin themselves!

With such qualities our factory owners of 1815 felt all too well the demoralization of that sad period. Political death is not far from moral death, and they could see it then. From their military life they generally preserved a sense of violence and not of honor. Thus they cared for neither men nor things nor the future, and they treated unmercifully two groups of individuals — the workers and the consumers.

Nevertheless, workers were still scarce at that time, even in the factories, which require so little training. Thus they were forced to pay high wages. In this way they enlisted men in town and country, made these recruits of labor march to the pace of the machine, and required that they, like it, be indefatigable. They seemed to apply to industry the great imperial principle: sacrifice men to shorten the war. Our national impatience, which often makes us barbarous toward animals, followed the authority of military traditions against our men; work had to move on the run at double time, and so much the worse for those who fell!

As for their sales, the manufacturers of that time acted as if they were in enemy territory; they fleeced the customer just as the female shopkeepers had fleeced the Cossacks in 1815. They sold at false weight, false dye, and false measure. Thus they played their cards with sleight of hand, and then pulled back after having shut France out of her best markets and having compromised her commercial reputation for a long time. Most serious of all, they performed for the English the essential service of estranging us from a whole world at the very least — the world of Spanish America, the imitator of our Revolution.

Their successors, who are either their sons or their principal workmen, now have a hard time with this reputation in every market. They are astonished and dismayed to find their profits so greatly reduced. Most of them would be delighted to retire if they could, but they are in it now and must go on — Forward march! Forward march!

In other countries, industry is based upon great financial resources, upon a mass of customs, traditions, and established patterns; it has a vast and regular trade for its foundation. But here in France, to be quite honest, it is a continuous battle. An enterprising worker who inspires confidence finds a sleeping partner, or a young man risks his father's savings. He has only a little capital in any case, whether from a loan or his wife's dowry. God grant that his efforts are between two crashes, for we have one about every six years (1818, 1825, 1830, 1836).

It is always the same story. A year or two after the crash a few orders come in, and they forget the past and hope for the future. The manufacturer believes he is off and running; he pushes, forces, and strains men and things, his workers and his machines; for a moment the commercial Bonaparte of 1820 reappears. Finally the warehouses are filled and the markets glutted, and he must sell at a loss. And do not forget that about every five years these expensive machines are worn out or made obsolete by some new invention. His profits, if any, must always go for new machinery.

The capitalist, instructed by so many lessons, now believes that France is more a manufacturing than a commercial nation and better suited to make than to sell. But he lends to the new manufacturer as if to a man embarking on a dangerous voyage. What security does he have? The most splendid factories are always sold at great loss, and that shiny machinery is good only for scrap metal in a few years. Therefore he lends not upon the security of the factory but upon the man himself. For the manufacturer has the sad advantage of being able to be imprisoned, and that gives value to his signature. The manufacturer is well aware that he has pawned his person and sometimes much more — the lives of his wife and children, the property of his father-in-law or of a trusting friend, perhaps even property for which he is only trustee, dragged on as he is by the frenzy of this terrible life. So there is no time for niceties. He must conquer or die, make a fortune or drown himself.

A man in this state of mind is not very tenderhearted. It would be a miracle if he were kind and gentle to his employees and his workers. See him as he strides through his vast factory with a hard and sullen look. When he is at one end, the workers at the other whisper to each other, "What a temper he has today! And did you see how he treated the foreman!" In fact he treats them all as he himself has just been treated. He has just returned from the local money market — to Mulhouse from Basle or to Déville from Rouen, for example. He bawls at them, and they are astonished. Little do they know that the Jew has just taken a pound of flesh from his body!

From whom will he get it back? From the consumer? He is on his guard. Once again the manufacturer falls upon the worker. Wherever there is no apprenticeship system, wherever apprentices are created imprudently and men come in crowds and offer themselves at a low price, then the manufacturer profits from the fall of wages.[1] Afterward overproduction forces him to sell even at a loss, and the deterioration of wages, which is death for the workers, no longer profits the manufacturer. The consumer alone gains from it.

The hardest factory owner was born a human being, however, and once he sympathized a bit with that crowd of men.[2] Gradually the preoccupation with business, the uncertainty of his posi-

[1] For a long time I refused to believe what I was told about the infamous frauds certain manufacturers practice upon the consumer as to quality of product and upon the worker as to quantity of work. I have been forced to change my mind. These charges have been confirmed by friends of manufacturers who have spoken of them to me with grief and humiliation, as well as by persons of note, both merchants and bankers. The reconciliation boards have no authority to repress these crimes; moreover, the worker does not dare complain. Such questions should be investigated by the attorney general.

[2] This gradual hardening of the heart and the ability to stifle the voice of humanity within, which one acquires little by little, are acutely analyzed by Mr. Emmery in his pamphlet *Amélioration du sort des ouvriers dans les travaux publics* (1837). He treats in particular those workers injured in dangerous tasks the contractors undertake for the government.

"A contractor whose heart is in the right place may once, or even several times at first, aid his unfortunate workers when they are injured. But when this happens often and the demands for relief are multiplied,

tion, and his risks and mental sufferings have made him indifferent to the material sufferings of the workers. He does not know them as well as his father did, who had been a worker himself.[3] He comes to regard this ever-changing crowd as numbers, as machines, though a less docile and less regular kind which future improvements will allow him to do without. They are the flaw in the system. In this world of iron where movements are so precise, the only defect is man.

It is curious to observe that the small number of owners who are interested in the condition of the worker's lot are either the very small manufacturers who live with him on a patriarchal footing, or at the other extreme the very large and powerful firms which are founded upon solid fortunes and are above all of the ordinary anxieties of trade. Everything between is a pitiless battlefield.

Thus it is well known that our prosperous manufacturers of Mulhouse have demanded a law to regulate child labor in opposition to their own interest. In 1836, when an experiment was made by one of them to give the workers healthy lodgings with little gardens, these same manufacturers of Alsace were moved by this

they become too burdensome. The contractor then makes a bargain with himself, wards off his first impulse toward generosity, gradually reduces the number of applicants, and diminishes in a more noticeable way the amount he gives in each case. The contractor finds that in his most dangerous workshops he receives no extra payment for the dangers involved, but that he must pay his workers higher wages for such work. Now these higher wages soon seem to him to be the price of the accidents that are feared. Additional aid and charity seem to him above his means. Moreover, the injured worker has not been in his service long enough; the injured worker is not one of the most skillful, or most useful, and so on and so on. Thus the heart hardens itself by habit, and often by necessity, and all charity is soon extinct. The little relief granted is no longer shared among all according to strict justice, and the only result of all the generous emotions which ought to be felt before such distressing sights is reduced to a few donations, which are granted arbitrarily and which are not calculated according to the real needs of starving families, but in the future interest of the enterprise and the contractor's business."

[3] The difference between father and son is that the latter, who was never a worker, knows less about the process of fabrication and is less acquainted with the limits of the possible and the impossible. Thus he is sometimes a harder taskmaster because of ignorance.

fine idea and generously subscribed two million francs. I have been unable to discover whatever became of that subscription.

The manufacturers would no doubt be more human if their families, often very charitable, were more familiar with the factory. They generally live apart and see the workers only from afar. They willingly exaggerate their vices, judging them almost always on the basis of the moment I spoke of earlier — I mean the moment they leave the factory, when freedom so long restrained finally escapes with noise and disorder. It often happens that the manufacturer and his family hate the worker because they think they are hated by him. I must say, contrary to common opinion, that they are frequently mistaken about this. In the great factories the worker hates the foreman, whose tyranny he feels directly, while that of the master is more remote and thus less odious to him. If he has not been taught to hate, he looks upon it as the tyranny of fate and is not aroused against it.

The problem of industry is greatly complicated for France by her external relations. In a sense she is blockaded by the unanimous ill will of Europe. Along with her old political alliances, she has lost all hope of opening new commercial outlets in the East or the West. Industrialism, which founded the present system on the strange supposition that our rivals the English would be our friends, finds that with this friendship it is blockaded and walled up as in a tomb. Of course our great agricultural and warlike France, with her twenty-five million men who listened to the manufacturers and upon their word and for their benefit stood back and did not retake the Rhine, now has the right to deplore such naïveté. Shrewder by far, she always believed that the English would remain English.

We must, however, make a distinction between the manufacturers. There are some who have not fallen asleep behind a triple line of customhouses and have nobly continued the war against England. We thank them for their heroic efforts to raise the stone under which she thought to crush us. Their industry struggles against England despite every disadvantage (often with expenses one-third greater!), and has nevertheless defeated her at several points — particularly those which required the most brilliant abilities and the most inexhaustible wealth of invention. Their industry has conquered through art.

It would take a whole book to appreciate the magnificent efforts of Alsace. Lacking the soul of the trader and without arguing about the expense, Alsace has used every means and every science to attain the beautiful, cost what it would. Lyons has solved the problem of continual metamorphosis, becoming ever more ingenious and brilliant. And what shall we say of that Parisian fairy who responds every moment to the most unpredictable turns of fancy?

Unexpected and surprising result — France sells! Excluded, condemned, and excommunicated — and still she sells. They come in spite of themselves, and in spite of themselves they buy.

They buy ... patterns, patterns to take home and copy, either successfully or unsuccessfully. An Englishman has declared before a parliamentary inquiry that he has a branch in Paris *to get patterns*. A few pieces of cloth purchased in Paris, Lyons, or Alsace, and then copied abroad, enable the English or German counterfeiter to flood the world. It is like the book trade: France writes and Belgium sells.

These products in which we excel are unfortunately those that change the most and are always requiring new production lines. For although art can add infinitely to the value of the raw material, so expensive an art leaves hardly any profit. England, on the contrary, possesses markets among the inferior nations of the five parts of the world, and manufactures uniform fabrics on a grand scale for long periods without any new lines or further research. Such products may be vulgar, but they are always lucrative.

Work, then, O France, to remain poor! Work and suffer, without ever tiring. The motto of your great factories, which are your glory and which impose your taste and sense of art upon the world, is this: Invent or perish.

∾

CHAPTER V

The Bondage of the Shopkeeper[1]

The man of labor, whether worker or manufacturer, generally looks upon the shopkeeper as a man of leisure. Sitting in his shop, what has he to do in the morning but read the newspaper, then chat all day, and lock up his till in the evening? The worker vows that if he can save a little, he will become a shopkeeper.

The shopkeeper is the manufacturer's tyrant. He gives him back all the meanness and vexation he has received from the customer. In the present state of society the customer is a man who wants to buy for nothing — a poor man who would ape the rich, or a man of new wealth who finds it hard to spend what he has just made. They require two things: a showy article and the lowest price. The quality of the object is secondary. Who will pay the price of a good watch? No one. Even the rich want nothing but a cheap and pretty watch.

The shopkeeper must outwit these people or fail. He is always waging a two-front war: a war of cheating and cunning against the unreasonable customer, and a war of vexations and outrageous demands against the manufacturer. Fickle, restless, and finicky, he conveys to the manufacturer day after day the most absurd whims of his master, the public. He drags the manufacturer right and left, changes direction every moment, prevents him from following up a single idea, and, in more ways than one, renders great invention almost impossible.

---

[1] Here I will treat the individual dealer, who is the usual trader in France, and not those large partnerships which so far exist only in a few large towns.

The main goal of the shopkeeper is to get the manufacturer to help him cheat the customer with petty frauds, and even great ones. I have heard manufacturers moan about the dishonorable things required of them. Either they become accomplices in the most flagrant frauds or they lose their business. It is not enough to alter the quality of their goods; they must also become forgers and use the trademarks of other well-known firms.

The repugnance for industry shown by the noble republics of antiquity and the haughty barons of the Middle Ages is certainly irrational, if by industry we mean those complex fabrications which require science and art, or large-scale wholesale trade which requires a great variety of knowledge, information, and negotiation. But this repugnance is quite reasonable when it relates to the ordinary practices of commerce and the miserable necessity of the shopkeeper to lie, cheat, and adulterate.

I do not hesitate in testifying that for a man of honor the position of the most dependent workingman is one of freedom compared with this. A serf in body, he is free in soul. For to enslave your soul and sacrifice your integrity, to be forced from morning to night to disguise your thoughts, is the lowest form of serfdom. Picture for yourself this shopkeeper who has been a soldier, who has preserved in everything else a feeling of honor, and who resigns himself to this. He must suffer a great deal.

What is strange is that it is precisely for honor that he lies every day — *to do honor* to his business. Dishonor for him is not falsehood, but bankruptcy. Rather than *fail,* he will be driven by commercial honor to the point where fraud becomes robbery and adulteration is poisoning. To be sure, it is a gentle poisoning, in small doses, which kills only in the long run. But if they pretend that they mix only inactive and inert materials with the products they sell, the workingman, who thinks he is restoring his forces, finds nothing at all there and can no longer regain his strength. He declines, exhausts himself, and lives, so to speak, on his capital, on the funds of his life which dwindle away little by little. In my opinion this adulterator, this seller of drunkenness, is guilty not only of poisoning the people but also of debasing them.

The weary workingman enters the bistro with confidence; he

loves it as his house of liberty. Well, what does he find here?
A disgrace! The alcoholic mixture sold to him under the name of
wine has an immediate effect that two or three times as much
wine would not produce. It mounts to the brain and troubles the
mind, the tongue, and the motions of the body. The tradesman
throws him into the street drunk and penniless ... Who is not
struck to the heart when on a winter day he sees a poor old
woman who has drunk this poison to warm herself and who has
then been pushed out in this state, a butt of ridicule for vicious
children? And the rich man passes by and says, "Here you have
the people!"

Every man who has or can borrow a thousand francs boldly
sets up shop. The workingman becomes a shopkeeper, that is to
say, a man of leisure. Since he used to live in the bistro, he opens
a bistro. He opens not far from his old haunts, indeed as near
as possible, in order to steal their customers. He flatters himself
with the sweet idea that he will ruin his neighbor. In fact he has
customers immediately — all those who owe the other and will
not pay. At the end of a few months the new man is old, and
others have set up around him. He declines and fails. He has
lost his money and what was worth even more — the habit of
working. Great is the joy of his competitors, who gradually end
in the same way. Others come, but he never reappears ... Sad
and miserable traffic, devoid of ingenuity and every idea but that
of preying one upon another.

When demand increases a bit, shopkeepers increase rapidly
and intensify competition, as well as envy and hatred. They do
nothing except stand at their doors with their arms folded, eye-
ing one another askance and watching to see if the faithless customer will enter another shop. Last year the shopkeepers of Paris,
eighty thousand in number, had forty-six thousand lawsuits before
the Tribunal of Commerce alone, not to speak of the other courts.
An awful number! How many quarrels and hatreds does it imply!

The special object of his hate, whom the licensed dealer pursues and has arrested when he can, is the poor devil who rolls
his shop along, stopping here and there for a moment. It is also
the sorry woman who carries her shop in a basket, and alas,

often a child as well! Let her not think of sitting down, let her be always moving on — otherwise she is arrested!

I really do not know whether that wretched shopman who has had her seized is more happy for being seated — never stirring, always waiting and unable to anticipate anything. For the shopkeeper hardly ever knows what his profit will be. Receiving his goods at second or third hand, he has no idea of the state of his own trade in Europe and cannot guess whether he will make a fortune or go bankrupt next year.

Several circumstances make the fate of the manufacturer and even the worker better than that of the shopkeeper in spite of their labor.

First, *the shopkeeper does not create*. He does not have the profound happiness worthy of man that comes from producing something, from seeing his work grow under his hand and assume a harmonious form. This progressive creation consoles the creator for his toil and boredom.

Second, and a terrible disadvantage in my opinion, *the shopkeeper must please*. The workman gives his time and the manufacturer his merchandise for so much money. Here is a simple contract that is not degrading. Neither has need to flatter. Neither is forced, often with broken heart and tearful eyes, to be suddenly amiable and gay like the lady behind the counter. The hapless shopkeeper, tormented to death about a bill that falls due tomorrow, must smile and give himself up by a painful effort to the babble of some young woman of fashion. She makes him unfold a hundred pieces, prattles for two hours, and leaves without a purchase. He must please, and so must his wife. He has put into his business not only his wealth, his person, and his life, but often his family as well.[2]

[2] Much has been said of the female silk worker, and of the clerk who made her pay with her person for his winking at her theft. People have also talked in the same manner of the female operative in cotton factories, but in my opinion they are mistaken; the manufacturer associates very little with his male and female workers. Last, it has been said that the country usurer often offers a delay at an immoral price. Why have they not spoken of the female shopkeeper, so exposed and obliged to please the purchaser, to talk so long with him, and who often finds her ruin there?

The man who is never offended on his own account will suffer constantly in seeing his wife or daughter at the counter. Even a stranger, a disinterested spectator, cannot observe without emotion the habits and domestic life of a respectable family entering business being violently deranged as their fireside is thrown into the street and their holy of holies is displayed in the shop window! The young lady listens with downcast eyes to the impertinent language of some improper customer. We return a few months after and find her bold.

But the wife contributes much more than the daughter to the success of the business. She talks gracefully, charmingly. Where is the harm in such a public life, before the eyes of the crowd? She chats, but she listens ... and to everybody other than her husband. That husband of hers has a moody mind and is not at all amusing. He is full of doubts and trifles, wavering in politics, discontented with the government and everything else, and discontented even with the discontented.

The wife is more and more aware that she has a tiresome task — twelve hours a day on the same spot, exposed behind the window with the goods. She will not always remain so motionless — that statue can come to life.

And now the husband's torments begin. The cruelest place in the world for a jealous man is a shop. Everybody comes, and everybody flatters the lady. The wretched man does not even always know whom to blame. Sometimes he goes mad or kills himself or her. Sometimes he takes to bed and dies. Unhappiest of all, perhaps, is he who resigns himself to his fate.

There was a man who died such a slow death, not from jealousy but from grief and humiliation as every day he was insulted and outraged in the person of his wife. I mean the unfortunate Louvet. After escaping the dangers of the Reign of Terror and returning to the Convention without any fortune, he set his wife up as a bookseller in the Palais Royal, the book trade being the only flourishing one at that moment. Unfortunately this ardent Girondin, just as opposed to the Royalists as to the Mountain, had a thousand enemies. The *gilded youth,* who had run away so quickly on 13 Vendémiaire, came to parade bravely before Louvet's shop, entered, sneered, and took their revenge on a woman. To the challenges of the infuriated husband they answered only with shouts of laughter. Louvet himself had armed them by printing in the account of his flight and misfortunes a thousand passionate details, doubtless indiscreet and imprudent, about his dear Lodoïska. One thing ought to have protected her and made her sacred for men of feeling: her courage and devotedness, for she had saved her husband. But our gallant gentlemen were not moved. They coldly carried on their cruel jests, and Louvet died from it. His wife wanted to die, but her children were brought to her and they condemned her to live.

಄

CHAPTER VI

The Bondage of the Official

As children grow up and the family and relatives begin to ask what is to be done with them, the liveliest and least disciplined seldom fails to say, "I want to be independent." He will go into business and find there the independence we have just examined. The other brother, the quiet, gentle boy, will become a government official.

At least every effort will be made in this direction. The family will make enormous sacrifices, often well beyond their means. Great efforts, and for what? After several years of schooling and ten years of college life, he will be appointed temporary clerk, and finally be a minor employee with a trifling salary. His brother, the man of commerce who has had very different adventures during that time, is full of envy and seldom loses a chance to allude to the unproductive classes "who comfortably fall asleep at the banquet of the budget." In the eyes of the businessman there is no producer but himself: the judge, the soldier, the teacher, and the official are all "unproductive consumers."[1]

The parents were well aware that public employment is not a lucrative career. But they wanted for their gentle, quiet child a safe, fixed, and regular livelihood. Such is the ideal of families after so many revolutions; such, in their opinion, is the lot of the official. Everything else comes and goes, varies and changes; the official alone escapes the vicissitudes of this mortal life, and is, as it were, in a better world.

I do not know if the official ever had this paradise on earth,

---

[1] As if justice, civil order, defense of the country, and public education were not also productions, and the greatest of all!

this life of immobility and sleep. Today, however, I see no man more constantly in motion. Without speaking of cutbacks and dismissals, which sometimes come and are always feared, his life is a series of changes, journeys, and sudden transfers from one end of France to the other for some electoral mystery or other. These inexplicable disgraces, which are called promotions, send him all the way from Perpignan to Lille for 200 francs more a year. All the roads are filled with officials traveling with their furniture; in fact many no longer keep any at all. Rather, they camp in inns for a year or less with their suitcases packed, and live a sad and lonely life in an unknown town. Toward the end, when they are just beginning to make friends, they are hurried off to the opposite pole.

They must beware of marriage; their situation would be even worse. For quite apart from the fact of this roving life, their salaries cannot support a family. Those like the judge, the junior officer, and the teacher, who are charged with men's souls and must uphold the honor of their position, will pass their lives, if they have no personal fortune, in a continual struggle full of miserable attempts to hide their wretchedness and clothe it in some imaginary dignity.

Have you not met several times in a stagecoach a respectable, serious, or rather sad-looking lady, modestly dressed if somewhat out of fashion, with one or two children, many trunks and cases, and a household of furniture on top of the coach? At the end of the journey you see her met by her husband, a brave and deserving officer who is no longer young. She follows him in a life of inconvenience and boredom from garrison to garrison. She sleeps on the road and eats in an inn, and then continues her journey. Nothing is sadder to see than these poor women sharing all the hardships of military life because of their affection and sense of duty.

The salaries of all government employees have changed very little since the Empire.[2] The fixed salary, which people consider

[2] They have improved in almost all the other states of Europe. Here in France they have increased for a small number of posts and lowered for others.

the official's supreme good fortune, is enjoyed by almost all of them. But as the value of money has fallen, the fixed figure is constantly declining in real value and representing less, as we noted in speaking of wages in industry.

France can boast of one thing. With the exception of a few high posts which are too well paid, her public officials serve the state for almost nothing. Yet for all that, I assert that in this much maligned country there are very few officials open to bribery.

I hear an objection. You say that many are corrupted by the hope of promotion, by intrigue, and by evil influences. I grant you this. And yet I will still maintain that among these poorly paid people you will not find any who take money, as they do in Russia, Italy, and so many other countries.

Look at the highest ranks. The judge who decides the fate and fortune of men, who every day has cases worth several millions in his hands, and who for his important, constant, and wearisome duties earns less than many a workman — this judge takes no bribe.

Now take the lowest, in a class where temptations are great. Take the customhouse officer. There are some, perhaps, who will accept a small tip for some small service, but never for anything the least suspected of fraud. Now, do you wish to know how much he gets for his thankless task? Six hundred francs a year, or something more than thirty sous a day, and the nights go unpaid. Every other night he is on the border or the coast with no shelter other than his cloak, exposed to the attack of the smuggler and the mighty gale that sometimes hurls him from the cliff into the sea. There on his lonely vigil his wife brings him his meager meal, for he is married, has children, and must feed four or five persons on his thirty sous!

A journeyman baker in Paris earns more than two customs officials, more than a lieutenant of infantry, more than many a judge and the majority of professors, and *as much as six local schoolmasters!*[3] Shame! Infamy! The nation that pays the least

[3] I mean the ordinary worker with average pay who is also employed throughout the winter. See an earlier note, p. 54.

to those that instruct the people — and let us blush to confess it — is France.

I speak of the France of today. On the contrary, the true France, that of the Revolution, declared that teaching was a holy office and that the schoolmaster was equal to the priest. It established as a principle that the first expense of the state was instruction. In its terrible poverty the Convention wished to give 54 million francs to primary education, and would certainly have done so had it lasted longer . . . A strange time, when men called themselves materialists, but which was in reality the apotheosis of thought, the reign of the mind.

I do not hide the truth. Of all the miseries of the present day there is not one which weighs more heavily upon me. The most deserving, the most miserable, the most neglected man in France is the local schoolmaster.[4] The state, which does not even know what its true instruments and its strength are, which does not suspect that its most powerful moral lever is this class of men, abandons them to the enemies of the state. You say that the teaching brothers of the church teach better. I deny it. But even if it were true, what is that to me? The local schoolmaster is France; the teaching brother is Rome, the stranger and enemy. Read rather their books, and follow their habits and their connections. They are flatterers of the university and all Jesuits at heart.

I have spoken elsewhere of the bondage of the priest. It is

___

[4] In his *Tableau de l'instruction primaire,* an official work of the highest importance which summarizes the reports of 490 inspectors who visited all the schools in 1833, Mr. Lorain cannot find expressions strong enough to describe the misery and contempt in which our teachers live. He states that some get *altogether* only 100 francs a year, and others only 50! Moreover, they have to wait a long time for payment, which often is not forthcoming! They are not paid in money, since every family sets apart the worst of the crop for the schoolmaster, who *goes on Sunday to beg at every door with a sack on his back.* He is not welcome when he claims his small lot of potatoes, for *they feel he is robbing the pigs!* Since these official reports, new schools have been erected, but the fate of the old masters has not improved. Let us hope that the Chamber of Deputies will grant this year the raise of 100 francs that was demanded in vain last year.

great and worthy of compassion. The serf of Rome, the serf of his bishop, he is in a position which almost always gives to his well-informed superior a mortgage on him. Well then, this priest, this serf, is the tyrant of the schoolmaster. The latter is not legally his subordinate, but he is his valet. The schoolmaster's wife, the mother of a family, must try to please the priest's housekeeper as well as some influential favorite in the congregation. This woman who has a family and has such a time making ends meet knows very well that a schoolmaster on bad terms with the village priest is a lost man! For the priest does not merely intimate that the schoolmaster is an ignorant fellow. Oh no, he is immoral, a drunkard, a ———. His children, alas! increasing year after year, testify vainly to his moral conduct. The teaching brothers alone are moral. Of course a few little lawsuits are brought against them, but they are soon hushed up.

Bondage, heavy bondage! I find it among the high and the low at every level, crushing the most worthy, the most humble, the most deserving! And I am not speaking of legitimate hierarchical dependence, of obedience to the natural superior. I speak of another kind, of an oblique, indirect dependence which weighs heavily from high to low, penetrating, questioning, spying, and attempting to master even the soul.

There is a vast difference between the shopkeeper and the official! The former, as we have said, must lie about the smallest matters for his external interest; but in what concerns his soul he often preserves his independence. It is precisely on this side that the official is attacked. He is troubled in affairs of the soul, and sometimes forced to lie about what concerns his religious and political faith.

The wisest of them work hard to be forgotten. They avoid living and thinking, pretend to be nothing, and play their game so well that at last they have no need of pretending. They actually become what they wished to appear. Our officials, who are nonetheless the eyes and arms of France, try not to see and try not to stir. A body with such limbs must be very ill indeed.

Is the unhappy man free in return for annihilating himself? Not always. The more he yields and the more he retreats, the more they require. They go so far as to ask him for what they call proofs of devotion, or "positive services." He might be promoted if he made himself useful, if he informed on so and so: "That fellow, for example, your colleague; is he a safe man?"

Here is a sick and tormented man. He goes home worn out and dejected. Gently questioned, he confesses what is the matter. And where do you think he finds support at this critical moment? From his family? Rarely.

It is a sad and cruel thing to say, but it must be said: a man today is not corrupted by the world he understands all too well, or by his friends ... for who has friends? No, most frequently he is corrupted by his own family. An excellent wife, worried about her children, is capable of anything to advance her husband and will even push him to base and cowardly acts. A devoted mother finds it natural that he should make his own fortune by proofs of devotion. The end justifies everything; how can one sin in serving a good cause? What will a man do when he finds temptation even in his family, which ought to protect him from it? What will he do when vice comes to him in the guise of virtue, filial obedience, and the respect of paternal authority?

This side of our morals is very grave. I know none more grim and depressing.

Still I will never believe that even with such means the baseness and servility of Jesuitism will ever triumph in France. There is an invincible repugnance for whatever is false and base in this noble country. The mass of men is good; do not judge it by the floating scum. The mass may waver, but it still has a strength which makes it secure — the feeling of military honor ever renewed by our heroic legend. Many a man about to fall pulls himself up without knowing why ... It is because he has felt on his face the invisible spirit of the heroes of our wars, the breath of the old flag!

Ah! the flag is my hope! May that flag save France, and the France of the army! May our glorious army, upon which the eyes of the world are fixed, keep itself pure! May it be iron against the enemy and steel against corruption! May a police spirit never enter there! And may it ever preserve a horror of traitors, villainous proposals, and underhanded means of promotion!

What a trust is placed in the hands of these young soldiers! What a responsibility for the future! On the day of the last great battle between civilization and barbarism (and who knows that it may not be tomorrow?), the Judge must find them above reproach, their swords pure and their bayonets gleaming without a stain! Every time I see them pass, my heart leaps up: "Here, and only here, force and mind, valor and right — those two blessings separated over all the earth — march hand in hand. If the world is saved by war, you alone will save it. Sacred bayonets of France, watch that nothing dims that light which shines down upon you and toward which no eye can gaze."

❧

CHAPTER VII

The Bondage of the Rich and the Bourgeoisie

The only people that has an important army is the one that counts for nothing in Europe. This phenomenon is not sufficiently explained by the weakness of a ministry or a government. Unfortunately it springs from a more general cause — the decline of the governing class, so new and so soon worn out. I mean the bourgeoisie.

To make myself clear I must go some way back in time.

The glorious bourgeoisie that shattered the Middle Ages and brought about our first revolution during the fourteenth century had the unusual characteristic of providing a means of introducing the people into the nobility. It was far less a class than a stepping-stone and a means of passage. Then, having finished its creation of a new nobility and a new monarchy, the bourgeoisie lost its mobility, became stereotyped, and remained a class which was all too often quite ridiculous. The bourgeois of the seventeenth and eighteenth centuries was a bastard being whom nature seems to have kept in a state of imperfect development. He was a graceless mongrel, neither high nor low, able neither to walk nor to fly, who was satisfied with himself and strutted about with much pretension.

Our present bourgeoisie, born in the short time since the Revolution, did not find nobles above them as they rose. They wanted so much the more to become a class all at once. They drew their lines as they were born, so well that they rather naïvely believed they could produce an aristocracy — as much as to say they could improvise an ancient lineage. This creation has been found to lack such antiquity, and it only wore itself out, as might have been foreseen.[1]

Though the bourgeoisie wish for nothing better than to be a separate class, it is not easy to define the limits of this class, to say where it begins or where it ends. It is not made up exclusively of those well off, for there are many poor bourgeois.[2] In the country the man who is a day laborer here is a bourgeois elsewhere because he has a little property there. Thus, thank God, the bourgeoisie cannot, strictly speaking, be opposed to the people, as some believe, which would be no less than creating two nations. Our small rural landowners, whether they are called bourgeois or not, are the people and the heart of the people.

Whether you extend or limit your definition of the bourgeoisie, the important point to note is that the bourgeoisie, which almost alone has taken all the initiative for the last fifty years, seems paralyzed now and incapable of action. A very recent class seemed destined to give it new life. I am referring to the industrial bourgeoisie, which was born in 1815 and strengthened in the struggles of the Restoration, and which more than any other group caused the July Revolution of 1830. Perhaps more French than the bourgeoisie properly called, it is bourgeois by interest and dares not stir. In any case, the bourgeoisie as a whole will not and cannot act; it has lost all motion. Half a century has thus sufficed to see the bourgeoisie spring from the people, rise by its

[1] Ancient France was divided into three classes; new France has only two — the people and the bourgeoisie.

[2] If you observe carefully how the people use this word, you will find that among them it does not mean riches as much as a certain standard of independence and leisure — a lack of worry about where they will find their daily bread. Many an artisan, who earns 5 francs a day, says without hesitation, *"My bourgeois,"* to the famishing rentier, who may receive an income of 300 francs a year and walks around in an old black suit coat in the middle of January. If a sense of security is the essential distinction of the bourgeois, should we include those who never know whether they are rich or poor — the commercial class — or those others who seem more firmly established but who, in order to purchase a situation, have made themselves the serfs of the capitalist? If they are not true bourgeois, they nevertheless adhere to the same class because of interest, fear, and the fixed idea of peace at any cost.

activity and energy, and then suddenly in the midst of its triumph sink back upon itself. There is no example of so rapid a decline.

It is not we who say so, but the bourgeoisie itself. The most melancholy confessions escape from it about its own decline and that of France, whom it drags down with it. Ten years ago a minister remarked before several persons, "France will be the first of the second-rate powers." This prophecy, so humble then, seems almost ambitious in our present circumstances. So rapid is the decline!

As rapid within as without. The progress of the evil shows itself in the discouragement of the very persons who profit by it. They can hardly be interested in a game in which nobody hopes to deceive anybody else any longer. The actors are almost as bored as the spectators; they yawn with the public, sick of themselves and disgusted to feel so low.

One of them, a man of wit, wrote a few years ago that great men were no longer necessary and that henceforth people could do without them. That saying hit home. But if he uses it again, he will have to extend it, and prove that mediocre men, real second-rate talents, are not indispensable either, and may be done without as well.

Ten years ago the press pretended to exert influence. It has laid aside that pretension. To speak only of literature, the press has come to feel that the bourgeoisie, who alone read since the people hardly read at all, have no need of art. It has consequently been able to remodel two expensive items without anybody complaining — art and criticism. It has used hack writers and novelists who only sell their names while third-rate craftsmen actually do their work.

The general decline is felt less because it is the same for everything. Everything sinks, so the relative levels are the same.

Who would say, quiet as we are today, that we used to be such a noisy people? The ear becomes gradually accustomed to quiet, and so does the voice. The diapason is changed. Many a man thinks he is shouting, but he is only squeaking. The only real noise comes from the stock exchange. He who hears it on the

spot and sees that agitation will all too easily imagine that this
torrent really stirs up the great stagnant swamp of the bourgeoisie.
That would be a mistake. It is doing too much wrong and too
much honor to the bourgeoisie to suppose they have such active
concern for material interests.[3] They are tremendous egotists, it
is true, but they are bound by habit and inertia to their first
gains, which they are afraid of risking. It is incredible how easily
this class resigns itself to mediocrity regarding everything,
especially in the provinces. They have only a little, and that
little only since yesterday. But provided they keep it, they settle
down to live without acting or thinking.[4]

The hallmark of the old bourgeoisie was security, and that is
what the new one lacks above all.

The bourgeoisie of the last two centuries, firmly established
on the basis of fortunes already old, on legal and financial offices
which were considered property, on the monopoly of the large
trading corporations and other great assets, believed itself as

[3] France does not have the business spirit, except in its English fits
(like that of Law and of the present moment), and these are extraordinary fevers. This is seen especially in the way in which the men who at
first seem the most eager generally stop early on the road to fortune.
The Frenchman who has gained in trade or otherwise an income of a
few thousand francs believes himself rich, and does nothing more. The
Englishman, on the contrary, sees in the wealth he has acquired the means
of growing richer; he continues in his work until he dies. He remains
chained to the oar, completely absorbed in his business. The only change
is the increased size of his operations. He does not feel the need of leisure, which would allow him to spend his time as he wished.

Thus there are very few rich men in France, if you exclude our foreign capitalists. These few rich people would almost all be poor in
England. And from our rich men you must deduct a number who make
a good figure, but whose fortune is at stake or mortgaged or quite
uncertain.

[4] I know a fairly large town near Paris that contains a few hundred
rentiers and men of property of from 4,000 to 6,000 francs a year, or a
little more. These men never think of going beyond that figure; they do
nothing and read no books and very few newspapers; they are interested
in nothing, never see each other, never get together, and hardly know
each other. The fascination of the Bourse is never felt there, although
unfortunately it is felt in the lower class — among the saving poor in
towns, for instance, and even in the country, where the peasant does
not even have a newspaper to warn him about this tricky business.

secure in France as the king. Its ridiculous side was its pride and awkward imitation of the great. This effort to rise higher in society than they could has even left its stamp in the emphasis and bombast which characterize most of the monuments of the seventeenth century.

The ridiculous side of the new bourgeoisie is the contrast between its military antecedents and its present timidity, which it does not hide at all and which it expresses on every occasion with unusual simplicity. Should three men be in the street talking together about wages, or should they ask the contractor who has grown rich on their labor for one sou, then the bourgeois is scared to death and cries out for strong measures.

At least the man of the old bourgeoisie was more consistent. He admired himself in his privileges, sought to extend them, and looked upward. His counterpart today looks downward; he sees the crowd rising behind him, just as he rose, and does not like it. He retreats and puts himself on the side of established power. Does he frankly admit his reactionary tendencies to himself? Only rarely, for his past is opposed to his development. Thus he remains almost always a set of contradictions. He is a liberal in principle, an egotist in practice. He wants and does not want. If there is anything French still within him, he quiets it by reading some innocently growling and peacefully warlike newspaper.

We must recognize that most of the time our governments have exploited this sad increase of fear, which in the end is nothing less than moral death. They have thought the dead easier to deal with than the living. To make the bourgeoisie fear the people, the government has constantly held up two petrifying Medusa's heads: the Reign of Terror and Communism.

History has not yet carefully examined that unique phenomenon, the Reign of Terror, which no man and certainly no party could now restore. All that I can say here is that behind the popular phantasmagoria, the directors of the operation, our grand Terrorists, were by no means men of the people. They were bourgeois and nobles, men with cultivated, subtle, bizarre minds — real sophists and scholastics.

As for Communism, which I shall discuss again in greater

detail, one point is all important. France is the last country in
the world in which private property will be abolished. If, as
someone of that school said, "Property is nothing but theft,"
then we have here twenty-five million thieves who are not about
to give up their loot.*

Nevertheless these two things provide excellent political machines to frighten those who possess and to make them act
against their principles, or to strip them of any principles. Look
at the way the Jesuits and their friends have used Communism,
especially in Switzerland. Whenever the party of liberty is gaining ground, they discover and then loudly publicize at just the
right moment some new atrocity or some nefarious plot which
horrifies the good men of property, Protestants and Catholics,
Berne as much as Fribourg.

No passion remains stationary, and fear less than any other.
So it must be nurtured and increased. Yet fear works in such
a way that it goes on magnifying its object and also weakening
the sick imagination of the fearful person. Every day brings some
new distrust. Today a certain idea seems dangerous, tomorrow
a certain man, a certain class. So they then shut themselves up
more and more. They barricade and solidly wall up their doors
and minds — no more daylight, not the slightest crack to let in
a ray of light.

There is no more contact with the people. Now the bourgeois
knows them only through the police reports. He sees them only
in his servant who robs him and laughs at him. He sees them
only through his window in the drunken man who goes past
shouting, falling, and rolling in the mud. He does not know that
the poor fellow is, after all, more honest than the wholesale and
retail poisoners who have brought him to that sad state.

Rugged work makes rugged men and coarse language. The
voice of the man of the people is rough; he has been a soldier and
always takes on a military energy. The bourgeois then concludes
that his habits are those of violence, and he is usually mistaken.
In nothing is the improvement of our age more visible than in

* This is how Proudhon had answered himself in his famous *What Is
Property?* in 1840.

this. Just lately, when the police rushed suddenly into the carpenters' lodge, broke open their strongbox, and seized their papers and meager savings, did we not see these brave men restrain their outrage and take the matter to the courts?

Generally the rich man is a man who has become rich, the poor man of yesterday. Yesterday he himself was the worker, the soldier, and the peasant he avoids today. I can better understand that the grandson, who was born rich, can forget all this; but that within a man's life, in thirty or forty years, he should disown himself is inexplicable. For heaven's sake, you are a man of our warlike times and have faced the enemy a hundred times. Do not fear to face your poor countrymen whom they have used to frighten you! What are the poor doing? They are beginning today, as you once began. That man who passes there is you yourself, only younger. That young draftee who goes away singing the "Marseillaise," is he not you who left as a boy in '92? Does not the officer in Africa, full of ambition and the breath of war, remind you of 1804 and the camp at Boulogne? The tradesman, the worker, the small manufacturer — they all strongly resemble those who, like yourself, sought their fortune about 1820.

These men are like you. If they can they will rise, and probably by better means since they are born in better times. They will gain, and you will lose nothing. Put aside that false notion that someone gains only when he takes from others. Every rising wave of the people brings with it a wave of new wealth.

Do you know the danger of isolating yourself and shutting yourself up so well? It is that you shut up nothing but a vacuum. By excluding men and ideas, you yourself dwindle away and are impoverished. You close yourselves up in your class and your little circle of habits, where the mind and personal activity are no longer necessary. The door is firmly barred, but there is no one inside. Oh, poor rich man! If you are now nothing, what do you want to guard so well?

Let us open your soul and see if it has any recollection of what was and of what remains. Is there any of the youthful enthusiasm of the Revolution? Alas, who would find the least trace of it?

The warlike strength of the Empire and the liberal aspirations of the Restoration are no more to be seen.

We have seen this man of today grow smaller with every step that seemed to lift him up. As a peasant, he had morality, sobriety, and thrift. As a workman, he was a good companion and a great help to his family. As a manufacturer, he was active, energetic, and filled with an industrial patriotism which struggled against foreign industry. But he has left all as he has risen, and nothing has taken its place. His house is full, his coffer is full, and his soul is empty.

Life is lighted and kindled by life, and it is extinguished by isolation. The more life mixes with lives different from itself and the more it joins itself with other existences, the stronger, happier, and more fruitful is its own existence. Descend the scale of animal creation to those poor beings which leave us in doubt as to whether they are plants or animals. You enter into solitude, for these miserable creatures have scarcely any connection with each other.

Stupid egotism! In what direction does the fearful class of rich men and the bourgeoisie turn its eyes? With what does it associate and ally itself? Precisely with what is most changeable — the political powers that come and go in this country, and the great capitalists who will take their bonds and bills and cross the Channel on the day of revolutions. Men of property, do you know what will not move any more than the land itself? It is the people. Trust in them.

Rich men, the safety of both France and yourselves depends on your not fearing the people, on your going to them, on your knowing them, on your laying aside the fables you have been told, which bear no relation to reality. You must understand one another, open your mouths and your hearts as well, and speak to one another like men.

You will go on sinking, weakening, and always declining if you do not summon and adopt all those who are strong and able. It is not a question of having more *qualified* people in the common sense of the word. It is of no consequence if an assembly that now has one hundred fifty lawyers had three hundred. The men educated by our modern scholastics will not regenerate the world. No, it is the men of instinct and of inspiration, who are either uncultivated or have different cultures (foreign to our ways of thought and which we do not appreciate) — these are the men whose alliance will bring life to the man of study and practical sense to the man of business. These qualities have certainly been lacking of late, as the present state of France shows all too clearly.

I really do not know what I ought to hope for from the rich and the bourgeoisie in the building of a large, honest, and generous association. They are very sick; people so far gone are not easily cured. But I must confess that I still have hope for their sons. Those young people, such as I see before my desk in our schools, have better tendencies. They have always welcomed warmly every sentence in favor of the people.

May they do more. Let them stretch out their hands and quickly join the people in a common regeneration. Let these rich youths never forget that they bear a heavy load, the life of their fathers, who in so short a time have risen, enjoyed, and fallen. These rich youths are exhausted from birth, and young as they are, they have need to grow younger by breathing the popular spirit. Their strength lies in their still being close to the people, their root, whence they have just sprung. Ah! May they return there with all their heart and sympathy and regain a little of the vitality which has been the genius, the wealth, and the strength of France since 1789.

Young and old, we rich and learned are worn out. Why not admit it at the end of this hard day's work which has lasted half a century? Even they who have passed through various classes and all sorts of trials, like myself for instance, have nonetheless lost on the way in their inner struggles a great part of their strength. It is late — I feel it; the evening is coming on. "Already longer shadows fall from the tops of the mountains."

Come on then, you young and strong! Come on, you working people. We will open our arms to you. Bring back a new warmth to us; let the world, let life, let learning begin again.

For my part, I fondly hope that my science, my dear study of history, will go on gathering new life in this popular life, and by means of these newcomers become the grand and beneficial thing I have dreamed of. The historian of the people will come from the people.

That man will certainly not love them more than I. My home and my heart, my life and my country, are among them. But many things have prevented me from drawing out the most creative element there. The entirely abstract education that is given us dried me up for a long time. It took many long years to efface the sophist that had been made of me. I became myself only by shaking off that foreign accessory; I have learned to know myself only by negative means. That is why, sincere and passionate after truth as I have always been, I have not attained the ideal of grand simplicity which I had before my mind. To you then, young man, to you will be given the gifts I have lacked.[5] Son of the people and less removed from them, you will come all at once upon the field of their history with their colossal strength and inexhaustible vitality. My streams will come of their own accord to lose themselves in your torrents.

I give you all that I have done. You will give me oblivion. May my imperfect history be swallowed up in a worthier monument, where learning and inspiration blend in better harmony, where among vast and penetrating research we feel everywhere the breath of immense crowds and the creative soul of the people.

[5] But I must first help and prepare this young man. That is why I continue my history. A book is the means of making a better book.

❧

CHAPTER VIII

Review of the First Part: Introduction to the Second

In glancing over this long ladder of society traced in a few pages, a host of painful ideas and a world of sadness beset me. So many physical pains are there! But how many more mental sufferings! And few are unknown to me. I know and I feel that I have had my full share. I must, however, put aside my own feelings and recollections and follow my little light through this cloud of mist.

My light from the very first, which will not deceive me, is France. The feeling for France, the devotion of the citizen to the native land, is my standard for judging these men and these classes. This is a moral, but also a natural, standard; for in every living thing each part derives its value primarily from its relation to the whole.

It is the same with nationality as with geology — the heat is below. Descend, and you will find it increases. In the lower strata it is burning hot.

The poor love France as if they were indebted to her and had duties toward her. The rich love her as if she belonged to them and had obligations to them. The patriotism of the first is the feeling of duty; that of the second is a demand and the pretension to a right.

The peasant, as we have said, has joined France in lawful wedlock. She is his wife forever; he is one with her. For the worker she is his beautiful mistress; he has nothing but he has France, her noble past and her glory. Free from local ideas, he adores the grand unity. He must be very miserable, enslaved by hunger and toil, when this sentiment fades within him. It never vanishes.

The unhappy bondage of personal interest is much greater when we move up to the manufacturers and shopkeepers. They feel themselves always in danger, and walk as if upon a tightrope. Bankruptcy! To avoid a partial bankruptcy they would rather risk a general one. They made and unmade the July Revolution.

And yet can we say that in this great class of several million souls the sacred fire is extinct, absolutely and irremediably? No, I would rather believe that the flame is in a latent state within them. Rivalry with the foreigner, the Englishman, will prevent them from losing the spark.

How cold it is if I go higher! It is like the cold of the Alps. I reach the region of snows. Moral vegetation gradually disappears, and the flower of nationality grows pale. It is like a world seized in a single night by a sudden frost of selfishness and fear. If I ascend one step higher, even fear ceases. There is the pure egotism of the calculator who has no fatherland, where people are no longer people but only numbers. There is a true glacier, abandoned by nature.[1] Let me come down. The cold is too great for me there, and I cannot breathe.

If, as I believe, love is life itself, there is very little life up there. It seems that as far as national sentiment is concerned, which makes a man extend his life throughout the grand life of France,

[1] These glaciers do not have the impartial indifference of those in the Alps, which accumulate life-giving waters only to pour them out indiscriminately among the nations. The Jews, whatever be said of them, have a country — the London Stock Exchange; they operate everywhere, but they are rooted in the country of gold. Now that an armed peace, that motionless war which devours Europe, has put the funds of every state into their hands, what can they love? The land of the status quo — England. What can they hate? The land of progress — France. Recently they thought to deaden her by buying up a score of men whom France refuses. Another mistake: from either vanity or an exaggerated feeling of security, they have taken kings into their band, mingled with the aristocracy, and by so doing have associated themselves with political risks. That is what their forefathers, the Jews of the Middle Ages, would never have done. What a decline in Jewish wisdom!

the higher one goes toward the upper classes, the less alive one becomes.

But, by way of compensation, are they above less liable to sufferings; are they freer and happier? I doubt it. I see, for example, that the great manufacturer who is so superior to the miserable little rural landowner is also and even more often than he the slave of the banker. I see that the petty shopkeeper who has risked his savings in trade and compromises his family (as I have explained), who dries himself up with anxious waiting, envy, and rivalry, is not much happier than the worker. And if the worker is a single man and can spare thirty centimes out of his four francs of daily wages for times of unemployment, then he is incomparably merrier than the shopkeeper, and more independent.

The rich man, it will be said, suffers only from his vices — but that is much in itself. Still we must also add his boredom and ennui, his moral decay, the feeling of a man who was once better and has life enough to feel his decline and see in his lucid moments that he is sinking into the miseries and follies of a petty mind. What can be sadder than to sink and never be able to rise again by any act of the will? From being a Frenchman he falls to the level of a cosmopolitan, of just any man, and from there to the level of a mollusk!

What have I tried to say in all this? That the poor man is happy? That all are equal before fate? That "things balance out in the long run"? God forbid I should uphold so false a thesis, so well fitted to kill the heart and reassure egotism! Do I not see, do I not know by experience, that physical suffering, far from excluding mental suffering, is generally allied with it — that these terrible sisters march together to crush the poor! See, for instance, the fate of the wife in our poorer quarters. She seldom brings a child into the world except to die, and she finds in material poverty an unlimited source of mental suffering.

Mentally and physically, contemporary society has above all others an affliction peculiar to itself: it has become extraordinarily sensitive. I believe that the ordinary ills of humanity have decreased, and history sufficiently proves this on the whole. However, these ills have decreased in a finite proportion while sensibility has increased infinitely. While the enlarged mind opened a new sphere to pain, the heart gave through love and family ties new hostages to fortune, dear opportunities for suffering which no one wishes to sacrifice. But how much more disturbing have they made life! People no longer suffer only from the present, but also from the future, from what might be. The soul, sore and aching in advance, feels and anticipates future ills and sometimes ills which will never come.

To top it off, this age of extreme individual sensibility is precisely that in which everything is done by collective means that are the least responsive to the individual. Action of every kind is centralized around some great force, and whether he likes it or not, man is drawn into this whirlwind. How little he weighs there, and what becomes of his dearest thoughts and deepest griefs in these vast impersonal organizations? Alas, who can tell? The machine rolls on, immense, majestic, and indifferent. It never knows that its small wheels, which withstand such heavy pressure, are living men.

But surely those moving wheels, which act under one and the same impulse, at least recognize each other? Surely their necessarily cooperative relationship must produce a mental and moral relationship? By no means. This is the strange mystery of this age: the period in which we act together the most is perhaps that in which our hearts are united the least. The collective means which place thought in common, circulate and diffuse it, have never been greater; yet never was isolation more profound.

The mystery remains inexplicable to all who do not observe the historical evolution of the system which gave it birth. This system can be called *Machinism*. Let me state its origin.

The Middle Ages laid down a formula of love, but it ended only in hatred. It consecrated inequality and injustice, which made love impossible. The violent reaction of love and nature called the Renaissance did not found a new order, and seemed a disorder. The world, for which order was a necessity, then said, "Well, let us not love; the experiment of a thousand years has been enough. Let us seek order and strength in the union of powers. We will find machines which will unite us together without love, which will frame and hold men so fast, so nailed and riveted and screwed together, that even though they detest one another, they will act together." And then once again they made administrative machines analogous to those of the old Roman Empire: bureaucracies like that of Colbert under Louis XIV; armies like that of Louvois in the same period. These machines had the advantage of employing man as a regular power, of employing life — minus its whims and inequalities.

Yet these machines still used men and retained something human. The marvel of Machinism would be to do without men. So let us seek powers which may act without us, like clockwork, once they are set in motion by us.

Set in motion by us? Here we still have man, and that is a defect. Let nature furnish not only the parts of the machine, but the power to make it go as well. It was then that these iron workers were created, which comb, spin, weave, and manufacture with a hundred thousand arms and a hundred thousand teeth. The power was taken from the elements, from water that falls or that — held captive and expanded in steam — moves and lifts with its mighty sigh.

There were also machines to make our social acts uniformly automatic, and to let us dispense with patriotism. There were more which multiplied monotonous products ad infinitum once they were built, and which, with the art of the day, exempt us from being artists every day. This is a great deal, and man no longer has much of a place in the system. Machinism, however, wants more; man is not yet mechanized profoundly enough.

He preserves his solitary reflection, his philosophical meditation, and the pure thought of Truth. There he cannot be reached, unless some latter-day scholastic succeeds in drawing him out of himself to entangle him in his formulas. Once he puts his foot on that wheel, which turns effortlessly, then the Thinking Machine, being enmeshed in the political machine, will roll on triumphantly and will be termed Political Science.

But imagination still remains free, "useless" poetry which loves and creates according to its own pleasure. But this serves no purpose and is a sad waste of forces! Are those objects which imagination pursues at random so numerous that one cannot, through careful classification, stamp for each class a mold into which we shall only have to pour, according to the wants of the day, such and such a novel or drama or any work that may be ordered? Then there will be no more men of literary labor, no more passion, and no more fantasy. The English economists have dreamed of an ideal industrial world with one single machine with one single man to set it going. How much finer is the triumph of Machinism to have mechanized even the winged world of fantasy and imagination.

Let us sum up this evolution: we have the State without the country, industry and literature without art, philosophy without inquiry, and humanity without man.

Why are we surprised if the world chokes and suffocates beneath this air machine? It has found a way to do without its soul, its life; I mean love.

Deceived by the Middle Ages, which promised union and did not keep its word, the world has renounced this goal and sought in its discouragement the art of not loving. Thus machines, even the finest industrial or administrative machines, have given man, among so many advantages,[2] one unfortunate ability — that of uniting forces without uniting hearts, of cooperating without loving, of acting and living together without knowing one another. The moral power of association has lost all that mechanical concentration has gained.

There is savage isolation even in cooperation itself, for it is a sterile contact without will or warmth, where the only heat is from the severity of the friction. The result is not indifference, as one might suppose, but antipathy and hatred. There is not merely the negation of society, but the opposite: society actively working to become unsociable.

Here before my eyes and in my heart I have the grand review of our miseries which the reader has shared with me. Well! I would swear on oath that among all these very real miseries,

---

[2] I have absolutely no intention of contesting these advantages (see above, pp. 43-45). Who would wish to return to those ages of impotence when man had no machines?

which I certainly do not underrate, the worst of all is the misery of the mind. By this I mean the incredible ignorance of each other which we all share, whether practical or speculative men. And the principal cause of this ignorance is that we believe there is no need to know one another. A thousand mechanical ways of acting without the soul allow us to avoid knowing what man is and to avoid seeing him as something besides a force or a number. Being numbers and abstractions ourselves, relieved of vital action through the aid of machinism, we feel ourselves declining every day and sinking to zero.

Hundreds of times I have observed the perfect ignorance of other classes in which every class lives — not seeing and not wanting to see. We, the cultivated minds, for example — what difficulty we have in recognizing any good qualities in the people! We blame them for countless things which depend almost entirely on their situation: an old or dirty coat, a binge after long abstinence, a crude expression, rough hands, and a thousand charges of the kind. And what would become of us if those hands of work were less rough? We limit ourselves to externals, to pitiful matters of form, and we do not see the good and great heart which is often beneath.

On their side, they do not suspect that an energetic soul may be found in a weak body. They laugh at the learned man for leading the life of a cripple. In their opinion he is a loafer. They have no idea of the powers of reflection, meditation, and the force of calculation increased tenfold by patience. Every advance that is not gained in war seems to them ill earned. How often have I noticed with a smile that the Cross of the Legion of Honor seemed to them out of place upon the breast of some puny man with a sad, pale face.

Yes, there is a misunderstanding here. They misunderstand the powers of study and persevering reflection by which discoveries are made. We misunderstand the instinct, the inspiration, and the energy which make heroes.

You may be sure that this is the greatest evil in the world. We hate one another, we despise one another; that is to say, we do not know one another.

The partial remedies that may be applied are no doubt good, but the basic remedy is a general one. We must cure the soul.

The poor suppose that if the rich were tied down by such and such a law, all would be done and the world would go well. The rich think that in bringing the poor back to some religious pattern, dead for the last two centuries, they are strengthening society. Fine partial remedies! Apparently they both imagine that these formulas, whether political or religious, have a mystical power to charm the world, as if their power were not in the harmony they find or do not find in the heart!

The evil is in the heart. So let the remedy be also in the heart! Lay aside your old formulas and recipes. Open your hearts and arms. Why, they are your brothers after all! Had you forgotten that?

I do not say that this or that form of association may not be excellent. But fundamentals, not forms, are the question. The most ingenious forms will not be of much help to you if you are unsociable.

Between men of study and reflection and men of instinct, who will take the first step? We, the men of study. On our side the obstacle (whether repugnance, laziness, or indifference) is trifling. On theirs it is truly serious. It is the ignorance which fate decreed; it is the suffering which closes and withers the heart.

No doubt the people reflect, and often more than we. Nevertheless their basic characteristic is their instinctive powers, which affect equally both thought and activity. The man of the people is above all a man of instinct and action.

The separation of men and classes is due principally to the absurd opposition between instinct and reflection that has been established in our time, in this age of machinism. It is due to the contempt reflection has for instinctive faculties, which it believes it can do without.

Thus I must explain what instinct and inspiration are, and the laws that they follow. Come with me in this investigation, I beg you, where we shall see the natural condition of my subject. The political city will not understand itself, its evils, and its remedies until it has seen itself in the mirror of the moral city.

PART TWO

❧

Of Freedom through Love:
Nature

∾

CHAPTER I

The Instinct of the People: A Neglected Question

About to begin this vast and difficult investigation, it is not very encouraging to realize that I am alone on this road and that there is no one to give assistance. Alone I am; but nonetheless I will go forward, full of courage and hope.

Some noble writers of artistic spirit, who had always drawn the manners of the upper classes, have remembered the people. They have undertaken through their benevolent attention to bring the people into fashion. They have gone out of their drawing rooms into the street and asked the passersby where the people lived. They were directed to the jails, the prisons, and the haunts of vice.

The result of this misunderstanding is very sad, for these writers have produced an effect contrary to that which they intended. In order to interest us in the people, they have chosen to draw and relate things which would naturally disgust and frighten us. "What! are the people like that?" cried with one voice the timid race of bourgeois. "Quick! We must increase the police and arm ourselves! Then shut the doors and bolt them tight!"

Close examination clearly shows, however, that these artists, famous dramatists before everything else, have depicted under the name of the people a limited class whose life — full of accidents, violence, and felonies — offered them easy picturesque effects and successful horror stories.

Everyone, whether criminologist, economist, or social commentator, has studied (almost exclusively) an exceptional people —

that classless class which frightens us every year with increase of crime and the number of recidivists. It is a well-known people, thanks to the publicity given our courts and the conscientious thoroughness of our trials, and it occupies the public's attention as it does in no other country in Europe. The secret trials in Germany and the rapid administration of justice in England do not give any sensational publicity to their criminals, who are either buried in prison or deported to the colonies. England, two or three times as rich as France in this respect, does not display her wounds.

Here, on the contrary, there is no class that obtains the honor of more complete publicity. This strange community, which lives at the expense of society, is passionately followed by society. There are newspapers to record their acts, arrange their words, and give them cleverness. There are heroes and famous men, men known to all the world by name, who come periodically before the courts to relate their campaigns.

This chosen tribe, which supplies almost all the models privileged to sit before these painters of the people, is drawn principally from the populace of large towns, and no class contributes more to it than the working class.

Here again our criminologists have led public opinion. Our economists have followed their lead and inspiration in studying what they call *the people*. For them *the people* is above all the worker, particularly the factory worker. This approach, which would not be out of place in England, where industrial population forms two-thirds of the whole, is singularly so in France — a great agricultural nation where this same class does not constitute a sixth of the population.[1] It is a numerous class, but a small minority nonetheless. Those who take it for their model have no right to use the caption "This is a portrait of the people."

Examine closely these witty and corrupt crowds of our cities which strike the observer so forcefully. Listen to their language, note their often very clever flashes of wit, and you will discover something which has gone unnoticed so far. You will see that

[1] And of this sixth the factory worker forms a very small portion.

these men and women, who sometimes do not even know how to read, still have in their own way highly cultivated minds.

Men who live together, in constant contact with one another, necessarily develop themselves through this simple contact — by the effect of this natural warmth, as it were. They give themselves an education — a bad one if you like — but still an education. The vitality alone of a great city means a person is taught every instant without even trying to learn anything.

One has only to go into the street and walk with his eyes open to become aware of a thousand new things. This city, this sight, is a school. They who live there do not live an instinctive and natural life. They are cultivated men who observe and reflect, for good or for bad. I find them often very subtle and even viciously cunning. The effects of refined cultivation are all too plainly visible.

If you want to find something in the world contrary to nature, directly opposed to all the instincts of childhood, look at that artificial creature called the street child of Paris.[2] Still more artificial is the youngest imp of Satan, that horrible boy-man of London who at twelve years of age traffics, thieves, drinks gin, and visits prostitutes.

Artists, such are your models. The bizarre, the exceptional, the monstrous — that is what you seek. Are you moralists or caricaturists? What difference is there now?

One day a man came to the famous Themistocles and offered a way to improve his memory. He answered bitterly, "Give me instead a way to forget." May God give me such an art, so that I may now forget all your monsters, your fantastic creations, and these shocking exceptions with which you confuse my subject. You go hunting in the gutters with a magnifying glass, and when you find some dirty, filthy thing, you bring it to us exclaiming, "Triumph! Triumph! We have found the people!"

To interest us in the people, they show them to us forcing doors and picking locks. To these picturesque descriptions they add

[2] It is a marvel of our national character that this abandoned child, incited to evil and overexcited in every manner, still retains good qualities such as wit and courage.

those profound theories by which the people, if we listen to them, justify for themselves in their own eyes this warfare against property. Truly it is a terrible misfortune, in addition to so many others, to have these rash friends. These acts and these theories are not at all of the people. The mass is doubtless neither pure nor irreproachable. Still, if you want to characterize them by the idea which dominates for the immense majority, you will find them occupied, quite to the contrary, in building through labor, economy, and the most respectable means the immense work which constitutes the strength of this country — the participation of all classes in property.

I said that I feel I am alone, and I should be sad indeed if I did not have with me my faith and hope. I see myself weak, both by nature and with respect to my previous efforts, in the presence of this immense subject. It is like standing at the foot of a gigantic monument which I must move all alone. Alas! how disfigured it is today, how loaded with foreign matter, moss, and moldiness, spoiled by the rain and mud and by the injuries it has received from passersby! The painter, the man of art for art's sake, comes and looks at it; what pleases him is precisely that moss. But I would tear it away. You, painter passing by, this is not a plaything of art — this is our altar!

I must dig away the earth and discover the deep foundation of this monument. The inscription, I see, is now quite buried and hidden far underground. I have neither mattock, spade, nor pick, but my fingernails will do.

Perhaps I shall be as fortunate as I was ten years ago when I discovered two curious monuments at Holyrood. I was in the famous chapel, long unroofed and exposed to rain and fog so that now all its tombs are covered with thick green moss. The memory of the old alliance between France and Scotland, so unfortunately lost, made me regret that I was not able to read anything on those tombs about the old friends of France. Mechanically I scraped away the moss from one of the stones, and read the inscription of a Frenchman who had been the first man to pave the streets of Edinburgh. My curiosity aroused, I went on to another stone with a death's head carved upon it. This marker, which had fallen over, was itself buried in a shroud of moldiness. I scratched with my nails, having no other instrument, and began to read something of a Latin inscription. After long study I at last deciphered four words almost effaced, words of serious import, well fitted to cause reflection and to raise suspicions of a tragic end: "Legibus fidus, non regibus" — Faithful to laws, not to kings.

And now I dig again. I would get to the bottom of this stone. But this time it is not a monument of hatred and civil war that I wish to excavate. On the contrary, what I want to find in descending below this sterile, cold ground are those depths where social warmth begins again, where the treasures of universal life are kept, and where the dried-up fountains of love will gush forth once more for all the world.

༄

CHAPTER II

The Instinct of the People: Weakened but Still Powerful

Criticism waits for my first word and then begins to speak. "In a hundred-odd pages you have drawn up a long balance sheet of social miseries, of the bondage attached to each condition. We have been patient in the hope that after the evils we would finally learn the remedies. For evils so real, so positive, and so carefully specified, we expect that you will offer something better than vague words, hackneyed sentimentality, or moral and metaphysical remedies. Propose specific reforms. Draw up, for every abuse, a clear formula of what must be changed and address it to the Chamber of Deputies. Or if you confine yourself to lamentations and reveries, you would do better to return to your Middle Ages, which you should never have left."

Well, it seems that special remedies have not been wanting. There must be some fifty thousand on our statute books. We add more to them every day, but I do not see that we are improving. Our legislative doctors treat each symptom which appears here or there as an isolated and distinct case, and expect to cure it by some local application. They understand neither the profound solidarity linking all the parts of the social body together nor the questions that relate to it.[1] Herodotus tells us that in the

---

[1] For instance, they have not wished to see that the question of prison reform is a corollary to the question of public instruction. Whether the question is to form or reform man, to raise or relieve him, it is not the mason but the teacher that the State should call upon: the religious, moral, and national teacher, who will speak in the name of God and in the *name of France.*

infancy of medical science the Egyptians had different physicians for each part of the body: one treated the nose, another the ear, a third the stomach, and so on. They did not worry whether their remedies harmonized; each of them worked apart, without disturbing the others. If after each separate member was cured, the man still died, that was his business.

I must confess that I have formed a different standard of medicine. It seemed to me that before trying every external and local remedy, it would be useful to inquire into the inner evil that produces all these symptoms. This evil is, in my opinion, the chill and paralysis of the heart, which creates unsociableness. This unsociableness is due primarily to the false notion that we may isolate ourselves with impunity, that we have no need of others. The wealthy and educated classes especially imagine that they gain nothing from the instinct of the people, that their book knowledge is sufficient for everything, and that men of action would teach them nothing. To enlighten them I am forced to explore what is creative in instinctive and active abilities. This is a difficult approach but a legitimate one, and none other has been so before.

I bring three things to this inquiry. When I said just now that I was alone, I was wrong.

First, I bring with me the observation of the present, which is all the more important in my case because it is not only from outside but also from inside. Son of the people, I have lived with them, I know them. They are myself. How could I, being at the center of things, go astray like the others and take the exception for the rule, or monstrosities for nature?

My second advantage is that thinking less about this or that innovation in manners, less about this or that special class of yesterday, and rather keeping myself in the rightful universality of the mass, I have no trouble linking its present state with its *past*. Changes in the lower classes are much slower than in the upper. I do not see this mass suddenly born at random, like some ephemeral monster bursting from the earth. Rather, I see it descending in lawful succession from the dawn of history. Life is less mysterious when we know the birth, the ancestors, and the antecedents, and when we have seen, so to speak, how the living being existed long before he was born.

Finally, taking this people thus in its present and its past, I am able to reestablish their necessary *relationships with other peoples,* whatever their degree of civilization or barbarism. All peoples explain and comment upon one another. To any question that you put to one, the other replies. For example, you consider certain habits of our mountaineers of the Pyrenees and Auvergne as gross; I look upon them as barbarous, and I understand and classify them as such, and know their proper place and value in the scale of general life. How many things half effaced in the manners of our people, seemingly inexplicable and devoid of all reason and sense, I have learned to see as being in harmony with primitive inspiration, and as being nothing else but the wisdom of a forgotten world . . . For some reason or other I could not leave such poor shapeless fragments that I met unnoticed at the side of the road. So I picked them up at random and filled the folds of my cloak with them. Later on closer examination I discovered with a religious emotion that what I had collected was neither stone nor flint, but the bones of my forefathers.

This analysis of the present in terms of the past and the comparative study of different peoples and different ages went beyond the scope of this little book. Nevertheless this method of analysis has helped me check and clarify my findings concerning our present customs, findings which are the product of observation, reading, and every kind of information.

Some will protest. "Is not this method dangerous in itself? Is not this analysis foolhardy? Do the people we see today possess any important tie to their original source? Now so very commonplace, do they resemble in the slightest those tribes which in their savage state still retain a poetic flame? We do not pretend that fecundity and creative power have always been lacking in the masses. In the savage or barbarous state they produce something, as the national songs of all primitive peoples testify. They also produce when transformed by culture, when they approach the higher classes and mingle with them. But a people which has neither primitive inspiration nor culture, which is neither civilized nor savage and stands in an intermediate state, both vulgar and rude — does not such a people remain *impotent?* The savages themselves, who are naturally gifted with much noble feeling and poetry, turn with disgust from our emigrants who are the offspring of these crude populations."

I do not dispute the state of depression, of physical and occasionally mental degeneration, in which the people are now found, especially in the towns. The whole mass of oppressive labors, all the burdens which in ancient times the slave bore alone, is now found parceled out among the free men of the lower classes. All share in the miseries, the commonplace vulgarities, and the ugliness of slavery. The most fortunate races — our handsome races of the south, for instance, so full of life and song — are sadly bowed down by work. The worst is that today the soul is often as crushed as the shoulders: misery, want, fear of the moneylender or the tax collector — what could be less poetic?

The people have less poetry in themselves and find less in the society that surrounds them. That society rarely has the kind of poetry they can appreciate — those piquant details that are picturesque or touching. Such poetry as this society has is of a high order, often with very complicated harmonies, which an inexperienced eye cannot discern.

The poor and lonely man, surrounded by immense objects and by enormous collective forces which hurl him along without his understanding them, feels himself weak and humiliated. He has none of the pride which formerly made individual genius so powerful. If no explanation is forthcoming, he stands discouraged before that grand society which seems to him so strong, so wise, and so learned. So he accepts whatever comes from that center of light, and without hesitation prefers it to his own conceptions. In the presence of this wisdom, the humble muse grows mute and dares not breathe. The village girl is overawed, silenced, or even made to sing an alien song. Thus we have seen Béranger, with his exquisite and nobly classic style, become the national songwriter, take possession of the entire people, and drive out the old village songs and even the ancient sea shanties sung by our sailors. Our worker-poets of late have imitated the rhythms of Lamartine, disinheriting themselves as much as they could and too often sacrificing whatever they might have of popular originality.

The fault of the people when they write is always to abandon their heart, which is where their force lies, and to borrow abstractions and vague generalities from the upper classes. They have a great advantage but do not appreciate it — that of not knowing the conventional language, of not being besieged and pursued as we are by ready-made sentences and formulas which present themselves of their own accord when we write and then take their places upon our paper. And yet this is precisely what our studious workmen envy in us and borrow from us as much as they can. When they write, they wear a suit and put on gloves, thus losing the superiority that strong hands and powerful arms give to the people when they know how to use them.

Well, what of it? Why ask men of action what their writings are? The true products of popular genius are not books but brave deeds, witty sayings, glowing and inspired language, just like I find every day in the street coming out of some vulgar mouth apparently the least likely to be touched by inspiration. Moreover, take the old clothes away from that man who is now so repulsive with his vulgarity and put him in uniform, with a saber, a gun, a drum, and a flag before him. You will not recognize him: he is another man. And where is the first fellow? Impossible to find him.

Yes, this depression, this degeneration, is only superficial. The foundation is intact. This race still has wine in its blood; even in those who seem the most burned out you will find a spark. There is always a military energy, always a brave recklessness, always a grand exhibition of independent spirit. This independence, which they do not know where to place (shackled as they are on every side), they too often throw into their vices, and then boast of being worse than they are. Exactly the reverse of the English.

Shackles without and a strong life boiling within — this contrast produces many false movements and discord in word and deed which is shocking at first sight. It also leads aristocratic Europe to delight in confusing the people of France with the imaginative and gesticulating peoples, such as the Italians, the Irish, the Welsh, and so on.

What distinguishes our people from them in a definite and distinct manner is that in their greatest excesses, in their wildest bounds of imagination, in what people are pleased to call their fits of Don Quixotism, they still retain their common sense. In their most exuberant moments, a firm, cool phrase shows that our man has not lost his balance and that he is not the dupe of his own excitement.

This is true of the French character in general. To turn to the people in particular, let us note that the instinct which dominates them gives them an immense advantage for action. Reflective thought reaches action only after passing through the process of deliberation and discussion; it has to pass so many things that frequently it never arrives. On the contrary, instinctive thought touches the act and is almost the act itself; it is almost at the same moment both thought and action.

The classes which we call inferior, and which follow instinct more closely, are for that very reason eminently capable of action and ever ready to act. But we cultivated minds chat, dispute, and spend all our energy in words. We unnerve ourselves through mental dissipation, through the vain amusement of running from book to book or of opposing them one to another. We show great anger about trifles and utter loud threats of action. But once said, we do nothing, we do not act. We pass on to other disputes.

They do not speak so much, or make themselves hoarse with shouting like learned men and old women. But should an opportunity arise, they make the most of it without making any noise and act with vigor. Economy in words encourages action in deeds.

With this in mind, let us take for our judges of these classes the heroic men of antiquity or the Middle Ages, and let us ask them which classes constitute the aristocracy. Without the least hesitation they will answer, "Those who act."

If you prefer to judge in terms of common sense and sound judgment, I do not know in what class we should find a more sensible man than the old French peasant. Without speaking of his shrewdness concerning his personal interest, he knows mankind well and understands the society he has not seen. He has great powers of inner reflection and a singular foreknowledge of natural occurrences. He comprehends the sky, and sometimes the land, better than a prophet of antiquity.

Beneath the appearance of a totally physical and vegetative life, these people think and dream; and what is dreaming in the youth becomes reflection and wisdom in the old man. As for us, we have all those advantages which can stimulate, sustain, and focus meditation. But being more wrapped up in life, in its pleasures and empty conversations, we can seldom reflect, and we wish to do so even less. The man of the people, on the contrary, is often sentenced to solitude by the nature of his work. Isolated by his work in the fields, isolated by noisy trades which create solitude in the midst of the crowd, he must necessarily turn his soul inward and converse with himself. If not, he will die of boredom.

The women of the people in particular, obliged more than any others to be the careful managers of the family and even of their husbands, forced every day to use on them infinite skills and virtuous schemes, occasionally attain with time an astonishing degree of maturity. I have seen some who toward the end of life — having preserved their best instincts through many hard trials, having always cultivated their minds through reflection, and being elevated by the natural improvement of a pure and devoted life — no longer belonged at all to their own class, nor, I think, to any other, for they were truly superior to all. They were endowed with extraordinary prudence and penetration, even in matters with which you would have supposed they had no experience whatever. They saw so clearly into probabilities that people would have easily believed they had the gift of prophecy. Nowhere else have I ever met with such a union of two things generally believed to be distinct and even opposed — worldly wisdom and the spirit of God.

∾

CHAPTER III

Do the People Gain Much by Sacrificing Their Instinct? Bastard Classes

This peasant we were discussing, this wise and careful man, has one fixed idea: his son shall not be a peasant, he shall rise, and he shall become a bourgeois. He succeeds only too well. You will have no difficulty recognizing his son, who finishes his education and becomes a "monsieur" — a priest, a lawyer, or perhaps a manufacturer. Red-faced and of hardy stock, he will dominate everything with his vulgar energy; he will be a great talker, a politician, a man of weight and grand views who no longer has anything in common with humble folk. You will find him everywhere in the world with his voice which drowns out everything, concealing under the finest white gloves the coarse hands of his father.

I am expressing myself badly; the father had strong hands, the son has coarse ones. The father, beyond a doubt, was more muscular and shrewd. He was much nearer the aristocracy. He did not talk so much, and he went straight to his goal.

Has the son risen by quitting his father's social rank? Has there been progress from one to the other? Yes, no doubt, as regards cultivation and knowledge, but not as far as originality and real distinction are concerned.

Everyone is changing his social rank today; they all rise, or think they rise. In the last thirty years, five hundred thousand workers have taken out licenses and become masters. The number of agricultural laborers who have become small landowners is incalculable. The liberal professions, as they are called, have recruited their members from the inferior ranks to an immense extent; they are now full to the brim.

A profound change in ideas and morality has been the consequence of all this. Man patterns his soul to his material situation. It is very strange: now we have the soul of the poor, the soul of the rich, the soul of the businessman. It seems that man is nothing but the accessory of material fortune.

There has been among the different classes not a union or an association but a rapid and crude mixing together. No doubt this was necessary to neutralize the otherwise insurmountable obstacles the new equality encountered. But this change has nevertheless had the result of stamping art, literature, everything, with great vulgarity. People living comfortably, even the rich, adapt themselves marvelously to cheap common articles; in many a house of great style you will find common, ugly, and tasteless articles. They want art — at bargain prices. The thing that makes true nobility, the power of sacrifice, is lacking in the man of new wealth. He is lacking it in art as well as in politics. He is unwilling to sacrifice anything, even in his own real interest. This moral weakness pursues him even in his pleasures and vanities and makes them vulgar and paltry.

Will this class of all classes, this bastard hodgepodge so quickly formed and already decaying, ever be productive? I doubt it. The mule is sterile.

One people which seems to me eminently bourgeois, in comparison to military ones such as the French, the Polish, and so on, is the English. They may enlighten us as to the future prospects of the bourgeoisie. No other people in the world had more class changes, and none has taken more pains to disguise as noblemen the man of new wealth and the son of the merchant. These men, who have renewed the entire English nobility in the last two centuries, have been determined to preserve, together with the names and arms, the venerable manors, the furniture, and the hereditary collections. They have gone so far as to copy the manners and characters of the ancient families whose homes they occupy. With unfailing pride they have represented and played those old barons in their attitudes, speech, and general manners.

Well, what have they produced with all this labor in the art of preserving tradition and manufacturing antiquity? They have created a sober and important nobility with great steadfastness of purpose, but with few resources and little political invention in the final count, and by no means worthy of the great position the British empire occupies and is destined to occupy hereafter. Where, I ask you, is the England of Shakespeare and Bacon? The bourgeoisie (disguised, ennobled, it makes no difference) have governed England ever since Cromwell: power and riches have increased beyond calculation; the average level of culture has risen; but at the same time, a certain sad uniformity has established itself among the gentlemen — a universal similarity of men and things. You can hardly distinguish in their elegant penmanship one letter from another, or in their towns one house from another, or in their people one Englishman from another.

To return to the larger question, I am inclined to think that in the time to come, great inventive originality will belong to men who will not be lost in that bastard mediocrity in which all native character is unnerved. Strong men will be found who will not want to rise, men born of the people who will wish to remain of the people. To rise to a comfortable position, all well and good; but to enter the bourgeoisie, to change their condition and habits, will not appear to them at all desirable. They will feel certain that they would gain little by it. Great stamina, the all-encompassing instinct of the masses, and moral courage — all that is better preserved in the workingman, provided that he is not crushed by work and that his life is not too hard and allows him some leisure.

I have before my eyes two instances of men who with great good sense had no wish to rise. One, a factory worker, intelligent and reflective, always refused to be a foreman, dreading the responsibility, the reproaches, and the unpleasant contact with the manufacturer and preferring to work in silence alone with his thoughts. His admirable inner peace, which recalled that of the mystic workmen of whom I have spoken, would have been lost if he had accepted this new position.

The other, the son of a shoemaker, having finished his classical education and even his study of the law, and after being admitted to the bar, accepted without a murmur meeting the needs of his family and resumed his father's trade. He showed that a strong mind can rise or descend with equal ease. His resignation has been rewarded. This man, who did not seek glory, has now received it through his son, who, endowed with a singular gift, found in his father's craft the sentiment of art and has now become one of the greatest painters of our age.

Continual changes of ranks, trades, and habits prevent all inner improvement; they produce only those mixtures which are at one and the same time vulgar, pretentious, and barren. If you were to change the relative values of the strings in an instrument under the pretext of improving them, and were to reduce them all to one common tonality, you would in fact have canceled them all and made the instrument useless and harmony impossible.

To remain yourself gives you a great power and a chance for originality. If fortune changes, so much the better; but let nature remain. The man of the people should consider well before he stifles his instinct in order to put himself in line with fine bourgeois minds. If he remains true to his trade and improves it, like Jacquard, or if from a trade he forms an art, like Bernard Palissy, then what greater glory could he have in this world?

∿

CHAPTER IV

The Simple Ones: The Child, the Interpreter of the People

Whoever wishes to understand the highest gifts of the people's instinct must pass over those mongrel, bastard, half-cultivated minds which share the qualities and defects of the bourgeoisie. He must search out and study, above all, the simple.

The simple are in general those who seldom divide their thought. Not being armed with the machinery of analysis and abstraction, they see everything as one, entire and concrete, just as life presents it.

The simple form a large people. There are the simple by nature and the simple by culture. There are the poor in intellect who will never draw distinctions, children who do not yet draw them, and the peasants and common folk who are not used to doing so.

The scholastic, the critic, the man of analysis and exceptions and distinctions, looks down on the simple. However, since the simple never divide things, they have the advantage of seeing things in their natural state, organized and living. Not inclined to reflection, they are often rich in instinct. Inspiration is not uncommon in these classes, and sometimes it is even a kind of prophecy. Among them are found persons quite apart who preserve in an ordinary common life what is the highest moral poetry — the simplicity of the heart. Nothing is rarer than the preservation of these divine gifts of childhood; to do so generally implies a special grace and a sort of sanctity.

Even to speak of it requires that same gift and grace. Knowledge and learning, it is true, by no means exclude simplicity, but they do not give it. Nor does willpower have much to do with it.

The great jurist of Toulouse, at the most difficult point in his work, pauses and asks his reader to pray that he may have a special light to guide him in such subtle matter. How much more do we need it — for myself, and for you, my friends, who read me! How great is our need to obtain, not the gift of subtlety, but on the contrary the gift of simplicity and a childlike heart!

The wise men must no longer be content to say, "Suffer the little children to come unto me." They must go to them. They have much to learn in the midst of these children. The best thing they can do is adjourn their studies, lock up their books, which have been of so little use to them, and go quietly among mothers and nurses to unlearn and forget.

To forget? No, rather more to reform their wisdom, to check it against the instinct of those who are nearer to God, and to correct it by placing it beside that small standard — and tell themselves that the knowledge of the three worlds does not contain more than what lies in a cradle.

To speak only of our present subject, nobody will really penetrate it if he has not studied the child. The child is the interpreter of the people. What am I saying? The child is the people themselves in their native truth before they are deformed; it is the people without vulgarity, rudeness, or envy, inspiring neither distrust nor repugnance. Not only does the child interpret them, but it also justifies and proves their innocence on many occasions. Many a word that you find crude and coarse in the mouth of a crude man, you find natural (as it truly is) in the mouth of your child; thus you learn to guard against unjust prejudices. The child, being like the people in a happy ignorance of conventional language, formulas, and ready-made sentences that dispense with imagination, shows you by its example how the people must constantly seek and find their language. Both the child and the people often find it with a happy energy.

It is, moreover, through the child that you may appreciate what is still young and primitive in the people, changed though they are. Your son, like the peasant of Brittany and the Pyrenees, speaks at every moment the language of the Bible or *The Iliad*. The boldest criticism of Vico, Wolf, or Niebuhr is nothing in comparison to the bright and profound flashes certain words of the child will suddenly open for you in the darkness of antiquity. How often in observing the historical and narrative form that it gives to even abstract ideas will you feel how infant peoples must have narrated their dogmas in legends, and made a history of every moral truth! Oh, wise men, it is here that we must hold our tongues. Let us form a circle and listen to this young teacher from bygone ages. He has no need to analyze what he says in order to instruct us, for he is like a living witness: "He was there and knows the story better."

In him, as in young peoples, everything is still concentrated in a concrete and living state. It is enough to look at him in order to be conscious of the singularly abstract state we have attained in the present day. Many hollow abstractions cannot stand this examination. Our children of France especially, who are so lively and talkative with their precocious common sense, are continually bringing us back to realities. These innocent critics never fail to embarrass the philosopher. Their simple questions too often present him with the insoluble heart of things. They have not learned, as we have, to turn aside difficulties and avoid certain problems which it seems philosophers have agreed never to meddle with. Their bold little logic always goes straight ahead. No sacred absurdity would have maintained itself in this world if mankind had not silenced the objections of the child. From four to twelve especially is their time of reasoning; between lactation and puberty they seem lighter, less material, and livelier of mind than they are afterward. An eminent grammarian, who always preferred to live with children, told me that he found in them a capacity for the most subtle abstractions at that age.

They lose infinitely in developing so fast, in passing so rapidly from the life of instinct to the life of reflection. Until then they were living upon the large fund of instinct; they were swimming in a sea of milk. When from that obscure and fruitful sea, logic begins to disentangle the strands of a few luminous nets, there is no doubt progress, a necessary progress which is a condition of life. But this progress is nevertheless a decline in one sense. The child now becomes man, and he was a little god.

Childhood and death are the moments when the infinite radiates grace in man, and you may take the word in either its artistic or theological sense. Grace, lively in the child that plays and makes an attempt at life; grace, austere and solemn in the dying man when life is ending: always grace divine. Nothing could make us better understand the truth of the great biblical saying: "You are gods, you shall be gods."

Apelles and Correggio studied constantly these divine moments. Correggio passed whole days in watching children play. Apelles, says one of the ancients, loved to paint only the dying.

On these days of arrival and departure, of passage between two worlds, man seems to hold them both together.[1] The instinctive life into which he is then plunged is like the dawn and the twilight of thought — more vague than thought, no doubt, but how much more vast! All the intermediate work of the reasoning and reflective life is like a thin beam which starts from obscure boundlessness and returns to it. If you want to feel this well, study closely the child or the dying man. Place yourself at his pillow, be silent, and observe.

Unfortunately I have had too many opportunities to contemplate the approach of death, and for those very dear to me. I remember especially a long winter's day that I passed between the bed of a dying woman and the reading of Isaiah.* This painful scene was that of a struggle between wakefulness and sleep, a fitful dream of one who rose and fell again. Her eyes swimming

---

[1] The horror of the fatal enigma, the seal that shuts the mouth at the very moment one knows what to say — all that has been grasped in a sublime work I discovered in an enclosed part of Père Lachaise, in the cemetery of the Jews. It is a bust by Préault, or rather a head, held and clasped in its shroud with its finger pressed upon its lips — a truly fearful work, whose impression the heart can scarcely withstand and which appears to have been sculptured by the great chisel of death.

* Michelet is probably referring to Madame Dumesnil. Her death in 1842 moved the historian greatly, as did those of his dear friend and intellectual companion Poinsot in 1821 and his first wife in 1839.

in the void expressed the uncertainty between two worlds with painful accuracy. Her vast and obscure thought retraced the life now passed and grew larger in the face of immense forebodings ... The witness of this great struggle, who shared this ebb and flow and all the anxieties, clung as in a shipwreck to the firm belief that the soul returning to our primitive instincts had already anticipated the unknown world in that return, and thus could not be going on to annihilation. Rather, everything suggested that she was about to endow with this double instinct some young existence that would resume more happily the work of life, and express the dreams, developing ideas, and mute desires which the departing soul had failed to realize.[2]

One thing always strikes us in observing children and the dying. It is the perfect nobility which nature then gives them. Man is born noble, and he dies noble. It takes the work of a lifetime to become coarse and ignoble and to produce inequality between men.

Look at that child whom his mother on bended knee so aptly calls her Jesus. Society and education have soon changed him. The infinite that was in him and made him divine is disappearing; he acquires character and individuality, it is true, but he contracts. Logic and criticism hew and sculpture without mercy what seems a block of stone before them; cruel sculptors, whose iron bites into material too tender, every stroke breaks off whole pieces! Alas! how meager and mutilated he is already! Where is now the noble

___

[2] "The ancestor joins the infant as it springs to life from its mother ...Lo! thou art now reborn, O my soul, to sleep anew in a human subsistence." (Indian laws, quoted in my *Origines du droit.*) Without admitting the hypothesis of the transmigration of souls (and still less that of the transmission of sins), one is much tempted to believe that our first instincts reflect the collective mind of our ancestors, which the young traveler brings with him as provisions for his journey. He adds much to them. If I lay aside theories and shut my books to consider nature, I see thought spring up within us like an obscure instinct that gleams through twilight and enlightens and develops itself by the light of reflection. Then it becomes a formula and is more and more accepted as one; it passes into our habits, into the things that are ourselves and that we no longer examine; then finally it is obscured once again and becomes a portion of our instincts.

fullness of his nature? The worst is that under the influence of so rough an education, he will not only be weak and sterile, but he will also become vulgar.

When we regret our childhood, it is not so much the life and years that were then before us. It is our nobility that we regret. We had then that simple dignity of the being that has not yet been bent — equality with all, and all young, all handsome, all free. Let us be patient, for that must return: inequality is only for life; equality, liberty, mobility — everything returns to us by way of death.

We persist in seeing childhood only as an apprenticeship for life, a preparation for living, but alas, the greater number of children do not live. We want them to be happy "later on," and to insure the happiness of those uncertain years, we crush them with boredom and sorrow during the brief moment already assured.[3]

No, childhood is not only an age, a stage in life; it is a people, the people innocent. The flower of the human race, which is generally short-lived, conforms to nature, to whose bosom it is soon to return. And nature is just what they want to subdue in it. Man, who himself retreats from the barbarism of the Middle Ages, still maintains that barbarism toward the child. Always he starts from the inhuman principle that our nature is bad, that therefore education is not wise conservation but reformation, and that art and human wisdom ought to punish and improve the instinct that God has given us.

[3] I do not speak of overloading with work, or of those innumerable and excessive punishments we inflict upon their flexible character which nature herself decrees, but rather of the silly cruelty which causes us to plunge a young being rudely and incautiously into cold abstractions, a young being that just came from the maternal bosom, is still warm, and wants only to unfold its blossoms.

CHAPTER V

૭

Is the Natural Instinct of the Child Perverse?[1]

Is human instinct depraved from the outset? Is man wicked from his birth? Can the infant that I hold in my arms be already among the damned as it springs from its mother's breast?

To this atrocious question, which is painful even to write, the Middle Ages will answer yes, without any pity or hesitation.

What! this creature that seems so innocent and disarmed, for whom all nature feels tender, whom the she-wolf or the lioness would come and suckle in the absence of a mother — this creature has only the instinct of evil and the breath of that which ruined Adam? Would it belong to the devil if we did not hasten to exorcise it? Even after, if it should die in its nurse's arms, it is judged, it is in danger of damnation, it may be cast to the black beasts of hell! For the church says, "Deliver not to the *beasts* the souls that testify for thee." And how could this little one testify? It can neither speak nor understand.

While visiting during August 1843 a few cemeteries in the neighborhood of Lucerne, I found a very simple and painful expression of such religious terrors. At the foot of every tomb there was, according to ancient practice, a vase of holy water to guard the deceased night and day, and to prevent the beasts of hell from coming to take away the body, from tormenting and worrying it, or from making it into a vampire.

[1] Inattentive minds will think this chapter is foreign to the subject, but it is the very heart of the matter. (See p. 149.)

Alas, as for the soul of the child, they had no means of defending it; this cruel fear was expressed in several inscriptions. I stood a long time before this one without being able to tear myself away: *"I am a child two years of age ... What a terrible thing it is for such a child to go to Judgment, and appear already before the face of God!"* I burst into tears; I had caught a glimpse of the abyss of a mother's despair!

The poor quarters of our cities, those vast dens of death where women are wretchedly fecund and give birth only to weep, give us at best a very imperfect idea of the perpetual mourning of the mother in the Middle Ages. Constantly pregnant through barbarous lack of foresight, she produced without rest or truce and in tears and desolation more children, more dead, *more damned!*

What a horrible age! It is a world of cruel illusions over which a hellish irony seems to hover! Man, the plaything of his fluctuating, divine, and diabolical dream! Woman, the plaything and sport of man, always a mother and always in mourning! And alas, the child, who plays for a day at the sad game of life, smiles, weeps, and disappears — unfortunate little shadows that come by millions and billions and remain only in the memory of a mother! Her despair shows itself especially in one thing: she easily abandons herself to sin and damnation; she willingly takes revenge for the man's brutality; she is unfaithful, weeping and laughing.[2] She is lost, but what does it matter if she rejoins her child?

The child that survived was scarcely more happy. The Middle Ages were a terrible schoolmaster for him; they put before him the most complicated symbol that was ever taught, the most inaccessible to the simple. This subtle lesson, which the Roman Empire in its highest wisdom had great difficulty comprehending, this child of the Barbarians, this son of the rustic serf lost in the forest, must learn and understand. He repeats it and learns it; as for understanding that thorny, Byzantine, and scholastic formula,

---

[2] The infidelity of woman is the basic theme of the Middle Ages. The eternal subject for jokes, those *merry* stories can only sadden him who knows and understands. They prove all too plainly the overpowering boredom of that age, the emptiness of those souls without any cure for their weakness, the moral prostration, the despair of virtue, and the abandonment of one's self and one's salvation.

that is more than rod, blows, and whippings will ever get from him.

The Church, democratic by her principle of election, was eminently aristocratic by the difficulty of her teaching, which only a few men could really attain. She damned the natural instinct as perverse and corrupt from the beginning, and made learning, metaphysics, and a most abstract formula the condition of salvation.[3]

All the mysteries of the religions of Asia and all the subtleties of the Western philosophers — in a word, all the difficulties of East and West that the world contains — all compressed and heaped together in a single formula! "Well, yes," says the Church, "it is the whole world in one immense cup. Drink it in the name of love!" And here in support of the doctrine she brings history and touching legends — the honey on the edge of the cup.

"Whatever it contains I will drink, if truly love is at the bottom" — such was the answer of the human race. Here was the real difficulty, the real objection, and it was love that made it, not hatred or human pride as they are ever repeating.

The Middle Ages promised love and did not give it. They said, "Love! love!"[4] Yet they consecrated a hateful civil order, with

[3] If some answer that uncultivated minds (which in that period means everybody, or nearly so) were exempted from understanding, then it must be admitted that so difficult an enigma imposed, upon pain of damnation, the general abdication of human intellect into the hands of a few learned men who believed they knew the meaning. And look at the result. Once the enigma was laid down and surrounded with commentaries just as obscure, mankind became silent and stood there mute and sterile. Throughout an immense period as long as the entire brilliant period of antiquity, from the fifth to the eleventh centuries, mankind scarcely ventured a few prayers and a few childish legends, and even that movement was stopped by the express prohibition of the Carolingian councils.

[4] They not only said so, but they sincerely desired it. This touching aspiring toward love is what constitutes the genius of the Middle Ages and insures them our eternal sympathy. I do not take back one word of what I said about the Middle Ages in the second volume of my *History of France*. But there I gave their spirit and their ideal. Today, in a book of practical interest, I can give only the real, the results. At the end of the same volume, printed in 1833, I had already noted the impotency of this system, as well as the hope that it might escape its ruin and suc-

inequality in the law, in the state, and in the family. Their too
subtle instruction, accessible to so few, had brought a new kind
of inequality into the world. They had put on salvation a price
rarely attained, the price of an abstruse learning, and thus they
weighed down the simple and the child with all the metaphysical
science in the world. The child, who had been so happy in antiquity, found its hell in the Middle Ages.

It required centuries for reason to shine forth, for the child
to reappear as he is, *an innocent*. It was hard to believe that man
was hereditarily a corrupt being.[5] It became difficult to maintain
in its barbarity the principle which damned the non-Christian wise
men, the simple and the ignorant, and the children who had died
without baptism. They even invented for children the palliative
of limbo, a somewhat milder little hell where they were always
to hover about weeping, far from their mothers.

But these were insufficient remedies, and the heart was not
satisfied. With the Renaissance burst forth the reaction of love,
in opposition to the harshness of their musty doctrines. It came
in the name of justice to save the innocents, condemned within
the system which had called itself one of love and grace. But that

---

ceed in transforming itself. On 11 May 1844 we saw how far we already were from the Middle Ages. On that day a member of the Chamber
of Deputies, a sincere and courageous orthodox Christian, deduced a
penal theory from the doctrine of Original Sin and the Fall. Even the
Catholics drew back from the idea.

[5] The embarrassment of theology is due especially to the progress of
civil law. As long as the law maintained in all its severity the concept of
lèse-Majesté, which through confiscation extended the penalty of the
father to the heir, theology could defend its law of divine high treason,
which damned the children for the sin of the father. But when law
became more merciful, it was more and more difficult to maintain in
theology — the world of love and grace — this horrible doctrine of the
inheritance of sin, which had been abandoned by human law. The
scholastics, Saint Bonaventura, Innocent III, and Saint Thomas, found
no way of softening the doctrine other than to exempt children from
everlasting fire, while *leaving them in other respects in damnation.*
Bossuet has shown very well, in opposition to Sfondrati, that this doctrine is not particular to the Jansenists, as some pretended to believe;
rather, it was the very doctrine of the Church, the Fathers (except
Gregory of Nazianzus), the councils, and the popes. Indeed, if they
exempt children from damnation, they also give up Original Sin and
the inheritance of crime, which is the basis of the whole system.

system, which was based entirely upon the two ideas of the damnation of all by one and the salvation of all by one, could not renounce the first without shaking the second.

Mothers began to believe again in the salvation of their children. From then on they have been saying, without asking whether or not they are perfectly orthodox, "They must be angels on high, as they were while here below."

The heart has prevailed, mercy has prevailed. Humanity is drawing further and further away from ancient injustice. It is now sailing in an opposite direction from the old world. And where is it going? Toward a world (we can well foresee it) which will condemn innocence no more, and where wisdom may truly say, "Suffer the simple and the little children to come unto me."

∾

CHAPTER VI

Digression: The Instinct of Animals: A Plea in Their Favor

However hurried I may be in this review of the simple, those humble children of instinct, my heart stops me and forces me to say one word about the most simple of all, the most innocent and perhaps most unfortunate. I mean the animals.

I just observed that every child is born noble. Similarly, naturalists have remarked that the young animal is more intelligent at birth and seems then to resemble the child. As the animal grows up, it becomes brutish and sinks into the beast. It seems that its poor soul succumbs under the weight of the body, and submits to the fascination of nature and the magic of the great Circe. Man turns away then and will no longer recognize a soul there. The child alone still feels through the instinct of the heart that there is a person in that despised being; he speaks to it and questions it. And the animal listens and loves the child.

What a dark mystery the animal is! What an immense world of dreams and dumb sorrows! But in place of language, signs all too visible express those sufferings. All nature protests against the barbarism of man, who disowns, debases, and tortures his inferior brother; she accuses him before Him who created them both!

Take an unbiased look at their gentle, musing air and at the attraction the most advanced among them visibly feel for man. Would you not say they are children whose development some evil fairy has prevented and who have not been able to unravel their first childish dream, or perhaps are chastised and humiliated souls under the curse of some passing fate? A sad spell in which the captive being of an imperfect form is dependent on all those who surround it, like a person asleep. But because he is as if asleep, he has access to a sphere of dreams of which we have no idea. We see the light side of the world, and the animal sees the dark. Who knows which side is more profound?

The East has maintained the belief that the animal is a soul asleep or under a spell; the Middle Ages returned to it. Religions and systems have not been able to stifle this voice of nature. India, nearer to the creation than we, has better preserved the tradition of universal brotherhood. She has inscribed it at the beginning and end of her two great sacred poems, the *Ramayana* and the *Mahabharata,* those gigantic pyramids before which all our petty Western productions must stand humble and respectful.* When you become tired of this disputatious West, give yourself the pleasure of returning to your mother, to that majestic antiquity so noble and so tender. Love, humility, grandeur — you will find them all united together, and in a sentiment so simple and so detached from all petty pride that there is never any need to speak there of humility.

India was well rewarded for her kindness to nature; for her, genius was a gift of pity. The first Indian poet sees two doves on the wing; while he is admiring their grace and amorous flight, one of them falls, struck by an arrow. He weeps, and without dreaming of it, his groans are measured by the pulsations of his heart and assume a rhythmical movement, and poetry is born.

---

* The *Ramayana,* the great epic of ancient India, was written in either the fifteenth or eleventh century B.C., according to differing opinions. It recounts the conquest of Hindustan by the Aryans and the expedition of Rama to Ceylon. The *Mahabharata* was written in perhaps the tenth century B.C.

Michelet's great admiration for these epics was not shared by his acquaintance Guizot, the ascetic history professor best known as the principal minister for Louis Philippe in the 1840s. (Guizot's general answer to the political and social problems of the day was summed up in his phrase "get rich.") One day when Guizot was criticizing the "over-exuberance" of this Indian poetry in a discussion at the Academy, Michelet suddenly exploded, "You cannot understand them! You have always hated life!"

Since that time, according to the *Ramayana,* the melodious doves are born again in the songs of man and love and fly two by two throughout the world.

Grateful nature has endowed India with another admirable gift, fertility. Surrounded with tenderness and respect, nature has multiplied for her, as for the animal, the spring of life by which the earth is renewed. There exhaustion is unknown. So many wars, so many disasters and servitudes, have not been able to exhaust the milk of the sacred cow. A river of milk is always flowing for this blessed land, blessed by its own goodness and by its gentle tenderness toward the lower creatures.

That touching union which at first bound man to the humblest offspring of God has been broken by pride. But not with impunity, for the earth rebelled and refused to nourish the inhuman races.

That world of pride, the Greek and Roman city, had contempt for nature; it valued only art and was impressed only by itself. That proud antiquity, wanting nothing which was not noble, succeeded all too well in suppressing everything else. Whatever seemed low or ignoble disappeared from its eyes; animals perished as well as slaves. Rid of both, the Roman Empire entered into the majesty of the desert. The earth, always giving and no longer renewing itself in the midst of so many monuments which covered it, became a garden of marble. Cities remained, but the country was gone; circuses and triumphal arches stayed, but cottages and laborers were no more. Magnificent roads were ever waiting for the traveler who passed no longer. Sumptuous aqueducts continued to carry rivers to silent cities, but they found no one there to quench his thirst.

In the face of growing desolation, only one man found in his heart a protest and a lamentation for all that was dying. Amid the devastation of civil wars in which both men and animals perished, only one found in the immensity of his pity tears for the laboring ox that had enriched ancient Italy. He consecrated a divine poem to these disappearing races.*

And then tender and profound Virgil! I who have been fed by

* This is a reference to Horace's *Odes,* XVI.

him and brought up as if seated on his knee, I am glad that this unique glory belongs to him — the glory of pity and excellence of heart. That peasant of Mantua, with the timidity of a virgin and long rustic hair, is nonetheless, without his having known it, the true high priest and prophet between two worlds and between two ages, halfway down the road of history. Indian in his tenderness for nature, Christian in his love for man, this simple man restores in his great heart the lovely universal city. There nothing having life is excluded, though each creature there wishes only that his own kind may enter in.

Christianity, in spite of its gentle spirit, did not renew the ancient union. It preserved a Jewish prejudice against nature; Judea knew herself, was afraid to love too much this sister of man, and fled from her with curses. Christianity, faithful to these fears, kept animal nature at an infinite distance from man and debased it. The symbolic animals which accompany the evangelists and the cold allegories of the lamb and the dove did not better the beast. The new benediction did not reach it; salvation did not come for the smallest and humblest of creation. The God Man died for man, not for them. Having no share in salvation, they remain beyond the Christian law, as do pagans and those impure, and are too often suspected of conniving with the principle of evil. Has not Christ in the Gospel permitted demons to dwell in swine?

We shall never know the terrors in which the Middle Ages lived for several centuries, ever in the presence of the devil, ever with the vision of the invisible evil one! What a wicked dream! What an absurd torture! And from it sprang a strange, fantastic life which would make us laugh every second if we did not feel it was too sad even for tears. Who then could have doubt of the devil? I have seen him, says Emperor Charles. I have seen him, says Gregory VII. The bishops who make the popes and the monks who pray all their lives declare that he is there behind them, that they feel him, and that he does not stir. The poor country serf who sees him in the form of a beast, sculptured above the church door, is afraid on his return to find him among his own beasts. At night, in the flickering light of the hearth, they take a fantastic aspect: the bull has a strange mark, the goat an equivocal look, and what must he think of that cat whose hair shoots out sparks in the dark as soon as he touches it.

It is the child that reassures the man. He fears those animals so little that he makes them his companions. He gives leaves to the ox, mounts the goat, and boldly handles the black cat. He does still better; he imitates them, counterfeits their voices — and the family smiles. "Why indeed should I be afraid of them; I was wrong. I am in a Christian house, with holy water and holy flowers; he would not dare approach. My beasts are God's creatures, innocents, children. Why, even the animals in the fields seem by their looks to know God; they live like hermits. That fine stag, for instance, who has the cross upon his head and who moves through the forest like a living forest, seems himself a miracle. The doe is as gentle as my cow, and she has small horns; had the mother been unable, the doe would have nursed my child." This last sentence, expressed in a historical form as was everything then, finally developed into the most beautiful legend of the Middle Ages. This is the legend of Geneviève de Brabant: the family oppressed by man is taken in by the animal; the innocent wife is saved by the innocent beast of the forest; thus salvation comes from the least and the humblest.

The rehabilitated animals take their places in the peasant family next to the child that loves them, just as poor relatives sit at the lower end of the table in a noble household. They are treated as such on great occasions, when they share the joys and sorrows and go in mourning or wear wedding dress (as was still recently the custom in Brittany). They say nothing, it is true, but they are docile and listen patiently; and man, as priest in his own house, preaches to them in the name of the Lord.

Thus popular genius, more simple and more profound than the sacred sophistry of priest and schoolman, brought about timidly but effectively the rehabilitation of nature! And nature was not ungrateful. Man was rewarded; those poor beings who have nothing gave treasures. The animal, as soon as it was loved, endured and multiplied. The earth became fertile again, and the world that seemed at an end grew rich and strong again because the blessing of mercy had fallen like dew upon it.

Once the family was made up this way, the next question was to take the entire family into the church, if possible. Now comes the difficulty! They are very willing to receive the animal, but only to sprinkle it with holy water, to exorcise it, as it were, and this only at the doorstep. "Simple man, leave your beast behind and enter alone. The entrance of the church is the divine Judgment that you see represented upon the doors: the law waits at the threshold; Saint Michael stands ready above with sword and scales. How can the animal you bring with you be judged, and saved or damned? Has that beast a soul? And what should we do with them, the souls of these beasts? Shall we open a limbo for them, as for little children?"

No matter, our man is obstinate; he listens respectfully but does not care to understand. He does not wish to be saved alone and without his own. Why should his ox and his ass not be saved along with Saint Paulin's dog? They have certainly worked as well!

"All right! I will be clever," he says to himself. "I will choose Christmas Day, when the Church gathers as a family, the day when God is still too young to be just. Right or wrong, we shall all go in; I, my wife, my child, and my ass. Yes, my ass too! He was at Bethlehem and bore our Lord. As a reward the poor beast ought to have his day. Besides, it is not quite certain that he is what he seems. He is at bottom malicious and lazy — just like me. If I were not also dragged to it, I would not work much either!"

It was a grand spectacle, far more touching than laughable, when the beast of the people was, in spite of the commands of bishops and councils, taken into the church. Nature, condemned and cursed, returned victorious under the humblest form that could gain pardon. She returned with the saints of paganism, between the Sibyl and Virgil. They met the animal with the sword that stopped him under Balaam. But that sword of the ancient law was blunted and frightened him no more; the law was near its end that day and was making room for grace. Humbly but assuredly the beast went straight to the manger. There he listened to the service and knelt in devotion like a baptized Christian. Then they sang to him and for him, partly in the language of the church and partly in the vernacular so that he might understand this comic yet sublime anthem:

On thy knees, and say Amen!
Put grass and hay aside today;
Amen once, and once again,
Leave the old things, and away!

The animal gained little from these amends.[1] The councils closed the church against him. The philosophers, who in pride and hardheartedness followed the path of the theologians, decided that he had no soul. So what if the animal suffers in this world? He must expect no recompense in a higher life. There is to be no God for him; man's merciful father is to be a cruel tyrant for whatever is not human! To create playthings, but these so sensitive; machines, but these so suffering; automatons who resemble humanity only in their ability to endure evil! Ah! may the earth lie heavy on you, you hardhearted men who could conceive this impious idea — you who pass such a sentence upon so many innocent but suffering creatures!*

Our age will have one great glory. It has produced a philosopher with a human heart. He loved the child and the animal. Previously the unborn child had excited interest only as an outline, as a preparation for life; but he loved it in itself, followed it patiently in its little obscure life, and discovered in its changes the faithful reproduction of animal development. Thus in the

---

[1] Popular genius did more for its protégé. Not stopped by the opposition of the church, it created for the animal a legal position, treated it as a person, and made it appear in court, even in the most serious criminal cases where it figured as a witness and sometimes as the prisoner. There is no doubt that such importance attributed to the animal contributed powerfully to its preservation and perpetuation, and consequently to the fertility of the land, which generally depends on the treatment the animal receives from man. This is, perhaps, the real reason why the Middle Ages always recovered after so many frightful devastations.

* Here, as elsewhere in this section of the book, Michelet is anticipating the famous "nature" books of his mature years, such as *The Bird,* *The Insect,* and *The Sea.* Temporarily discouraged after 1851 by "the hard and savage history of man," Michelet found solace in the observation of nature.

bosom of woman, in the true sanctuary of nature, the mystery of universal brotherhood has been discovered. Thanks be to God!

This is the true rehabilitation of inferior life. The animal, that serf of serfs, finds himself once more related to man — the lord of this world.

May the latter now resume with a more gentle feeling the great work of the education of animals, which formerly gained him the dominion of the globe and which he has abandoned for two thousand years to the great detriment of the earth. May the people learn that their prosperity depends on their merciful treatment of this poor inferior people. May knowledge remember that the animal is more closely related to nature and was her prophet and interpreter in antiquity. She will find a voice of God in the instinct of these simplest of the simple.

❧

The Instinct of the Simple and the Instinct of Genius: The Man of Genius Is Preeminently the Simple, the Child, and the People

I have read in the life of a great doctor of the Church that after his death he returned to his monastery and honored with his apparition, not the most distinguished of his brethren, but the least so, the simplest. This half-witted fellow received from the doctor the favor of dying three days later, when his face shone with a truly heavenly joy. The life of the saint concludes, "One might apply to him the words of Virgil: 'Little child, know thy mother by her smile!' "

It is a remarkable fact that most men of genius have a particular fondness for children and the simple. On their side, these folk, generally timid in public and dumb in the presence of men of wit, feel completely safe with men of genius. That power which overawes everybody else gives them confidence. They feel that there they will not be met with mockery, but with benevolence and protection. And so they find themselves truly in their natural state. Their tongues are untied, and it becomes clear that these people, who are called simple because they are ignorant of conventional language, are often all the more original, highly imaginative, and endowed with a singular instinct for grasping obscure and distant relationships.

They compare and connect very willingly, but they seldom divide or analyze. Not only does every kind of division trouble their minds, but it pains them and seems to dismember reality. They do not like dissecting life, and everything seems to them to have life. All things, whatever they may be, are for them organic beings which they are very careful not to alter in the slightest way. They draw back the moment it is necessary to disturb by analysis anything that shows the least appearance of vital harmony. This disposition usually implies natural gentleness and goodness of heart, and thus we call them *good folk.*

Not only do they not divide, but as soon as they find anything divided or partial, they either neglect it or mentally rejoin it to the whole from which it is separated; they reconstitute this whole with a rapidity of imagination that could not be expected from their natural slowness. They are as powerful in putting things together as they are powerless in separating them. Rather, it seems on looking at so easy an operation that it is neither power nor impotency, but a necessary condition inherent in their existence. In fact it is by virtue of this that they exist as *simple ones.*

A hand appears in the light. The reasoner concludes that no doubt there in the shadows is a man whose hand alone he sees; from the hand he infers the man. The simple one does not reason and does not infer; seeing the hand, he immediately says, "I see a man." And so he does in fact, with the eyes of the mind.

Here they both agree. But on a thousand occasions the simple one, who sees by means of a part a whole unseen by others and who by a sign divines and affirms a being still invisible, is laughed at or passes for a fool. To see what appears to the eyes of nobody is second sight. To see what seems to be coming or about to be is prophecy. Here are two things which amaze the crowd and bring the derision of learned men, and which are generally a natural gift of simplicity.

This gift is rare among civilized men, but it is common among simple peoples even if they are savages or barbarians.

The simple sympathize with life and have as their reward this magnificent gift: the slightest sign permits them to see and to foresee life itself. That is their secret relationship with the man of genius. They often attain without effort and by mere simplicity what he obtains by the power of simplification which is within him; thus they who are the first of men and they who are the last meet on common ground and understand one another. Their mutual understanding is due to one thing — their common sympathy for nature and life, which causes them to delight only in a unity that lives.

If you study seriously the life and works of that mystery of nature called the man of genius, you will generally find that he preserved the gifts of the simple while he was acquiring the gifts of the critic.[1] Those two men, opposed to each other elsewhere, are in harmony within him. At the moment when his inner criticism seems to have urged him to infinite division, his simplicity still maintains unity. It always preserves for him the sentiment of life and keeps it indivisible. But though genius has both these powers, its love of living harmony and its tender regard for life are still so strong that it would sacrifice study and knowledge themselves if they could be obtained only by dissecting reality. Of the two men within him, he would reject the one who divides and keep the simple one with his ignorant power of divination and prophecy.

This is a mystery of the heart. If genius, through all the fictitious divisions and subdivisions of knowledge, always preserves within itself a *simple* being who never agrees to unalterable division and who always tends toward unity and is afraid to destroy that unity in the smallest living thing, it is because the characteristic of genius is the love of life itself — the love that causes life to be preserved and the love that produces it.

The crowd, which sees all this confusedly from the outside without being able to account for it, occasionally finds this great man a *good* man and a *simple* man. They are astonished at the contradiction. But there is no contradiction: simplicity and goodness are the basis of genius and its primary cause; through them the man of genius taps the creativity of God.

[1] Genius has, I know, a thousand forms. The one I am presenting here is certainly the most original and the most creative, and that which most frequently characterizes great inventors. La Fontaine and Corneille, Newton and Lagrange, Ampère and Geoffroy Saint-Hilaire, were at one and the same time the most simple and the most subtle of men.

This goodness, which gives him respect for tiny beings neglected by others and which sometimes stops him suddenly so that he will not crush a blade of grass, is the amusement of the crowd. The spirit of simplicity, which never allows his mind to be shackled by divisions, which by a part or a sign makes him see or foresee a whole being or a system that no one yet comprehends — this wonderful faculty is precisely what causes the astonishment and almost the scandalization of the vulgar. It raises him above the world, as it were, and sets him beyond opinion, place, and even time . . . though he alone will leave a mark there for the future.

The mark he will leave is not the work of his genius alone, but that life of simplicity, childhood, goodness, and holiness to which all ages will come to seek a sort of moral regeneration. This or that discovery of his will become perhaps less useful in the progress of the human race; but his life, which in his lifetime seemed his weak side and in which envy found its satisfaction, will remain the treasure of the world and the eternal festival of the heart.

Certainly the people are quite right to call this man simple. He is preeminently the simple — the child among children — the people more than the people themselves. Let me explain.

The simple man has his unintelligent side, his confused and undecided views amid which he wavers and searches about while following several roads at once, abandoning the character of a simple man. The simplicity of genius, which is true simplicity, never has any of these uncertain views; it applies itself to objects like a powerful light that is not deflected, because it pierces and traverses the whole.

Genius has the gift of childhood, but as the child never has. This gift, as we have said, is the vague, powerful instinct which reflection soon channels and defines so that the child soon becomes a questioner and a faultfinder full of objections. Genius preserves the native instinct in its grandeur and its strong impulsiveness, together with the divine grace of bright and perennial hope, which unfortunately the child loses.

The people, in the highest sense of the concept, are seldom found among the people. When I observe them here or there, they are not the people but a certain class or some partial manifestation of the people, altered and ephemeral. The people exist in truth and in their highest power only in the man of genius; in him resides their great soul. And all the world marvels to see the inert masses vibrating at his slightest word, the roar of the ocean hushed before his voice, and the wave of the populace prostrate at his feet. But why is that so strange? That voice is the voice of the people; mute itself, it speaks in that man and God with him. It is then we may truly say, "The voice of the people is the voice of God."

Is he God or is he man? To express the instinct of genius, must we seek out mystic names like inspiration or revelation? That is the tendency of the vulgar; they must forge gods for themselves. "Instinct? Nature? Hardly!" they say. "Were it but instinct, we would not be carried away by it. It is inspiration from above; it is the well-beloved of God; it is a God, a new Messiah!" Rather than admire such a man and recognize his human superiority, they make him into God's emissary, or even God himself if necessary. Everyone says to himself that it required nothing less than a supernatural light to dazzle them so.

So they set above nature and beyond science and observation him who was true nature, him whom science ought to observe of all others. They exclude from humanity him who alone was *man*. This man of men is sent back to heaven by this imprudent adoration, banished from the land of the living, where he had his roots. Ah! leave him among us, him who is the essence of life on earth. Let him remain man; let him remain the people. Do not separate him from the children, the poor, the simple — where his heart is —to exile him upon an altar. Let him be enveloped by the crowd whose spirit he is; let him plunge into full creative life, live with us, suffer with us. He will gain from his participation in our sufferings and weaknesses that strength which God has placed within and which will be his very genius.

∾

CHAPTER VIII

The Birth of Genius: A Model for the Birth of Society

If perfection is not found here below, what approaches it most closely from all we can see is the harmonious and creative man who manifests his inner excellence by a superabundance of love and strength, and who proves it not only by fleeting actions but also by immortal works through which his great soul will remain united with all mankind. His superabundant gifts, his fecundity, his lasting creation, are apparently the sign that we should find in him the fullness of nature and the model of art. And the art of society — the most complicated of them all — should consider carefully whether this masterpiece of God, whose rich diversity is harmonized in creative unity, could not throw some light upon the subject of its investigations.

Permit me, then, to dwell upon the character of genius, to penetrate its inner harmony, and to consider the wise economy and intelligent policing of this great moral city which rests in the soul of man.

Genius, that inventive and generating power, supposes, as we have already explained, that the same man is endowed with two powers, that he combines what may be called the two sexes of the mind — the instinct of the simple and the reflection of the wise. In a way he is man and woman, child and adult, barbarian and civilized, people and aristocracy.

This duality — which astonishes us and often causes the vulgar to regard the genius as a bizarre phenomenon, a real monstrosity — is what gives him in the highest degree the normal and legitimate character of man. To tell the truth, he alone is man, and there are no others. The simple man is half a man, the critic is half a man, and they have no power of procreation; still less do those of mediocrity, whom we might call *neuter* since they are of neither sex. He alone who is complete, he alone can procreate. He is charged with carrying on divine creation. All the others are sterile, except for those moments when by means of love they reconstitute for themselves a sort of double unity; their natural aptitudes passed from generation to generation remain powerless until they meet the complete man, who alone has fertility.

It is not that the spark of instinct and inspiration has been lacking in all these men, but that reflection soon freezes or obscures it in them. It is the privilege of genius to have inspiration act before reflection, to have its flame burn suddenly and with all its energy. In other men everything emerges slowly and in succession, and the intervals sterilize them. Genius fills up the intervals, joins the ends together, and annihilates time — it is a lightning flash of eternity. Such rapid instinct thus touches the act and becomes the act itself; the idea thus concentrated springs to life and procreates.

Some are now vulgar who also received at the outset this creative duality of two persons, of the simple and the critical, but whose natural spite quickly destroyed the harmony. With their very first steps toward knowledge came pride and subtlety, and the critical killed the simple. Reflection, idiotically proud of her precocious virility, despised instinct as infantile. Vain and aristocratic, she mingled as soon as she could with the glittering crowd of sophists, and wincing under their sneers, denied the humble relations which connected her too closely to the people. She has gone beyond them; fearful of their derision, she set about the impious task of ridiculing her brother. Well! she will remain alone, and by herself she does not produce a real man, for the men she makes are impotent.

The genius knows nothing of this sad policy. He has no thought of stifling his inner flame for fear of the world's laughter; he does not even hear it. In him reflection is neither bitter nor ironic, and she treats tenderly the *infancy* of instinct. That instinctive half must be spared by the other; feeble and vague, it is subject to tumultuous emotions since it is full of aspiration and blinded by love, and thus it rushes forth to meet the light. Reflection knows well that if she is superior by already possessing light, she is inferior to instinct with regard to creative heat and the concentration of vitality. The question between them is one of age rather than of dignity. Everything begins in the form of instinct. The reflection of today was the instinct of yesterday. Which is worth more? Who can say? Perhaps the youngest and weakest has the advantage.

The creativity of genius, let me repeat, undoubtedly depends to a large measure on the goodness, gentleness, and simplicity of heart with which the genius welcomes the feeble attempts of instinct. He welcomes them within himself in his internal world, and quite as much in the external world of man and nature. On all sides he sympathizes with the simple, and his easy indulgence is continually evoking from limbo new germs of thought.

They fly to him of their own accord. Innumerable things, which had no form yet and were floating about alone and abandoned, come toward him without fear. And he, the man with the piercing look, does not care to examine whether they are shapeless or coarse, but welcomes them, smiles at them, delights in their vivacity, and pardons and encourages them. From this clemency he receives a unique advantage: everything comes to enrich him, aid him, and strengthen him. And for all others the world is a sandy desert where they seek and do not find.

Into such a soul, full and overflowing with the living gifts of nature, how could love fail to enter? Some well-loved thing springs up . . . and no one can say from where it came. It is loved, and that is enough. It will grow and live in him as he also lives in nature, welcoming all that comes, thriving on everything, enlarging and improving itself, and becoming the flower of genius as he himself is the flower of the world.

What a sublime type of adoption! That living speck, which a bit ago still seemed obscure until gazed upon by the paternal eye, gradually acquires form and vitality and bursts forth in splendor — a great invention, a work of art, a poem. What a fine and noble creation, and how I admire the result! But oh how much more I would have liked to follow it in its transformation and in the tender incubation under which its life and heat began![1]

Mighty men, in whom God accomplishes these great things, deign to tell us yourselves what was the sacred moment when the invention or the work of art flashed forth for the first time! What were the first words in your soul with that new being? What dialogue took place within you between old wisdom and young creation? What tender reception was given? How did the former encourage the latter, still rude and rough, and fashion it without changing it, and how, far from restraining its liberty, did it do everything to make it free and truly itself.

Ah! if you revealed these things, you would enlighten not only art, but the art of intellect as well — the art of education and of public policy. If we knew the education that genius gives to the well-beloved of his thought, how they live together, and how he encourages it, without injuring its originality, by giving it kindness and gentleness to develop according to its own nature, then we would have at one and the same time the rule of art and the model of education and civic instruction.

Gift of God, it is there we must behold you! It is in that superior soul, where wisdom and instinct are in such close harmony, that we must seek the model for every social effort. The soul of the man of genius, that soul unquestionably divine since it creates like God, is the inner city on which we must model the outer one so that it too may be divine.

This man is harmonious and productive when the two men

[1] It is extremely regrettable that men of genius efface the successive steps in the development of their creation! They seldom keep the series of sketches which have prepared the way. With great effort, you may get some idea of what I mean in the series of pictures of a few great painters who were constantly painting their thoughts, and thus fixed each stage of their development in immortal works. Thus it is not impossible to follow the birth of an idea in Raphael, Titian, Rubens, and Rembrandt. To speak only of the latter, his "Good Samaritan," "Christ at Emmaus," "Lazarus," and finally "Christ Consoling the People" indicate the successive degrees by which the great artist, touched by the new spectacle of profound modern miseries, conceived and developed his idea. In the last expression of it, which is so strong and so popular, the work and the workman have attained an unheard-of degree of tenderness.

who are in him — the simple and the reflective — understand and aid each other. Well, society will be in its most harmonious and productive form when the cultivated and reflective classes, welcoming and accepting the men of instinct and action, receive heat from them and give light in return.[2]

"But look at the difference!" some will say. "Do you not see that in the soul of a single man, the inner city is always composed of one and the same; between two persons so closely related, reconciliation is easy. But in the political city, how many different and discordant elements there are, how varied are the opposing forces! The data are here infinitely more complex. Indeed, of the objects compared, one is almost the opposite of the other: in one I see only peace; in the other, only war."

Would to heaven that this objection were reasonable and that I might accept it! Would to heaven that discord were found only in the outer city, and that in the inner city, in the apparent unity of the individual, there were truly peace! I feel quite the contrary. The general battle of the world is far less discordant than the one I bear within me: the struggle of myself with myself, the combat of *homo duplex* — of two-sided man.

This warfare is visible in every man. If there be truce and peace in the man of genius, that is due to a great mystery — the mystery of the inner sacrifices his opposing forces make to one another. Never forget that the basis of art, like that of society, is sacrifice.

This struggle is very handsomely rewarded. The work, which one would think inert and passive, modifies its workman. The work improves him morally, and thus rewards the tender care with which the great artist cherished it when it was young, weak, and still unformed. He made it, but it makes him; and as it grows, it makes him very great and very good. If the whole world with its miseries, necessities, and calamities did not oppress him,

[2] Extend this to the great society of the human race. Some nations are in the instinctive state, relatively speaking; others are in the state of reflection. When they come in contact, the cultivated nations ought to make in the name of humanity and their own interests an art and a language for this meeting, in order to get along with the nations that have only the barbarous instinct.

we would see that there is no man of genius who is not a hero, because of the excellence of his heart.

All these inner trials, of which the world knows very little, preserve the genius from every paltry feeling of pride. If in the name of his work he rejects the stupid jeers of the vulgar, it is indeed on account of his work and not for his own sake. The inner man remains heroically meek, ever the child, the simple, the people. However great his achievement, he is on the side of the little ones. He lets the crowd of vain and subtle men go on wandering in the void, rejoicing in jeers, sophisms, and negations. Let them triumph and run about as much as they please in the ways of the world. He stands there calmly, where all the simple ones will come, at the steps of the Father's throne.

And it is through him that they will come. What other support, what other protector, do they have? He is the common heritage of this disinherited people, and their glorious indemnification. He is the voice of these mutes, the power of these powerless souls, and the belated fulfillment of all their aspirations. In him they are finally glorified, and by him they are saved. He pulls them and lifts them all up from the long chain of classes and conditions into which they are divided: women, children, the ignorant, the poor in intellect, and with them our humble fellow workmen who have only pure instinct, and last of all the countless forms of inferior life as far as instinct extends.

They all claim kinship with the Simple One at the gate of the City into which they all must enter sooner or later. "What do you want here? Who are you, poor simple ones?"

"We are the younger brothers of the eldest born of God."

༆

CHAPTER IX

Review of the Second Part: Introduction to the Third

The feelings of my heart have carried me far afield, perhaps too far.

I wanted to characterize the popular instinct, and show that it is the fountain of life where today's educated classes must seek to recapture their youth. I wanted to prove to these classes, born yesterday and yet already worn out, that they need to draw near to the people from whom they have sprung.

The people are disfigured by their misfortune and corrupted by their own progress, so that in order to uncover their true genius, I have found it essential to study them in their purest form — the people as children and simple ones. It is there that God preserves for us the source of living instinct, the treasure of eternal youth.

But it has happened that these simple ones and children, whom I summoned into my book to bear witness for the people, have put in their own claims — and I have listened to them. I have vindicated, as best I could, the simple from the contempt of the world. I have asked on behalf of the child why the cruelty of the Middle Ages is still practiced against him.

What! You say you have rejected in belief and in life the cruel fatalism which supposed that man is depraved at birth for a crime he did not commit? And yet when it is a question of the child, you begin with this idea: you chastise the innocent; on the basis of a hypothesis which is abandoned day by day, you establish an education of punishments. You stifle and gag the young prophet, this Joseph or Daniel who alone can solve your enigma and explain your forgotten dream.

If you maintain that the instinct of man is evil and corrupted at birth, that man is worth only as much as he is chastised, corrected, and metamorphosed by learning or scholastic training, then *you have condemned the people,* both the people as children and the peoples who are still children, though often called savages or barbarians.

This prejudice has been deadly for all the poor sons of instinct. It has made the cultivated classes disdain and despise the uncultivated classes. It has inflicted upon children the hell of our education. It has sanctioned against infant nations a thousand stupid and harmful fables which have contributed a good deal to the self-righteousness of our self-proclaimed Christians in their extermination of these peoples.

My book wished to encompass these peoples, whether savages or barbarians, and shelter the few that remain. Soon it will be too late; the work of extermination goes on rapidly. In less than half a century, how many nations have I seen disappear! Where are our allies, the Highlanders of Scotland, now? An English bailiff has driven away Robert Bruce and the people of Fingal. Where are our other friends, the Indians of North America, to whom our old France had so kindly stretched forth her hand? Alas, I have just seen the last of them exhibited as a sideshow at fairs. In their cruel ignorance the Anglo-Americans, those traders and puritans, have just finished driving back, starving, and annihilating these heroic races, who leave forever a void upon the earth and a regret for all mankind.

In the face of these devastations and those in the north of India, in the Caucasus, and in Lebanon, may France understand in time that our interminable war in North Africa is due mainly to our being ignorant of the genius of these peoples. We remain ever aloof and do nothing to dispel the mutual ignorance and misunderstandings it causes. The other day they admitted that they were fighting against us only because they believed we were the enemies of their religion, which is the Unity of God; they did not know that France and almost all Europe had thrown off the idolatrous beliefs which obscured that Unity during the Middle Ages. Bonaparte told them so at Cairo; who will repeat it now?

The mist between the two shores will lift some day, and we will know each other. Africa, whose races so closely resemble those of our South; Africa, which I occasionally recognize in my most distinguished friends of the Pyrenees and of Provence — Africa will do France a great service and explain to her many of her traits that are despised and misunderstood. We shall then better comprehend the rough vigor of our mountaineers and the inhabitants of our least racially mixed provinces. For as I said before, many a custom which is found rude and gross is actually barbarous, and it ties our people to those populations who are no doubt barbarous but by no means vulgar.

Barbarians, savages, children, even the people (for the most part), all have this common misery: their instinct is misunderstood, and they themselves do not know how to explain it to us. They are like those mutes who suffer and die in silence. And we hear nothing, we hardly know it. The man of Africa starves upon his devastated store of grain; he dies, and without complaint. The man of Europe works himself to death, ends up in a hospital, and no one even knows it. The child, even the rich child, languishes and cannot complain; nobody will listen to him. The Middle Ages are finished for us, but they continue for him in all their barbarity.

What a strange sight! On one hand there are beings full of youthful vitality but who seem under a spell and cannot communicate their thoughts and sufferings. On the other hand there are those who have collected together all the instruments that humanity has ever forged for analysis and expression of thought — languages, classifications, logic, and rhetoric — but life is feeble in them. They must get the mutes, whom God filled so abundantly with his vigor, to share a little of what they were given.

Who would not do something for this great people, which

aspires to rise from low and obscure regions and which ascends, groping in the dark, without even a voice to groan? But their silence speaks.

It is said that when Caesar was coasting along the shores of Africa, he fell asleep and had a dream; he saw a vast army, weeping and stretching their hands toward him. On awaking, he wrote down upon his tablets Corinth and Carthage, and he rebuilt those cities.

I am not Caesar, but how often I have dreamed Caesar's dream! I saw them weeping, I understood their tears. "Urbem orant." They want their city! They ask the city to receive and protect them. And I, a poor solitary dreamer, what could I give to that great silent nation? All that I had — my voice. May it be their first admission into the City of Right, from which they have been excluded until now!

In this book I have given a voice to those who as yet do not even know whether they have a right in the world. All who groan or suffer in silence, all who are aspiring and struggling toward life, these are my people. They are the people! Let them all come with me.

Why can I not expand the City so that it may be solid! It shakes and crumbles to pieces as long as it is incomplete, exclusive, and unjust. Its justice is its solidity. But if it wants to be only just, it will not even be just. It must be holy and divine, founded by Him who alone can found.

It will be divine if instead of jealously shutting its gates, it will call all who are the children of God, the least, the most humble, and woe unto him who will be ashamed of his brother! Let all without distinction of class or classification, weak or strong, simple or wise, bring here their wisdom or their instinct. Those weak and incapable ones, those miserable persons who can do nothing for themselves, can do much for us. They have in them a mystery of unknown power, a hidden creativity of living springs in the depths of their nature. In summoning them, the City calls the life which alone can renew it.

Then after this long separation, may man have a happy reconciliation here, with both his fellow man and nature. May every kind of pride cease, and may the City of Protection extend from heaven to the abyss, vast as the bosom of God!

For my part, I swear that if anyone remains behind whom the City still rejects and does not shelter with its right, I will not enter but will remain on the threshold.

∾

PART THREE

Of Freedom through Love: Our Native Land

CHAPTER I

༄

Friendship

It is a great glory for our old communes of France to have been the first to find the true name of our native land. In their simplicity, full of good sense and profound feeling, they called it the *friendship*.[1]

The native land, the fatherland, is indeed the great friendship which contains all the others. I love France because she is France, and also because she is the country of those whom I love and have loved.

Our country, the great friendship in which all our attachments center, is at first revealed to us by those attachments; then she in her turn generalizes, extends, and ennobles them. The friend becomes a whole people. Our individual friendships are like the first steps in that great initiation, the stations through which the soul passes and climbs little by little until she recognizes herself and loves herself in that better, more disinterested, and more exalted soul which we call *la patrie* — the native land.

I say disinterested because wherever this soul is strong, it causes us to love one another in spite of clashing interests, differences of conditions, and inequality. Rich and poor, great and small, we are all elevated by it above the petty miseries of envy. It is truly the *great* friendship because it makes us heroic. They who are united in it are firmly united; their attachment will last as long as the native land. It is as indestructible as their immortal souls.

[1] The native land, *la patrie*, was then only the local commune. They said the *friendship* of Lille, the *friendship* of Aire, and so on. See my *History of France*, vol. V.

Though it passed from the world and from history and became entombed in the bosom of the earth, it would survive as friendship.

To listen to our philosophers, it would seem that man is such an unsociable being that it would be extremely difficult, and would require all the efforts of art and meditation, to invent the ingenious machine that would bring man together with man. But for my part, I see at a glance that even from his birth he is a sociable being. Before he has his eyes open, he loves society; he weeps as soon as he is left alone. Why should we be surprised at this? On the day we call his first day, he leaves a society already quite old, and so pleasant! There he began, and now nine months old he must forsake it, experience loneliness, and grope about in search of a shadow of the dear union he had but has lost.

He loves his nurse and his mother, and hardly distinguishes them from himself. But how delighted he is the first time he sees another, a child of his own age, who is himself and yet not himself! Scarcely will he know anything like that moment again in the most joyous moments of love. His family, his nurse, even his mother for a time, all give way before the *comrade* — he has made him forget everything.

It is there we are forced to see how little inequality, that stumbling block of politicians, embarrasses nature. On the contrary, she amuses herself in all such affairs of the heart, playing with the differences and the inequalities which would seem likely to create insurmountable obstacles to union. Woman, for instance, loves man just because he is stronger. The child often loves his friend because he is superior. Inequality pleases them as an opportunity for devotion, as a chance for emulation and a hope of equality. The dearest wish of love is to make the other equal; its fear is to remain superior — and preserve an advantage that the other has not.

The singular character of the beautiful friendships of childhood is that inequality encourages them enormously. Inequality must be there in order to have aspiration, exchange, and mutual aid. Observe these children: what makes their friendship delightful to them is, following the analogy of character and behavior, the inequality of their minds and their education; the weak follows the strong without servility or envy; he listens to him with rapture and imitates him with joy.

Whatever may be said to the contrary, friendship, even more than love, is a means of progress. Love, like friendship, is doubtlessly a step forward, but it does not cause those whom it unites to emulate each other. Lovers differ in sex and in nature; the less advanced cannot change much in order to resemble the other; the effort of mutual assimilation stops short very quickly.

The spirit of rivalry, so soon awakened in little girls, begins late among boys. It requires the school, the college, and all the efforts of the master to arouse its sad passions. Man, in this respect, is born generous and heroic. He must be taught envy, for he does not know it by himself.

How right he is and how much he gains this way! Love does not count or measure or try to calculate a rigorous mathematical equality which is never attained. It much prefers to go beyond that. Most frequently it creates, in opposition to the inequality of nature, an inequality in an inverse sense. Between man and woman, for instance, it causes the stronger to wish to be the servant of the weaker. As the family grows and a child is born, the privileged place falls to this newcomer. The inequality of nature favored the stronger, the father; the inequality substituted by love favors the weaker, then the weakest, and makes the last first.

Such is the beauty of the natural family. And the beauty of the adoptive family is to favor the adopted son, the son of choice, who is dearer than those of nature. The ideal of the City that should be pursued is the adoption of the weak by the strong — inequality, but for the advantage of the weak.

Aristotle says very well in opposition to Plato, "The City is not made of similar but rather dissimilar men." To which I add, "Dissimilar, but harmonized by love and made more and more alike." Democracy is love in the City and common bonds.

The common bonds of patronage, whether Roman or feudal, were artificial and the result of circumstances.[2] It is to man's natural and invariable relations that we must return.

What are those relations? You do not need to search very far for them. Just look at man before he is enslaved by passion, broken by a harsh education, and soured by rivalry. Take him before love and before envy. Now what do you find in him? Something that is the most natural of all things, something that is first and hopefully last as well — friendship.

I shall soon be an old man. Besides my own age, I have two or three thousand years of history weighing upon me, with countless events, passions, and thoughts — my life and that of the world are all mixed up together. Well, among these innumerable great events and great sufferings, one thing which is ever young, fresh, and flourishing dominates and triumphs — my first friendship!

I remember it well, much better than my thoughts of yesterday.* There was an enormous, insatiable desire for communications, confidences, and mutual revelations, and neither words nor paper would suffice. After the longest walks, one would still see the other home and then vice versa. What a joy it was when day returned to have so much to say! I would leave early, full of strength and liberty, impatient to talk, to resume the conversation, and to share so many confidences. "What secrets? what mysteries?" you say. Why, some fact of history, for example, or some verse of Virgil I had just learned.

---

[2] The patronage of antiquity and the Middle Ages will not and should not return. We feel we are equals. Moreover, character and originality lost immensely in those relations of strict dependency in which man always had his eyes fixed on man, and became his shadow and poor copy. The long common table — where the baron sat near the fire, and where the line stretched from the chaplain to the seneschal to the other vassals as far as the door where the little kitchen-boy standing to serve used to eat — was a school where imitation mastered all. Each studied and copied his neighbor of the rank above. Their feelings were not always servile, but their minds were. This servility of imitation is doubtless one of the causes which retarded the Middle Ages and kept them sterile for so long.

* In this passage Michelet is referring to his friend Poinsot, the medical student. Poinsot's death in 1821 after a year of continuous companionship overwhelmed Michelet with grief.

How often did I mistake the hour! At four or five o'clock in the morning I went and knocked, got someone to open the door, and awoke my friend. How can I paint with words the light and vivid dawn of those mornings when my life seemed to fly, and I felt I lived at dawn. Today I still have this sensation in the early morning and in springtime.

It is an age to be regretted, a true paradise on earth knowing neither hatred nor contempt nor baseness. It is a time when inequality is completely unknown and society is still truly human and truly divine.

All that passes quickly. Different interests arise, then competition and rivalry. And yet something of it would still remain if education strove to unite men as much as it does to separate them.

If only the two children, the poor one and the rich one, had been sitting on the benches of the same school, if only they commonly considered themselves connected by friendship though separated by careers, they would do more good between them than all the politicians and all the moral lessons in the world. They would preserve in their disinterested, innocent friendship the sacred bond of the City. The rich man would know life and inequality, and would shudder at it. All his efforts would be to share with his poor friend. The poor man would show greatness of heart, and console him for being rich.

How can we live without knowing life? And we can know it only at the price of suffering, working, and being poor. Or else one makes himself poor through sympathy and compassion, and willingly participates in the toil and suffering.

What can a rich man know, even with all the learning of the world's schools? The very fact of his living an easy life causes him to be ignorant of its great and profound realities. Never digging deeply or forcefully, he runs and glides along as if on ice; he never penetrates anything and always remains on the surface. In his rapid external and superficial existence he will reach his end tomorrow, and will depart just as ignorant as he came. What he lacked was a solid point of departure, where he might anchor his soul and then dive deeply into life and knowledge.

Quite the opposite, the poor man is fixed on one obscure spot, unable to see either heaven or earth. He lacks the power to rise up, to breathe, and to behold the sky. Riveted to this spot by fate, he needs to expand, to generalize his existence and even his sufferings, and to live away from this spot where he suffers. For he has an infinite soul and needs to give it infinite expansion. But he is totally lacking in resources. As for the laws, they will accomplish little; he must have friendship. The man of leisure, culture, and reflection must put this captive soul in rapport with the world again. Should he change it? No, only help it to be itself, and remove the obstacle that prevented it from unfolding its wings.

All that would become easy if each of the two understood that he can find his emancipation only through the other. The man of learning and culture, who is today the slave of abstractions and formulas, will recover his liberty only by contact with the man of instinct. His youth and his life, which he expects to renew by foreign travel, are there near him in what is society's youth. I mean in the people. The poor man, on the other hand, for whom ignorance and solitude are like a prison, will extend his horizon and find pure air again if he will accept learning and respect the accumulated works of humanity and all the efforts of man before him, instead of belittling them out of envy.

I must admit that this assistance, this vigorous and serious reciprocal instruction they will find in each other, supposes true magnanimity in both men. I am calling for heroism. Yet what appeal is more worthy of man? And what is more natural once he returns to himself and, with the grace of God, rises once again?

The heroism of the poor man is to sacrifice envy. It is to be sufficiently above his own poverty that he does not even wish to inquire whether those riches are honestly or dishonestly acquired. The heroism of the rich is to know the rights of the poor man, and still to love him and go to him.

"Heroism! Why, is not this the most simple duty?" No doubt; but it is precisely because it is a duty that the heart tightens and contracts. Sad infirmity of our nature: we seldom love anyone but him to whom we owe nothing, the abandoned and disarmed inoffensive being who claims no right against us.

The heart must expand on both sides. They have taken democracy by right and duty, by the law — and they have had only the dead law. Well, let us retake it by grace!

You say, "What does that mean to us? We will make such wise laws, so cleverly drawn up and arranged, that there will be no need to love." But to wish to have wise laws and to obey them, you must first love.

"How is love possible? Do you not see the insurmountable barriers that our interests raise between us? Amid the overwhelming competition in which we are struggling, can we indeed be so simple as to help our rivals, or lend a hand today to those who will be our rivals tomorrow?"

What a sad confession! For a little money, for some miserable place that you will soon lose, you give up the treasure of man and all that is good and great within him — friendship, your native land, and the true life of the heart!

Oh, you miserable man! So near and yet so far from the Revolution! Have you already forgotten that the foremost men in all the world — those young generals with their tremendous energy and their furious rushing toward an immortal death they all competed for, those desperate rivals of that lovely mistress Victory, who kindles in hearts the most passionate love — felt no jealousy! That glorious letter, by which the conqueror of the Vendée shielded with all his virtue and popularity the man who was already to be dreaded, the conqueror of Arcola, and pledged his person for him, will last forever.[3] Ah, what a great time and

---

[3] It is known that Bonaparte had become suspect while acting as lord and arbiter of Italy. There, without consulting anybody, he granted or refused armistices which made peace or war, and sent funds directly to the army of the Rhine without the intervention of the treasury. A report was spread that he was to be arrested in the midst of his army. In order to justify him, Hoche wrote a letter to the Minister of Police that was made public. There he charged the royalists with the reports circulated. "Why is Bonaparte the object of the fury of those gentlemen? Is it because he defeated them in Vendémiaire? Is it because he dissolved the armies of the kings, and furnished the Republic with the means of gloriously ending

what great men: you were true conquerors to whom everything was forced to yield! And you conquered envy as easily as you subdued the world! Noble souls, wherever you be, give us for our salvation a breath of your spirit!

---

this war? Ah! brave young man, where is the republican soldier that does not burn to imitate you? Courage, Bonaparte, lead our victorious armies to Naples, to Vienna. Answer your personal enemies by humbling the kings, by giving a new luster to our arms, and leave the care of your glory to us!"

∾

CHAPTER II

Of Love and Marriage

One must have very little idea of the importance of such a subject to try to treat it in a few pages. I shall content myself with making a single observation which is essential in the present state of our manners.

Indifferent as we are to our country and the world, and being neither citizens nor philanthropists, there is only one thing in which we pretend to discard our selfishness. This is the family. To be the good father of the family is a virtue to be displayed, and often profitably so.

Well, it is time to admit it: among the upper classes the family is dangerously ill. If things go on as they are, the family will be impossible.

People have blamed the men, and not without reason. I myself have spoken elsewhere of their materialism, their harshness, and the singular lack of skill which causes them to lose their dominant position of the first days. However, it must be admitted that the women are especially at fault. I mean the mothers. The education they give, or allow to be given, to their daughters has made marriage an intolerable burden.

What we see reminds us all too much of the last years of the Roman Empire. The women having become heiresses, knowing they were rich and becoming patronizing to their husbands, rendered the condition of the latter so miserable that no pecuniary advantage or imperial decree could force men to submit to the degrading servitude. They preferred flying to the desert, which became inhabited.

The state, afraid of depopulation, was obliged to favor and regulate inferior relations, which were the only ones accepted by men. It would perhaps be the same in these days if our more commercially minded society did not speculate upon marriage. Modern man accepts out of greed or poverty the chances which disgusted the Romans. It is a dangerous speculation! The young wife knows she brings much, but she has learned nothing of the value of money and spends still more. Judging by recent events and reversals of fortune, I would be tempted to say that if you want to ruin yourself, you should marry a rich woman.

I know all the inconveniences of choosing a woman of inferior condition and education. The first is that we isolate ourselves as we leave our customary acquaintances and lose our position in society. Another is that we marry not only the woman but also her family, whose habits are often crude. We certainly hope to raise this woman, to make her like ourselves and for ourselves. But it often happens that even with a happy instinct and some willingness, she is not capable of being raised. And these tardy educations that we try to give to the strong races of the people, who are harder and less malleable, seldom have any impression upon them.

Having acknowledged these inconveniences, I am forced to come back to the far more serious problem, the problem of the "brilliant" marriages of the present day. It consists simply in the fact that life is impossible in them.

That life consists in beginning every evening after the day's work a still more fatiguing round of amusements and pleasures. There is nothing like this in the other countries of Europe, and nothing like this among the people. The Frenchman of the richer classes is the only man in the world who never rests. This is perhaps the main reason why our new rich, our bourgeoisie, a class created but yesterday, is already worn out.

In this age of work where time is of incalculable value, serious productive men who want results cannot accept so enormous an expenditure of life as a condition of marriage. The night spent in promenading a woman prematurely destroys the next day.

At night a man needs his home and his rest. He returns full

of cares; he ought to be able to collect his scattered thoughts and confide his ideas, his plans, his anxieties, and the struggles of the day — to have a home where he may pour out his heart. He finds a woman who has done nothing and who is in a hurry to use her energy, all ready, dressed up, and impatient. How can he speak to her? "That is fine, dear; but it is late and we are behind time. Tell me all that tomorrow."

So he goes, if he does not wish to confide her to the care of her friend, an older lady who is all too often a depraved mischief-maker who will find no pleasure greater than to set the young wife against her tyrant, compromise her, and launch her into the saddest follies. No, he cannot leave her with such a guide. He will take her himself, and starts off.

How envious he is to see the workman returning home late. It is true the workman has tired himself out during the day, but he is about to find rest, a home, a family, and finally sleep, that legitimate happiness God gives him every evening. His wife expects him; she counts the minutes. The table is set, and the mother and child are watching for him. If that man is worth much at all, she will center her vanity on him and admire and revere him. And how careful she is! I see her keeping the smaller portion of their scanty meal for herself without him noticing it. She is reserving for the husband, who works harder, the wholesome food that will recruit his strength.

He retires to sleep, and she puts the children to bed. Then she works far into the night. Early in the morning, long before he opens his eyes, she is up. Soon everything is ready — the warm food he eats at home and that which he takes with him. He goes off with his heart satisfied after kissing his wife and sleeping children, with no worries about what he is leaving.

I have said it and will say it again: happiness is there. She feels that she is supported by him, and she is happy; he works so much the better as he knows he works for her. Such is true marriage. Monotonous happiness, some will say. No, the child gives it variety. If the supreme spark were added, if the workman — with a little security and leisure — had some moments of a higher life, and if he took his woman as a partner on such occasions and nourished her with his own spirit, it would be too much. We would only pray to heaven for an eternity of such life as that here below.

Sad victim of greed, you might have had that happiness. But you sacrificed it. The humble girl you loved, who loved you, but whom you have forsaken — well may you regret her! Was it wise, leaving honor and humanity aside, to crush the poor creature and break your own heart in order to marry slavery? The money you sought will slip away by itself; it will not stay in your hands. The children of this union without love, conceived in calculation, will bear witness to the inward divorce this marriage contained; they will not have the heart to live.

Was the difference so great between those two girls? Both, after all, are of the people. The richer one has for her father a workman who has become wealthy. There is no great gulf between the true unadulterated people and the mixed people of the bourgeoisie.

If the bourgeoisie wishes to recover from its premature exhaustion, it should be less fearful of uniting with families that are today what they themselves were yesterday. That is the path to strength, beauty, and a bright future. Our young men marry late, already worn out, and generally take a sickly young lady. Their children die or live in poor health. After two or three generations our bourgeoisie will be as puny as our nobility before the Revolution.

And not only is the body failing, but so is the mind. How can we expect a series of works or important business achievements or any grand invention from a man who has sold himself into marriage for money, and is the slave of a woman and a family, ever obliged to disperse his efforts and throw his time to the four winds? Imagine what must become of a nation in which the governing classes consume themselves in vain words and empty agitation. For life to be creative there must be tranquillity of mind and the heart at rest.

A remarkable fact of our time is that the women of the people (who are by no means coarse like the men, and who feel the need of delicacy and distinction) listen to men above them with a confidence they did not have before. They saw the nobility as an insurmountable barrier to love, whereas wealth does not seem to separate the classes. Wealth counts for so little when one loves! How touching is this trust of the people, who in their best, most amiable, and most tender part thus draw nearer to the upper ranks of society and bring with them vigor, beauty, and moral grace! Ah! woe to those men who betray such trust. If they are incapable of feelings of remorse, they will at least suffer regret in the realization that they have lost what is worth all the treasures of the world and of heaven and earth — to be loved!

CHAPTER III

෬

Of Association

I have long studied the ancient guilds and associations of France. In my opinion the finest of all is that of the fishing nets of the coasts of Harfleur and Barfleur. Each of these vast nets (six hundred feet long) is divided into several portions, which are passed through inheritance to the girls as well as the boys. The girls who inherit this right do not go fishing, but they assist by mending their share of the nets they entrust to the fishermen. The beautiful and prudent girl of Normandy thus spins her dowry. Her portion of the net is her fief, which she administers with as much care as the wife of William the Conqueror. Being twice an owner, by right and by work, she must know all the details of the expedition; she understands its dangers, helps choose the crew, and shares the anxieties of this hazardous life. And she often risks more than net on the voyage. For it often happens that he whom she chose for her fisherman at the departure chooses her for his wife on his return.

A true country of wisdom! Normandy, which in so many things has served as a model for France and England, appears to me to have formed here a type of association more worthy than any other of being studied with care in the future.

This association is quite different from the associations of cheesemakers in the Jura, where, after all, they join only in the risk and the profit.[1] Each brings his milk for the common cheese

---

[1] Often mentioned by Fourier. I am a man of history and tradition; therefore I have nothing to say to the man who boasts that he proceeds by way of *absolute eccentricity*. This book of the people, founded particularly on the idea of the fatherland, which is to say on devotion and

and shares proportionately in the sale. This collective economy requires no moral union; it puts egotism at its ease and can be reconciled with all the hardheartedness of individualism. It does not seem to me to deserve the handsome title of "association."

That of the fishermen of Normandy unquestionably does, however, for it is moral and social quite as much as economic. There we have as a basis a young, serious, honest girl who out of her work, her nightly task, and her savings enters into partnership with young men, and stakes her fortune on their ship before she stakes her heart. She has a right to know, to choose, and to love the skillful and successful fisherman. Here is an association truly worthy of that name. Far from excluding the natural association of the family, it prepares that tie — and by so doing it contributes to the grand association, that of the native land.

Here my heart almost stops, and my pen falls . . . I must confess that the country and the family do not benefit much from it now. Those net associations will soon exist only in history; on many parts of the coast they are already replaced by what takes the place of everything — the bank and the usurer.

Noble race of Norman seamen, you who were the first to discover America, who founded the colonies of Africa and conquered the Two Sicilies and England, shall I no longer find you save in the Bayeux tapestry?* Who is not touched to the quick in passing

sacrifice, has nothing to do with the doctrine of *passionate attraction.* I nevertheless seize this opportunity to express my admiration for so many clever, profound, and sometimes very practical views, and my tender admiration for this misinterpreted genius whose whole life was occupied with the happiness of mankind. Someday I will speak about him according to the dictates of my heart. For the moment I note only the singular contrast between his boast of materialism and his self-sacrificing, disinterested, and spiritual life! This contrast has very recently reappeared, to the glory of his disciples. While the friends of virtue and religion and their necessary supporters, the born custodians of public morality, were secretly enlisting in the band of those who play the sure thing, the disciples of Fourier — who speak only of interest, money, and enjoyments — have ground interest under foot and courageously struck the Baal of the Bourse. The Baal? No, the Moloch, the idol that was devouring men.

* This tapestry, on display in Bayeux, France, is a long narrow band of more than fifty scenes which recount the Norman Conquest of

from our cliffs to the Downs of England, from our languishing coasts to those so teeming with life on the other side, from the inertia of Cherbourg to the terrible burning activity of Portsmouth? And what do I care if Le Havre is filled with American vessels engaged in a transit trade which passes through France without benefiting France, and sometimes even harming her!

Oh, what a heavy curse this is! A truly severe punishment for our insociability! Our economists declare that nothing may be done for free association. Our academics strike the word from their lists of prizes. This name is that of a crime, punishable by our penal code. A single association remains lawful — the increasing intimacy between Saint-Cloud and Windsor Castle.*

Commerce has formed a few societies, but only for a kind of war — to absorb the minor trades and destroy small tradesmen. They have done much harm and gained little profit. The large partnership companies created in this hope have had indifferent success. They are not advancing; as soon as a new one is formed, the others suffer and decay. Several have already failed, and those which remain have no tendency to expand.

As far as the country is concerned, I see that our ancient agricultural communities of Morvan, Berri, and Picardy are gradually breaking up and are calling upon the tribunals to legalize their dissolution. They had lasted for ages; several had been very prosperous. Those cloisters of married workers, which united a score of families related by blood under the same roof and under the direction of an elected chief, possessed beyond all doubt great economic advantages.

If I pass from these peasants to the most cultivated minds, I see hardly any spirit of association in literature. The men the most naturally brought together by their pursuits and mutual esteem and admiration nevertheless live apart. The nature of genius itself is of little use in bringing hearts together. I know here four or five men who are certainly the aristocracy of man-

---

England in 1066. Woven by Saxon masters soon after the victory, it is both a work of great artistry and a priceless commentary on life in the eleventh century.

* That is, between the reigning houses of France and England.

kind, and who have no peers or judges except themselves. These men who will live forever would have bitterly regretted not having known each other if they had been separated by centuries. They are living at the same time in the same city in the same neighborhood, but never see each other.

In one of my pilgrimages to Lyons, I visited some weavers, and according to my custom I inquired about their hardships and what might be done. I asked them especially whether they could not associate for certain material, economic purposes, whatever their differences of opinion might be. One of them, a man full of good sense and high moral character who saw that I was investigating sympathetically and in good faith, allowed me to carry it further than I had yet done. "The problem," he said at first, "is the partiality of the government for manufacturers." "And what else?" "Their monopoly, their tyranny, their unreasonableness..." "Is that all?" He was silent for a minute or two, and then with a sigh he uttered a serious confession: "There is another problem, sir. *We are unsociable.*"

Those words pierced straight to my heart and struck like a sentence of death. How many reasons I had to suppose this was just and true! How many times it has come back to me! "What!" I said to myself, "is France, that country famous above all others for the extraordinarily sociable gentility of its manners and genius, is that France irrevocably divided, and forever? If it is so, have we still any chance of living; have we not already perished even before death? Is the soul dead within us? Are we worse than our fathers, whose pious associations are constantly being lauded? Is love, is brotherhood, forever gone from this world?"

Plagued by such somber thoughts, I resolved like a dying man to ascertain whether I was dying. I considered seriously not the highest or the lowest, but one man, neither good nor bad, a man in whom several classes are represented, who has seen and suffered, and who in spirit and heart certainly carries within himself the thought of the people...That man, who is no other than myself, though living alone and in voluntary seclusion, has nevertheless remained sociable and sympathetic.

There are many others in the same situation. An immutable, unalterable fund of sociability sleeps here in the depths of society, held completely in reserve. I feel it everywhere among the masses whenever I go to them and listen and observe. But why should we be surprised if this instinct for easy sociability, so discouraged of late, has tightened up and drawn back? After being deceived by different political parties, exploited by the industrialists, and treated with suspicion by the government, it now neither stirs nor acts. All the powers of society seem directed against the sociable instinct! To unite stones and divide men is all they know.

Patronage by no means makes good what is missing in the spirit of association. The recent appearance of the idea of equality has stifled (for a time) the idea that preceded it — benevolent protection, adoption, and paternalism. The rich man has sternly said to the poor one: "You claim equality and the rank of brother? Well, so be it! But from this moment on you will get no help from me. God imposed the duties of a father upon me; by claiming equality you yourself have freed me from them."[2]

Among the French we run far less chance of being mistaken or misled than among any other. There is no social comedy or outward difference to create an illusion as to their sociability. They do not have the subdued manners of the Germans. They are not like the English, ever with their hats off before all who are rich or noble. If you speak to them and they answer you civilly and cordially, you may believe that they are honestly paying tribute to the person and very little to your position.

The Frenchman has passed through many trials, so much revolution and warfare. Such a man is most certainly hard to guide and hard to unify and associate. Why? Precisely because as an individual he has a great deal of intrinsic worth.

You are making men of iron in your war in Africa, for it is a very personal war which compels each man to rely only upon

[2] The task of the world and its salvation will be to recover the harmony of these two ideas. Brotherhood and fatherhood, two words irreconcilable in the family, are not at all so in civil society. As I have already said, the civil society finds the model that harmonizes these ideas in the moral society that every man bears within him. See the end of Part Two.

himself. No doubt you are right to want to have them and to shape them so, on the eve of the crises we must expect in Europe. But at the same time, do not be very surprised if those lions who have just returned keep something of a savage independence, even as they submit to the curb of the law.

And I must warn you that these men will take to association only through the influence of the heart and through friendship. Do not think that you will yoke them to a negative society in which the soul will have no place, or that they will live together without loving one another because of prudence and natural gentleness of character, as the German workmen in Zurich do, for instance. The cooperative society of the English, who unite perfectly well for a specific purpose while hating and thwarting one another in areas where their interests differ, does not suit our Frenchmen a bit better. France must have a society of friends; it is to her disadvantage commercially, but her social superiority will not accept any other. Union is effected here neither by weakness of character and community of habits nor by the greed of hunters who group together like wolves after prey. The only union possible here is the union of minds.

There is scarcely any form of association that is not excellent if this condition exists. The main question for this sympathetic people is that of persons and moral dispositions: "Do the members of the association love and suit one another?" That is what must always be asked in the first place.[3] Unions of workers will be

---

[3] In association, form is no doubt important, but it is still only a secondary consideration. Thus it seems sheer madness to me to re-establish the ancient forms with their guilds and monopolies, to pick up the old chains in order to walk better, and to undo the work of the Revolution and destroy without much thought what was demanded for so many centuries. On the other hand, to imagine that the State, which does so little by itself, could perform the functions of universal manufacturer and trader — is this anything but entrusting everything to the public official? Is this official an angel? When invested with this strange power, will he be less corrupt than the manufacturer or the tradesman? What is certain is that he will never be as active.

As for *community*, three words will suffice. *Natural* community is a very ancient, barbarous, and unproductive state. *Voluntary* community is a fleeting exuberance, a heroic emotion which marks a new faith and soon declines. *Forced* community, imposed by violence, is impossible at

formed, and they will last if they love one another; societies of foremen will live in equality as brothers, but there must be great mutual love.

To love one another is not simply to have feelings of mutual goodwill. The natural attraction of similar types and tastes will not suffice. To love, a man must follow his nature, but his heart must be in it. That is to say, he must ever be ready for sacrifice, for sacrifice that equals the devotion of nature.

What could you expect to do in this world without sacrifice?[4] It supports everything; without it the world would soon fall to pieces. Even with the best instincts, the most upright persons, and the most perfect natures (such as are not seen here below), everything would perish without this ultimate remedy.

"Sacrifice one's self for another!" What a strange unheard thought that will scandalize our philosophers. "Sacrifice one's self for whom? For a man we know to be worth less than ourselves? Why, I would lose an infinite value for the sake of this nothing!" Indeed this is a value that each of us seldom fails to attribute to himself.

This is a real problem, and I do not try to hide it. People seldom sacrifice themselves for anything but what they believe to be infinite. For sacrifice they must have a God, an altar; a God in whom men recognize themselves and love one another. How then could we sacrifice ourselves? We have lost our Gods!

Was the Logos, the God word, in the form in which it was considered by the Middle Ages, this necessary tie? Universal history is ready here to answer no. The Middle Ages promised union and gave only war. It was necessary that God should have a second

a time when property is infinitely divided, and nowhere more impossible than in France. So to return to the forms of association which are possible, I think they ought to be *divided according to the different professions,* which are more or less complicated and require more or less unity of direction. They should also be divided according to the different countries and the diversity of national genius. This basic observation, which I shall someday develop, might be supported by an immense number of facts.

[4] No period has furnished such famous examples. In what age were such great armies with so many millions of men ever seen to suffer and die so meekly and silently without revolt?

period and appear upon earth in his incarnation of 1789. He then gave to association its broadest and truest form, what alone can still unite us, and through us save the world.

Oh, glorious mother France! You who are not only our own, but who are destined to carry liberty to every nation, teach us to love one another in you!

CHAPTER IV

Our Native Land. Are Nationalities about to Disappear?

National antipathies have decreased, the law of nations has become more humane, and we have entered an era of goodwill and brotherhood if we compare today with that period of hate known as the Middle Ages. Nations have already been brought together to some extent by interests, and they have copied each other's fashions and literature. Is that to say that nationalities are on the decline? The question requires careful examination.

It is quite clear that internal dissension is declining in every nation. Our French provincialism is rapidly disappearing. Scotland and Wales have joined the British union. Germany is seeking her own, and believes herself ready to sacrifice to it a long list of conflicting interests which have kept her divided thus far.

This sacrifice of the different internal nationalities to the great nationality which contains them undoubtedly strengthens that nationality. It may perhaps efface those strikingly picturesque details which characterized a people in the eyes of the superficial observer; but it strengthens their basic genius and permits them to develop it. It was at the moment when France had suppressed in her bosom every conflicting France that she gave her lofty and original revelation. She found she was herself, and even as she was proclaiming the future common rights of all the world, she distinguished herself from the rest of the world more than she had ever done before.

We may say the same of England: with her machinery, her

fleets, and her fifteen million workers, she differs from all other nations today much more than in the time of Elizabeth. Germany, who in the seventeenth and eighteenth centuries was groping around to find herself, has at last discovered herself in Goethe, Schelling, and Beethoven; only since then has she been able to aspire seriously for unity.

Nationalities are so far from disappearing that I see them every day developing profound moral characteristics, and becoming individuals instead of collections of men as they once were. It is the natural progress of life. Every man at his origin feels his genius confusedly; in his early years he seems to be any man. Then as he advances, he begins to understand himself and goes on developing his character by his acts and works; he becomes gradually an individual, leaves his class, and merits a name.

The belief that nationalities are about to disappear can only be the result of two misunderstandings. First, to ignore history and know it only through shallow formulas, like the philosophers who never study it, or else through literary commonplaces in order to prattle about it, as women do. With such a knowledge of history they see nationalities in the past as a small obscure point which they may blot out if they wish. Nor is this all. Second, we must also be as ignorant of nature as of history and forget that national characteristics are not derived from momentary whims, but are profoundly influenced by climate, food, and the natural productions of a country. These characteristics may be modified somewhat; they are never erased. Those who are not bound by either physiology or history, and who constitute humanity without inquiring about either man or nature, may at their leisure efface every frontier, fill up the rivers, and level the mountains. I warn them, however, that the nations will still remain, unless they intend to eradicate the cities, those great centers of civilization where nationalities have concentrated their genius.

Toward the end of the second part of this work I said that if God has put the model for the political City anywhere, then in all probability it was in the moral City — I mean in the soul of man. Well, what does this soul do first? It finds a certain fixed position, meditates there, and forms for itself a body, a dwelling place, a set of ideas. And then it can act. In the same manner the soul of a people ought to make for its organism a central point; it should establish itself in one place, concentrate and meditate there, and put itself in harmony with some set of natural surroundings: the seven hills for that little Rome, for instance, or for our France the ocean, the Rhine, the Alps, and the Pyrenees, for those are our seven hills.

Every life finds power in defining itself, in carving for one's self a piece of time and space, and in feeding on something of its own in the midst of indifferent and dissolving nature, which always wishes to mix things together. To do this is to exist — to live!

A mind fixed on one point will go deeper and deeper. A mind floating in space disperses itself and fades away. Look at the man who shares his love with many: he dies without having known love; let him love but once and long, and he will find in that one passion the infinity of nature and all the progress of the world.[1]

The Fatherland, the City — far from being opposed to nature — is for that soul of the people which dwells there the single and all-powerful means of realizing its nature, because it supplies both a vital point of departure and freedom to develop. Imagine the Athenian genius without Athens: it floats, wanders, is lost, and dies unknown. But set in the narrow though creative framework of such a city, built on that exquisite land where the bee gathered the honey of Sophocles and Plato, the mighty genius of the incredible city of Athens accomplished in two or three centuries as much as a dozen nations of the Middle Ages did in a thousand years.

The most powerful means employed by God to create and develop distinctive originality is to maintain the world harmoniously divided into those grand and beautiful systems which we call nations, each of which opens to man a different field of action

[1] The native land or fatherland, which the Dorians so appropriately termed the motherland, is the love of loves. She appears to us in our dreams as a young, adored mother, or as a powerful nurse who suckles us by the millions. A poor image! Not only does she nourish us, but she contains us within herself: *in her we move and have our being.*

and is a living education.[2] The more man advances, the more he enters into the spirit of his country and the better he contributes to the harmony of the globe; he learns to recognize his country, in both its absolute and its relative values, as a note in the grand concert; through it he himself participates and loves the world. The fatherland is the necessary initiation to the fatherland of all mankind.

Thus union is always advancing without any danger of ever attaining unity, since every step every nation takes toward harmony makes it more original in itself.[3] If the impossible occurred and diversities were to disappear, if unity were established with every nation singing the same note, then the concert would be at an end; a too perfect harmony would be nothing but meaningless noise. The world, monotonous and barbarous, might then perish without even causing a regret.

Nothing will perish, I am sure of it, neither the soul of man nor the soul of the people: we are in too good hands. On the contrary, we shall continue living more and more; that is to say, strengthening our individuality and acquiring a more powerful and more productive originality. God preserve us from losing our individual identity in Him! And remember that if no soul perishes,

[2] Everything in the nation contributes to this education. No object of art, no branch of industry however luxurious, and no form of exalted culture is without action and influence upon the mass, even the lowest and poorest. In this great body of the nation, spiritual circulation is always going on, insensibly rising and falling to and from the highest and lowest. One idea comes through the eyes (fashions, shops, museums, and so on); another through conversation and language, which is the great depository of general advancement. Everyone receives the thought of everyone else — without analyzing it perhaps, but they receive it all the same.

[3] To the extent that a nation comes into possession of its own genius, and reveals and establishes it through its achievements, it has less and less need to oppose it to that of other nations in war. Its originality, every day better secured, shines forth better in production than in opposition. The diversity of nations was manifested violently by war, and is displayed still better when each nation lets its great voice be heard distinctly. They all used to shout in the same note; now each sings its own part: gradually harmony develops, and the world becomes a lyre. But the price of this harmony is diversity.

how could those great souls of nations, with their vivid genius, their history rich in martyrs, and abounding with heroic sacrifices of certain immortality, ever perish? When one of them is momentarily eclipsed, the whole world is sick in all its nations, and the heart of the world which responds to nations aches with pain. That suffering I see in your own heart, my reader, is Poland and Italy.

Nationality, the fatherland, is ever the life of the world. If it were dead, all would be dead. Ask especially the people; they feel it, and they will tell you so. Ask science and history, ask the experience of mankind. Those two grand voices are in unison. Two voices? No, two realities: what is and what was, both opposed to empty abstraction.

On this belief I set my heart and wrote my history; I was firm upon that rock and needed nobody to confirm my faith. But I have gone among the crowds and have questioned the people, young and old, great and small. I have heard them all give witness for their native country. That is the living core which dies last in them. I have found it among the dead, in those cemeteries called jails and prisons. I have opened the hearts of the men there, and in those dead men where the breast was empty, guess what I found. France, once again France, the last spark which might perhaps have given them life again.

Do not say, I beg you, that it is nothing at all to be born in the country surrounded by the Pyrenees, the Alps, the Rhine, and the ocean. Take the poorest man, starving in rags, the man you suppose to be concerned solely with material wants. He will tell you it is a rich inheritance to participate in this immense glory, in this unique legend which constitutes the talk of the world. He knows quite well that if he were to go to the most remote desert of the globe, under the equator or the poles, he would find Napoleon, our armies, and our grand history to shelter and protect him. He knows that children would come to him, that old men would hold their peace and ask him to speak, and that to hear him only mention those names they would kiss the hem of his garment.

For my part, whatever happens to me while on this side of the grave — riches or poverty, joy or sorrow — I shall ever thank God for having given me this great France for my native land. And this is not only on account of the many glorious deeds she has performed, but especially because I see her both as the representative of the liberties of all the world and as the country that links all the others together by sympathetic ties, the true introduction to universal love. This last feature is so strong in France that she has often forgotten herself. We must, at present, remind her of herself, and implore her to love all nations less than herself.

No doubt every great nation represents an idea important to the human race. But great God! how much more true is this of France! Suppose for a moment that she were eclipsed or had perished; the sympathetic bond of the world would be loosened, broken, and probably destroyed. Love, which is the life of the world, would be wounded in its most vital part. The earth would enter into an age of ice which other worlds nearby have already entered.

I had, on this very subject, a horrible dream in broad daylight which I must relate. I was in Dublin, near a bridge, and walking along the quay. I was looking at the river gliding along, sluggish and narrow between wide sandy banks, very much as we see our own near Notre Dame, and I thought I was by the Seine. The quays were very similar, with the exception of the absence of the fancy shops, the monuments, the Tuileries, and the Louvre. It was almost Paris — without Paris. A few poorly dressed persons were crossing the bridge, not in the blouses we wear but in old stained coats. They were arguing violently in a harsh, guttural, and very barbarous tone with a dreadful, ragged, humpbacked man whom I still see before my eyes. Other persons were passing along, miserable and deformed.

As I looked at them, a strange idea took possession of me and terrified me — that all those figures were Frenchmen. It was Paris; it was France — a France grown ugly, brutal, and savage. In that moment I experienced how terror can make us believe almost anything, for I made no objection. I said to myself that another 1815 must have happened, but long, long ago; that centuries of misery had oppressed my irrevocably doomed country; and that I had returned to take my share in that world of suffering. Those centuries weighed on me like a mass of lead; so much in two minutes! I stood nailed to the spot, unable to stir. My fellow traveler shook me, and then I collected myself a little. But I could not quite banish from my mind that terrible dream and could not shake a terrible dejection. As long as I remained in Ireland, it filled me with an overpowering melancholy, which has come back to me with all its vividness as I write these lines.

CHAPTER V

France

The head of one of our socialist schools of thought said a few years ago, "What is a fatherland?"

Their cosmopolitan utopias of material enjoyments seem to me, I must confess, a prosaic commentary on Horace's ode: "Rome is tumbling down, let us fly to the fortunate islands," that sad song of abandonment and despondency.

The Christians who came next, with their heavenly fatherland above and their universal brotherhood here below, nonetheless gave the deathblow to the empire by this beautiful and touching doctrine. Their brothers of the north soon came and put the rope round their necks.

We are not the sons of a slave without a country and without gods, as was the great poet just quoted; we are not Romans of Tarsus, like the apostle to the Gentiles. We are the Romans of Rome, and the Frenchmen of France. We are the sons of those who have done the work of the world through the efforts of a heroic nationality, and founded for every nation the gospel of equality. Our fathers did not understand brotherhood in the sense of being a vague sympathy which induces one to accept and love everything, and which mixes, bastardizes, and confounds. They believed that brotherhood was not the blind hodgepodge of existences and characters, but much more the union of hearts. They preserved for themselves and for France the originality of devotion and of sacrifice which no one disputed with them; alone France watered with her blood the tree that she planted. It was a glorious opportunity for the other nations not to leave her stand-

ing alone. They did not imitate France in her devotion. Do they
want France to imitate them in their egotism and their immoral
indifference now, and since she failed to lift them up, to descend
to their level?

Who would see without astonishment the same people that recently raised the beacon of the future toward which the eyes of
the world are turned, now walking with its head down on the
road of imitation? For what is that road? We know it all too well,
since many nations have followed it: it is simply the road to sui-
cide and death.

You poor imitators! Do you really believe you are imitating?
You take from a neighboring people this or that which is a living
thing among them, and you place it on yourselves no matter what,
in spite of the repugnance of a frame that was not made for it.
But it is a foreign body that you are grafting to your flesh, an
inert, lifeless thing. It is death that you are adopting.

And what if this thing is not only foreign and different, but
even hostile! What if you will go and seek it precisely among those
whom nature has given you for adversaries, those whom she has
made the exact opposite of you? What if you ask a renewal of
life from the negation of your own life? What if France, for
example, marches directly against her history and her nature, and
goes and copies what may be called Anti-France — England?

It is not a question of national hatred or blind malevolence.
I have the esteem that I should for that great British nation, and
have proved it by studying that country as seriously as any man
of the present day. The result of this very esteem and study is the
conviction that the progress of the world depends on these two
nations' not losing their respective qualities in some muddy mixture. These two opposing magnets act inversely, and the current
from their positive and negative poles must never be confused.

The element which was least compatible with us — the English
— is precisely the one we have preferred. We have adopted it
politically in our constitution on the faith of the doctrinaires who
copied without understanding. We have adopted it in our literature, without seeing that the foremost genius that England has
had in our time is he who has the most strongly condemned it.

Finally, and this is an incredible and ridiculous thing, we have copied the English in our art and fashion. And that stiffness and awkwardness, which is neither external nor accidental but based on a profound physiological mystery — we copy even that.

I have now before me two French novels written with great talent. Well, guess who is the ridiculous man in these works. The Frenchman — always the Frenchman! The Englishman is the admirable fellow — the invisible yet ever-present Providence who saves everything. He arrives just in time to right all the follies of the other. How? Because he is rich. The Frenchman is poor, and poor in intellect as well.

Rich! Is that, then, the cause of this strange infatuation? The rich man (for the most part the Englishman) is the well-beloved of God. The freest and strongest minds find it difficult to guard themselves from a predisposition in his favor. The women find him handsome, the men want to believe he is noble. His sorry nag is even taken as a model by our artists.

Rich! Go on and confess that this is the hidden cause of this universal admiration. England is the rich nation; never mind her millions of beggars. For any superficial observer who does not look at other men, she presents an unparalleled spectacle in the most enormous accumulation of wealth that has ever existed. A triumphant agriculture, so much machinery, so many ships, so many bursting warehouses, and that stock exchange, the mistress of the world — gold flows there like water.

Ah! France has nothing like that; it is a country of poverty. A comparison of all that one has and all that the other has not would not really lead us too far. Yet England can ask France with a smile: what, after all, are the visible results of your activity, and what has come from so much labor, motion, and effort?[1]

[1] The material products of France, the durable results of her work, are nothing compared to the nonmaterial results. These results were mostly acts, movements, words, and thoughts. Her written literature (which is, however, the first of all, in my opinion) is far, very far, below her oratory and her brilliant, fruitful conversation. Her manufactures of every description are nothing when compared to her action. For machines, she had heroes; for systems, inspired men. "But are not

Look at poor France! Like Job she is sitting on the ground among her friends, the nations who come to comfort her, question her, better her, and work out her salvation, if they can.

"Where are your ships and machinery?" says England. "Where are your systems? Don't you at least have works of art to show, like Italy?" says Germany.

Kind sisters who come thus to comfort France, let me answer your questions. She is ill, you see; her head is drooping and she will not speak.

If we could pile up all the blood, the gold, and the efforts of every kind that each nation has spent unselfishly and only for the good of the world, then France would have a pyramid that would reach to heaven. And you, O nations, the sum of all your sacrifices put together would reach the knee of a child!

So do not come and tell me how pale France is. She has shed her blood for you. Or how poor she is! For your sake she has given without counting.[2] And having nothing left, she has said, "Gold and silver have I none; but such as I have I give unto

these words and acts unproductive things?" Yet that is precisely what places France very high. She has excelled in things of movement and grace, in those which serve no purpose. Above everything material and tangible are found the imponderables, the intangibles, the invisibles. So never class France according to material things — by what is touched and seen. Do not judge her as you would another by way of what outward misery you see. France is the country of the mind, and consequently the one that is least affected by the material aspect of the world.

[2] I am writing here in milder form a thought that tore at me the first times I crossed the frontier. Once, especially, as I was entering Switzerland, I felt wounded to the heart by it. To see our poor peasants of Franche-Comté so miserable, and then suddenly, after passing a stream, the people of Neufchâtel so comfortable, so well clothed, and so clearly happy! What, then, is at the bottom of those two principal loads, the debt and the army, that are now crushing France? They are two sacrifices that she is making to the world as much as to herself. The debt is the money she pays the world for having given it her principle of salvation and the law of liberty that it copies while slandering her. And the army of France? It is the defense of the world, the reserve that it keeps for the day when the barbarians will arrive, when Germany, ever seeking her unity (since the time of Charlemagne), will either have to follow us or turn against liberty as the vanguard of Russia.

you." So she gave her soul, and that is what you are living on.[3]

"You mean she still has what she has given away?" Oh, you nations! Listen carefully and learn what you never would have learned without us: "the more you give, the more you keep!" Her spirit may sleep within her, but it is still whole and ever on the point of a mighty awakening.

For a very long time I have been France, living with her day by day for two thousand years. We have seen the worst days together, and I have come to believe that this is the country of invincible hope. God must certainly reveal more to her than to any other nation, for she sees in the darkest night when others see nothing. During that dreadful darkness which often prevailed in the Middle Ages and after, no one could make out the sky; France alone saw it.

Such is France. With her, nothing is finished; everything is always beginning again. When our Gallic peasants drove away the Romans for a moment and established the empire of Gaul, they stamped their coin with the first and the last motto of this country — *Hope!*

[3] No, it is not the industrial machinism of England, or the scholastic machinism of Germany, that gives life to the world. It is the breath of France in whatever state she may be, the latent heat of her Revolution that Europe always carries within her.

᭜

CHAPTER VI

The Superiority of France, as Both Dogma and Legend. France Is a Religion

The foreigner thinks he has exhausted the subject when he says with a chuckle, "France is the infant of Europe."

If you give her this title, which is not the least in the eyes of God, you must confess that it is the infant Solomon sitting in judgment. Who but France has preserved the tradition of the law? And ecclesiastical, political, and civil law: the throne of Papinianus and the chair of Gregory VII.

Rome is nowhere but here. To whom have the pope, the emperor, and the kings of Europe turned for justice ever since the time of Saint Louis? Who could not recognize the theological papacy in Gerson and Bossuet, the philosophical papacy in Descartes and Voltaire, and the political and civil papacy in Cujas and Dumoulin, in Rousseau and Montesquieu? Her laws, which are only those of reason itself, impose themselves even upon her enemies. England has just given our civil code to the island of Ceylon. Rome held the pontificate of the Dark Ages and the kingdom of the obscure. France has been the pontiff of the Age of Enlightenment.

This is not an accident of recent developments or a chance result of the Revolution. It is the legitimate consequence of a particular history tied to the general history of the last two thousand years. No other people has anything like it. The grand human movement — so clearly seen in the languages — from India to Greece to Rome continues on from Rome to us.

Every other history is mutilated: ours alone is complete. Take the history of Italy, and the last centuries are missing. Take the history of Germany, or of England, and the first are gone. Take that of France, and you know the world.

And in this great tradition there is not only a connected series of events but there is also progress. France has continued the Roman and Christian work that Christianity had promised, and France has delivered. Brotherly equality had been postponed to the next life, but she taught it as the law on earth to the whole world.

This nation has two very powerful qualities that I do not find in any other. She has both the principle and the legend: the idea made more comprehensive and more humane, and the tradition more connected and coherent.

This principle, this idea, which was buried in the Middle Ages under the dogma of grace, is called brotherhood in the language of man.

This tradition flows from Caesar to Charlemagne to Saint Louis, from Saint Louis to Louis XIV and Napoleon, and it makes the history of France that of humanity. It perpetuates the moral ideal of the world in various forms — from Saint Louis to the Maid of Orléans, and from Joan of Arc to our young generals of the Revolution. The saint of France, whoever he may be, is the saint of all nations. He is adopted, blessed, and lamented by all mankind.

An American philosopher has said impartially that "for every man the first country is his native land and the second is France."* And how many men prefer to live here than in their own country! As soon as they can break for a moment the thread that binds them, they come here like poor birds of passage to settle, take refuge, and at least enjoy a moment's vital heat. They tacitly confess that this is the universal fatherland.

This nation, considered thus as the asylum of the world, is much more than a nation. It is a living brotherhood. No matter

* Tom Paine, 1737-1809.

what weakness France may fall into, she contains at the heart of
her nature this undying principle which still preserves special
chances of recovery for her. When France remembers what she
was and must be — the salvation of mankind — she will gather
her children around her and teach them France as faith and as
religion, and she will find herself alive again and as firm as the
earth.

I know this is a serious proposition, and I have thought about
it a long time. It contains perhaps the regeneration of our country. Ours is the only country that has the right to teach itself such
a lesson, because it is the one that has most identified its own
interest and its own destiny with those of humanity. It is the only
one that can do so because its great national yet universal legend
is the only complete and connected one, and thus the one whose
historical development best answers the demands of reason.

And this is not fanaticism. It is the overly condensed summary
of a considered judgment based on long study. It would be very
easy for me to show that the other nations have only special legends, which the world has not accepted. And these legends are
often made up of isolated, individual stories that have no connection to each other, like points of light separated in space.[1] The
national legend of France is an immense, unbroken stream of

---

[1] To speak first of that great German nation, which seems the richest
in legends: those of Siegfried the invulnerable, Frederick Barbarossa, and
Goetz with the iron hand are poetic dreams which turn life back to the
past, to the impossible, and to vain regrets. Luther, rejected and spat
upon by half of Germany, has not been able to leave a legend. Frederick
the Great, hardly a German but a Prussian (which is very different) —
a Frenchman, moreover, and a philosopher — has left the trace of
strength but nothing for the heart, nothing as poetry or national faith.
   The historical legends of England, the victory of Edward III and that
of Elizabeth, present a glorious fact instead of a moral model. One type,
thanks to Shakespeare, has remained powerful in the English mind and
influences it all too much — that of Richard III. It is certainly curious
to observe how easily their tradition has been broken up; it seems as
though three different nations had sprung up at three different times.
The ballads of Robin Hood and others, which comforted the Middle
Ages, finish with Shakespeare; Shakespeare is silenced by the Bible,
Cromwell, and Milton. They in turn have been effaced by industrialism
and the half-great men of recent times. Where is their complete man on
whom a legend might be founded?

light, a veritable Milky Way which the world has always fixed its eyes upon.

By race, language, and instinct, Germany and England are strangers to the great Romano-Christian and democratic tradition of the world. They share a certain part of it, but without successfully bringing it into harmony with their foundations, which are quite exceptional. They adopt it obliquely, indirectly, awkwardly — are in it, but still not in it. Look at those nations carefully. You will find that in both their physical and mental endowments there is a discord between life and principle which France does not have, and which ought to prevent the world from ever seeking its models and lessons there (even if intrinsic value is not considered, but only form and style).

France, on the contrary, is not a mixture of two principles. In her the Celtic element has combined with the Roman, and the two are one. The Germanic element, which some people are always talking about, is really imperceptible.

She proceeds directly from Rome, and she ought to teach Rome — its language, its history, and its law. Our education is quite right in doing so. It is at fault only in not imbuing this Roman education with the sentiment of France; it lays such scholastic stress on Rome, which is the means, that it conceals France, which is the goal. This goal should be pointed out to the child at the very beginning, so that he starts out from the France which is himself, and comes back by way of Rome to the France which is still himself. Only then can our education form a harmonious whole.

When this people returns to itself, it will open its eyes and consider itself, and it will understand that the first institution that can make it live and endure is this harmonious education, which would found the country in the very heart of the child, and which should be given to *everyone*. There is no other salvation. We have grown old in our vices and do not wish to be cured. If God saves this glorious but unfortunate country, he will save it through the children.

∾

Faith in the Revolution. This Faith Has Withered and Has Not Been Transmitted by Education

The only government that devoted itself heart and soul to the education of the people was that of the Revolution. The constituent and legislative assemblies laid down the principles to be followed with admirable clarity and truly humane feeling. Then the Convention — in the midst of its terrible struggle against the world and against France, whom it saved in spite of herself, when personal dangers were everywhere and its forces were decimated and mutilated in a slow death — never gave up and obstinately pursued the holy and sacred object of the education of the people. In those stormy nights when the deputies met with their weapons in hand, prolonging each session which might be the last, the Convention nevertheless took the time to call forth every system and to examine them all. "If we establish education, then we shall have lived long enough," said one of its members.

The three projects adopted are full of good sense and grandeur. First they organized the high and the low, the normal schools for training teachers and the elementary schools. They kindled a bright flame and transported it instantly into the vast depths of the people. After this they were less pressed, and could fill up the intervening space with the central schools and the colleges where the rich may be educated. Nevertheless, everything was created uniformly and harmoniously; they knew then that a living work is not made bit by bit.

That moment will be always remembered! It was two months after 9 Thermidor. They were beginning to believe in life again. France — risen from the grave and suddenly mature with the experience of twenty centuries — that enlightened yet bloody France, called all her children to receive the sovereign instruction of her vast experience. "Come and look at me," she said.[1]

When the chairman told the Convention simply and sincerely, "Time alone could be the professor of the Republic," whose eyes were not filled with tears? They had all paid dearly for the lesson of the time; they had all passed through death, and not all had escaped!

After those great trials there seemed to be a moment of silence for all human passions; one might have thought that there was no longer any pride, self-interest, or envy. The leading men in the state and in science accepted the most humble positions of public instruction. Lagrange and Laplace taught arithmetic.

Fifteen hundred students — grown men who were in some cases already famous — came as a matter of course to take their seats at the normal school and to learn to teach. They came as they could, in the depth of winter, in that moment of poverty and famine. Above the ruins of all material things hovered the majesty of the mind, alone and without a shadow. Men of creative genius

---

[1] And the principal lesson of that experience is that human blood has a terrible power against those who have shed it. It would be too easy for me to prove that France was saved *in spite of* the Reign of Terror. Those terrorists have done us an immense disservice that still lasts. Go into the poorest cottage of the most distant region of Europe, and you will find the memory of it and its curse. Kings have put to death in cold blood upon their scaffolds, in their Spielbergs, their *presides,* their Siberias, and so on, a much greater number of men. Yet what does that matter? The victims of the Reign of Terror still remain forever bleeding in the thoughts of people. We ought never to lose an opportunity to protest against those horrors, which were not *ours* and which cannot be attributed to us. The enthusiastic vigor of our armies alone saved France. The committee of public safety no doubt seconded that enthusiasm, but precisely because of the excellent military administrators it had within itself, men whom Robespierre detested and would have put to death had he been able to do without them. Our purest generals found in Robespierre and his friends only malevolence, distrust, and obstacles of every kind.

took their turn in the chair of the great school. Some, like Berthollet and Morveau, came to found chemistry and to open and
penetrate the inner world of the body; others, like Laplace and
Lagrange, strengthened the system of the world through their
calculations and put the earth on a firmer basis. Never did power
of the mind seem more irresistible. Reason yielded obediently to
reason. And how great was the heart's part in it when among
those matchless men, each of whom appears but once in a mil-
lennium, there was seen a most precious head which had nar-
rowly escaped the scaffold — that of good Haüy, saved by
Geoffroy Saint-Hilaire!

A great citizen, Carnot — the man who organized victory, fore-
saw Hoche and Bonaparte, and saved France in spite of the Reign
of Terror — was the real founder of the Polytechnic School. They
learned as they fought, and completed three years of lectures in
three months. At the end of six, Monge declared that they not
only had received the knowledge of the day but had advanced it.
Watching the uninterrupted inventions of their teachers, the students went on to invent as well. Imagine the spectacle of a Lagrange who suddenly stopped short in the middle of his lecture
and was lost in thought. The room waited in silence. Finally he
awoke and told them of his glowing new discovery, barely formed
in his mind.

Everything was lacking, except genius. The pupils could not
have come if they had not been given four sous a day. They received their food with the food of the mind. One of the masters
(Clouet) would accept only a nook of ground in the sandy plains
of the Sablons as his salary, and lived on the vegetables he grew
there.

What a fall after that time! A moral fall and an intellectual
fall just as great! After the reports made to the Convention, read
those of Fourcroy and Fontanes and you sink in a few years from
manhood to old age, doddering old age.

Is it not heartbreaking to see that heroic, disinterested enthusiasm decline and fall so soon? The glorious normal school bears
no fruit. We can hardly be surprised at this when we see that
man is taught so little, when the humane sciences renounce and

contradict each other as if they were ashamed of themselves. The professor of history, Volney, taught that history *is the science of dead facts* and that there is no living history. Garat, the professor of philosophy, said that philosophy *is only the study of symbols* — which is another way of saying that philosophy is nothing. Symbols versus symbols, mathematics had the advantage, as well as the related disciplines such as astronomy. So in the great school that was to diffuse its spirit throughout the world, revolutionary France lectured on the fixed stars and forgot herself.

In this supreme effort of the Revolution to found an education, we especially see that it could be only a prophet and would die in the desert without having seen the promised land. How could it have been otherwise? The Revolution had to do everything, for it found nothing ready and no aid in the system that had gone before. It had entered into possession of an empty world *because there had been no heirs.* I will show someday on unequivocal evidence that it found nothing to destroy. The clergy was finished, the nobility was finished, and royalty was finished — and the Revolution had nothing at all to put in their places. The Revolution was caught in a vicious circle. To make the Revolution required men, but it would have taken the Revolution to have already made such men. There was no help to make the passage from one world to the other! An abyss to be spanned and no wings to fly across.

It is sad to see how very little the guardians of the people, royalty and clergy, have done to enlighten them in the last four centuries. The church spoke to them in a learned language they no longer understood. She made them repeat by heart that prodigious metaphysical doctrine, the subtlety of which amazes the most cultivated minds. The State had done only one thing and that very indirectly; it had brought the people together in camps and grand armies where they began to understand themselves. The legions of Francis I and the regiments of Louis XIV were schools where they formed themselves spontaneously without any instruction, acquired common ideas, and gradually rose to the sentiment of their native land.

The only direct instruction was that which members of the

bourgeoisie received in the colleges, and which they followed up as lawyers and men of letters. It was a verbal study of languages, rhetoric, literature, and the study of the laws, which was not learned and precise like that of our ancient jurists but of a so-called philosophical nature and full of shallow abstractions. Being logicians without metaphysics and jurists without law and history, they had faith only in symbols, forms, figures, and phrases. Substance, life, and the feeling of life were always missing in them. When they arrived at the great theater where vanity fights to the death, one could see all the bad qualities that scholastic subtlety can add to a bad nature. These dreadful *abstractors* of ultimate essences armed themselves with five or six formulas which they used like so many guillotines to *abstract* men.[2]

It was a terrible moment when that great assembly, which had made the Reign of Terror with terror itself under Robespierre, raised her head and saw all the blood she had shed. She had never lost faith when the whole world and even France were leagued against her; she had continued with only thirty departments and still saved everything. She had never lost faith even in the face of personal danger, when she no longer held even Paris and was forced to arm her own members, who were almost her only defenders. But in the presence of that blood, before all those dead men who were rising from their tombs, before that host of

[2] The genius of the inquisition and the police, which Robespierre and Saint-Just shared, has astonished many people. It does not surprise those who are acquainted with the Middle Ages and so often find there the temperament of the inquisitor and the bloodthirsty quibbler. This affinity of the two periods has been noted with much penetration by Edgar Quinet in his work on Christianity and the French Revolution (1845). Two men of scrupulous equity who were inclined to judge their enemies favorably, Carnot and Daunou, were in perfect agreement in their opinion of Robespierre. The latter has often told me that except in the last moment when necessity and peril made him eloquent, the famous dictator was a second-rater. Saint-Just had more talent. Those who wish to make us believe that they were both innocent of the last excesses of the Reign of Terror are refuted by Saint-Just himself. On 15 April 1794 (so short a time before 9 Thermidor!), he deplores their criminal *indulgence*. "In recent days the courts have granted acquittals to an increasing degree ... What have the tribunals been doing for two years? Have people spoken of their justice? Instituted to maintain the Revolution, *their indulgence* has left crime free everywhere ..."

released prisoners who came to judge their judges, she felt faint and began to abandon her task.

She did not take the step which would have given her the future. She did not have the courage to put her hand upon the young world that was rising. In order to take hold there, the Revolution ought to have taught one and only one lesson: the Revolution.

To do so it would have been necessary not to deny the past but, on the contrary, to challenge it, seize it again, and make it her own as she was doing with the present: to show that she possessed along with the authority of reason the authority of history and all our historical nationality, that the Revolution was the overdue though just and necessary manifestation of the genius of this people, and that it was only France herself having finally discovered her right.

She did nothing of the kind. Abstract reason was all she called upon, and it did not support her in the face of those terrible realities which rose against her. She doubted herself, abdicated, and passed away. She had to die and descend into the tomb in order that her living spirit might spread throughout the world. She was ruined by her defender Napoleon, but she received his homage in the Hundred Days. She was ruined by the Holy Alliance, but the kings based their compact against her on the social doctrine that she laid down in 1789. The faith she did not have in herself conquers those who have fought against her. The sword they plunged into her heart works miracles and heals. She converts her persecutors and teaches her enemies. Why did she not teach her children?

∾

CHAPTER VIII

No Education without Faith

The first question of education is this: do you have faith? Do you infuse faith?

The child must believe.

The child should believe the things he can prove by reason when he is a man.

To make a child a reasoner, a wrangler, and a critic is absurd. To be constantly digging up all the seeds we have sown — what crazy agriculture! To make a child learned is absurd. To load his memory with a chaos of useful and useless knowledge; to load him down with the undigested mass of a thousand things all ready-made, not living but dead, and with dead fragments without his ever seeing the whole: you are murdering his mind.

Before he can grow, he must first *exist*. We must create and strengthen the living germ of the young being. The child *exists* at first by faith.

Faith is the common source of inspiration and action. There is nothing great without it.

The Athenian had the faith that all human culture had descended from the Acropolis of Athens, and that his Pallas had sprung from the brain of Jupiter and had produced the light of art and science. That faith was realized. That city with her twenty thousand citizens has flooded the world with her light; though dead, she enlightens it still.

The Roman had the faith that the living and bleeding head found under his Capitol promised that he should be the head and the judge of the world. That faith was realized. If his empire has passed away, his law remains and continues to rule the nations.

The Christian had the faith that a God in the form of a man would make a nation of brothers, and would sooner or later unite the world in one and the same heart. That has not yet been realized, but it will be by us.

It was not enough to say that God was made man. Stated in such general terms, this truth has not been productive. We must see how God has manifested himself in the man of every nation, how in the variety of national geniuses the Father has responded to the needs of his children. The unity that He ought to give us is not a monotonous unity, but a harmonious unity in which all varieties love one another. Let them all love, but let them all remain. Let them go on increasing in splendor to better enlighten the world. Let man be accustomed from childhood to recognize a living God in his native land!

Here some will raise a serious objection. "How can I give a faith which I scarcely have? My faith in my native land, like my religious faith, has grown weak within me."

If faith and reason were contradictory things and there were no reasonable means of obtaining faith, we would be forced, like the mystics, to stop short and sigh and wait. But the faith worthy of man is a loving faith in what is proved by reason. The object of such faith is not this or that accidental miracle, but the permanent miracle of nature and history.

To put our faith in France again and to hope for her future, we must go back into her past and fathom her natural genius. And if you do so seriously and sincerely, you will see that this consequence inevitably follows. From the past you will deduce the future; the mission of France will rise before you and appear in full light. You will believe, and you will love to believe. Faith is nothing more.

How could you resign yourself to your ignorance of France? Your origin is in her; if you do not know her, you will know nothing of yourself. She is all around you and touches you on every side; you live in her, because of her, and will die with her. May you both live by faith!

She will return to your heart if you look at your children. That young world, so good and so docile, wishes to live and asks for the life of faith. You have grown old in your indifference; but which of you could wish his son to be dead in the heart, without a country and without God? These children hold the souls of our ancestors, and they are our country, old and new. Let us help it to know itself, and it will give us back the gift of loving.

As the poor man is necessary to the rich, so is the child necessary to the man. We give him still less than we receive from him.

Young people, you who will soon take our place, I must thank you. Who more than I has studied the past of France? Who should have known her better after so many personal trials which revealed her trials to me as well? And yet I must say that in my solitude my soul was languishing, either carried away by trifles and curiosities or else soaring toward the ideal and not treading the ground. Reality escaped me, and our country, which I have always pursued and loved, was still far below. She was my subject and goal, an object of science and study. Then she stood alive before me. "In whom?" In you who read me. In you, young people, I saw my country and her eternal youth. How could I fail to believe in her?

∿

CHAPTER IX

God in Our Native Land.
The Young Country of the Future:
The Country of Sacrifice

Education, like every work of art, demands first of all a strong, simple sketch. There must be no subtlety and no minutiae, nothing that presents any difficulty or raises an objection. Education must begin with a great, healthy, lasting impression that will found the man in the child and create the life of the heart. First, God revealed in love and nature by the mother. Afterward, God revealed by the father in the living country, in her heroic history and the feeling of France.

God and the love of God. Let the mother take the child on Saint John's Day — when the earth performs her annual miracle, when every plant is in flower, when every plant seems to grow while you behold it — let her take him into the garden, kiss him, and talk to him tenderly. "You love me, you know only me. Well, listen: I am not all. You have another mother. All of us — men, women, children, animals, plants, everything that lives — we all have a tender mother who is always sustaining us, invisible yet present. And we love her, my dear child, and we embrace her with all our hearts."

Nothing more for a long time. No metaphysics that destroy the impression. Let him brood over that sublime and tender mystery which a whole life will not be able to explain. That is a day he will never forget. Throughout all the trials of life and all the intricacies of science, amid all his passions and stormy nights, the gentle sun of Saint John's Day will always shine in the depths of his heart with the immortal light of the purest and very best love.

Some day later, when he is just beginning to be a man, let his father take him: it is a great public festival, and there are immense crowds in Paris. He leads him from Notre Dame to the Louvre and the Tuileries and to the Arc de Triomphe. From some roof or terrace he shows him the people, the army passing by with its bayonets flashing and glittering, and the tricolored flag. In those moments of expectation before the great parade, in those fantastic moments of illumination when tremendous silence suddenly stills that dark ocean of people — let him lean down and speak to him. "Look, my son, look: there is France; there is your native land! All this is like one man — with one soul and one heart. They would all die for a single man, and each one ought also to live and to die for all. Those men passing by, who are armed and now departing, they are going away to fight for us. They are leaving their father and their aged mother who will need them. You will do the same, for you will never forget that your mother is France."

If I know anything at all about human nature, this will make a lasting impression. He has seen the fatherland. That God, which is invisible in his supreme unity, is visible in his members and in those great works where the life of the nation is deposited. It is really a living person that this child touches and feels on all sides; he cannot embrace her, but she embraces him, warms him with her great soul diffused throughout that multitude, and speaks to him through her monuments. It is a wonderful thing for the Swiss to be able to regard his canton in a single look, to embrace from the heights of his Alps his beloved country and carry away her image with him. But it is truly great for the Frenchman to have the glorious and immortal fatherland focused at one point. All ages and all places are mixed together, and he can follow from the Baths of Caesar to the Column of Victory, from the Louvre to the Champ de Mars, from the Arc de Triomphe to the Place de la Concorde, the history of France and the world.

Still it is in the school, the great national school we will create someday, that the child will receive the strong and lasting knowledge of his country. I am speaking of a truly common school, where children of every class and condition will come for a year or two to sit together and learn nothing but France before any special education begins.[1]

We rush to place our children in schools and colleges among children of our own class, whether bourgeoisie or people; we avoid every mixture and are quick to separate the poor and the rich at that happy time when the child himself would not have felt these vain distinctions. We seem to be afraid of their really knowing the world in which they must live. By this premature separation we prepare that hatred which springs from ignorance and envy, and that internal warfare which plagues us later on.

If inequality must remain among men, how I would wish that childhood might at least be able to follow its instinct for a moment and live in equality! Oh, that these innocent little men of God, devoid of envy, might preserve for us the touching ideal of society in their school! And it would be a school for us as well; we should go and learn from them the vanity of ranks, the silliness of rival pretensions, and all the true life and happiness of having neither an upper nor a lower class.

There our country would appear young and delightful in all her variety and all her harmony — a wealth of characters, faces, and races, a rainbow with a hundred colors. Every rank, every fortune, and every dress; velvet and cotton, brown bread and dainty cake: all together on the same benches . . .

Let the rich child learn there while still young what it is to be poor. Let him suffer from inequality, learn to share, and strive already to reestablish equality as best he can. Let him find on those wooden benches the city of the world, and begin there the city of God! For his part, let the poor child learn, and perhaps remember, that if the rich man is rich, it is not his fault: he was

[1] The special education of the college or workshop would come afterward. The workshop would have been tempered and regulated by the school; the college would have been tempered by those first years when the child would learn only as much grammar as he could understand. More exercise and recreation and less useless writing. Mercy, mercy for little children!

born that way, and his riches often make him poor in basic values — poor in willpower and moral strength.

It would be a wonderful thing if all the sons of the same people were thus united, at least for a time, and could see and know one another before being corrupted by poverty and wealth, before the age of envy and egotism. The child would receive an indelible impression of his country, since he would find it in the school not only as study and instruction but as a living country, a country of children like himself, a better city before the City, a city of equality where all would be seated at the same spiritual banquet.

And I would hope that he would not only learn and see his native land, but would feel it as Providence and recognize it as his mother and nurse by its strengthening milk and its life-giving heat. God forbid that we should send a boy away from school or refuse him spiritual food because he lacks that of the body. Oh, how impious is the avarice that would give millions for buildings and priests — that would be rich only to endow from a deathbed — and yet would haggle with these little children who are the hope, the lifeblood, and the heart of hearts of France!

I have said elsewhere that I am not one of those who are always weeping — first with the healthy worker who earns five francs a day, and then with the poor woman who gains but ten sous. So impartial a pity is no pity. Women must have asylums, free convents, temporary workshops, and they must not be starved any longer in the old convents. And we must all be fathers to the little children and open our arms to them; the school must be their asylum, a pleasant, generous asylum. Let them be comfortable in school and go of their own accord; and let them love that house of France as much as or more than the paternal home. If your mother cannot support you, if your father treats you ill, if you are naked or hungry, then come, my dear son: the doors are all wide open, and France is on the threshold to embrace and welcome you. That great mother will never blush at the cares of a wet nurse; with her own heroic hand she will make for you the soldier's soup; and if she did not have something to cover and warm your frozen little limbs, she would even tear off a shred of her old flag!

Comforted and caressed, happy and free of mind, let the child find on those benches the food of truth. Let him know above all that God has had the grace to give him for his native home a land that proclaimed and sealed with her blood the law of divine equity and fraternity, and that the God of nations has spoken through France.

The first lesson is the country as a doctrine and as a principle. Then the country as a legend: our two redemptions, by the holy Maid of Orléans and by the Revolution; the enthusiasm of 1792; the miracle of the young flag; our young generals admired and mourned by the enemy; the purity of Marceau; the magnanimity of Hoche; the glory of Arcola and Austerlitz; Caesar and the second Caesar, in whom our greatest kings reappeared in still greater form. Further back, the glory of our sovereign assemblies; and the pacific and truly humane genius of 1789, when France offered so generously peace and liberty to all. And above all else, the supreme lesson: the immense capacity, the devotion, and the sacrifice that our fathers displayed; and how France has so often given her life for the world.

Child, let this be your basic gospel — your staff of life and the nourishment of your heart. You will remember it amid the toils and troubles which will soon be yours. It will be a powerful cordial which will comfort you on many occasions. It will charm your memory in the long days of labor and in the boredom of the factory; you will find it again as a cure for your homesick heart on your tiresome marches across Africa, and on those watches when you stand a solitary sentinel two steps from the barbarians.

The child will know the world, but he must first know himself — the best part of himself. I mean France. The rest he will learn from her. It is up to her to initiate him and tell him her tradition. She will tell him the three revelations she has received: how Rome taught her the Just, Greece the Beautiful, and Judea the Holy. She will connect her ultimate lesson with the first his mother gave him: his mother taught him *God;* his great mother will teach him the doctrine of love, the *God within man* of Christianity. And then she will show how love that was impossible in the barbarous and malevolent times of the Middle Ages was written into law *by the Revolution,* so that God within man might be made manifest.

If I were writing a book on education, I would show how general education, which is interrupted by the special education of the college or the workshop, ought to be resumed under the flag for the young soldier. This is the way the country ought to pay him for the time he gives her. When he returns home, she ought to follow him, not only as a law to govern and punish him, but also as a secular providence to increase his religious and moral culture through meetings, public libraries, theaters, and holidays and musical festivals of every kind.

How long should a man's education last? Just as long as his life.

What is the first part of public policy? Education. The second? Education. And the third? Education. I have grown too old in the study of history to believe in laws when they are not carefully prepared, and when men have not been raised to love and desire the law. Make fewer laws, but strengthen the principle of laws through education. Make them practical and applicable. Make men, and all will be well.

Politicians promise us order, peace, and public security. But what is the purpose of all these blessings? To let us enjoy ourselves? To sleep in an egotistical tranquillity, and to relieve us from working together and loving one another? Let them perish if that is their aim. As for myself, I would rather believe that if such order and great social harmony has a purpose, it is to aid our unfettered progress and to favor the improvement of all by all. Society ought to be only an initiation from birth to death, an education that embraces our life in this world and prepares the lives to come.

Education — a word so little understood — is not only the instruction of the son by the father, but equally, and sometimes even more, the teaching of the father by the son. If we recover from our moral decline, it will be through and for our children. The worst man wants his son to be good; he who would sacrifice nothing for humanity or for his country will still do it for his family. If he has not lost his moral sense as well as his mind, he pities that child who runs the risk of being like him. Search deeply into that soul: everything is ruined and empty; yet at the very depth you will almost always find a solid bottom of paternal love.

Well, then! In the name of our children, we must not allow our country to perish. Do you want to leave them a shipwreck and receive their curse — and that of the future and that of the world, lost perhaps for a thousand years if France succumbs?

You can save your children, and with them France and the world, in only one way. You must give them faith.

Faith in devotion, in sacrifice, and in the grand association where all sacrifice themselves for all — I mean our native land.

I know very well that this is a difficult lesson. Words alone will not suffice; there must be examples. The strength and generosity of sacrifice, so common among our fathers, seems lost with us. This is the true cause of our evils, our hatred, and that inner discord which weakens this country almost to death and makes it the laughingstock of the world.

If I take aside the best, the most honorable men, and question them a little, I see that although each of them appears disinterested, he has at bottom some petty thing which he would not sacrifice for anything. Ask him for everything else. A man who would give his life for France will not give up some amusement or habit or vice.

There are still some pure men among the rich, whatever may be said to the contrary. But what about the proud? Are they also pure? Will they take off their gloves to lend a hand to the poor man who is crawling along the rough path of fate? And yet I tell you, sir, if your white, cold hand does not touch that strong, warm, and living one, it will perform no works of life.

Our habits, far dearer than our enjoyments, must nonetheless be sacrificed in a short time. An age of warfare is coming.

And the heart has its habits and tender ties, which are now so well mingled with its living fibers that they have become other living fibers. It is hard to pluck them out. I have felt this occasionally in writing this book, where I have wounded more than one who was dear to me.

First I had to say "Begone!" to those Middle Ages where I

have passed my life, and whose touching though impotent aspirations I have reproduced in my histories. For today impure
hands are dragging them from their tomb and placing that stone
before us in order to make us stumble on the path of the future.

I have also sacrificed another religion — the humanitarian
dream of philosophy, which believes it can save the individual
by destroying the citizens, denying the nations, and renouncing
the fatherland. The fatherland, my fatherland, can alone save
the world.

From the poetic legend to logic, and from there to faith and
the heart — such has been my road.

In that very heart and faith I found ancient and respectable
things which protested, as well as those friendships which formed
the last obstacles. But they could not stop me in the face of my
country in danger. May she accept this sacrifice! All I have in
this world — my friendships — I offer them up to her, and give to
my country the beautiful name handed down by ancient France.
I lay them all on the altar of the *Great Friendship!*

Index

Africa, 88, 150-51, 174, 207
Ampère, André, 140
Apelles, 122
Apprenticeship, 42, 53-55
Arc de Triomphe, 204
Ardèche, 30
Aristotle, 159
Athens, 180, 200

Balzac, Honoré de, 7
Barbarians, 18
Bayeux tapestry, 171
Beethoven, Ludwig van, 179
Beghards, 47
Belgium, 68
Béranger, Pierre Jean de, 5, 111
Berri, 172
Berthollet, Charles, 196
Blanc, Louis, 54
Boisguilbert, Pesant de, 27, 29
Bossuet, Jacques, 128, 190
Bruce, Robert, 150
Burgundy, 37

Caesar, Julius, 152, 191, 207
Carnot, Lazare, 196, 198
Caucasus, 150
Chamber of Deputies, 108
Champ de Mars, 204
Charlemagne, 133, 191
Cherbourg, 172

Chilperic, 14
Christianity, 133-34, 185, 191, 201, 207
Church, 127-28, 135
Clouet, Louis, 196
Colbert, Jean Baptiste, 96
College of France, xiii, 17
Column of Victory, 204
Communism, 86-87
Convention, 78, 194, 196
Corneille, Pierre, 140
Correggio, Antonio, 122
Cossacks, 63
Courier, Paul Louis, 37
Crime, 32, 103-4
Cromwell, Oliver, 192
Cujas, Jacques, 190

Dagobert, 14
d'Alba, Andrieu, 15
Daunou, Pierre, 198
Descartes, René, 190
Drunkenness, 49, 70
Dublin, 183
Dumesnil, Madame, xxi, 122
Dumoulin, Charles, 190
Dürer, Albert, 19

Edward III, 192
Egyptians, 109
Elizabeth I, 192

England: culture of, 6, 116-17, 192-93; decline of, 50, 104; and France, xxx, 20-21, 67-68, 175, 186; wealth of, 85, 178-79, 186-88

Family, xvii-xviii, xxix, 10-11, 55-57, 73-74, 76, 159, 165-68
Faucher, Léon, 53-54
Fontanes, Louis de, 196
Fourcroy, Antoine de, 196
Fourier, François, 170-71
France, 29, 175, 182, 203; in Africa, 150; army of, 80-81, 204; economy of, 42-43, 64-67, 85; international position of, xxx-xxxi, 20-22, 67; landholding in, 26-31, 35; Michelet's love of, 92, 157, 177, 182-84, 209-10; mission of, 178, 185-86, 192-93, 201-2; and the Revolution, 7-8, 21-22, 78
Franche-Comté, 188
Francis I, 197
Frederick Barbarossa, 192
Frederick the Great, 192
Fredogonda, 14
French character, 112, 116
French Revolution, 22, 26, 63, 175, 189-91; and education, 78, 194-99, 207-8; understanding of, xxii, 8, 163-64
French Revolution of 1830, 83, 93

Garat, Dominique, 197
Gaul, 189
Geneviève de Brabant, 134
Germany, 6-7, 38, 188, 192; and liberty, 21, 104, 192-93; and unification, 20, 178-79
Gerson, Jean de, 190
Goethe, Johann Wolfgang von, 60-61, 179
Goetz von Berlichingen, 192

Greece, 190, 207
Gregory VII, 133, 190
Gregory of Nazianzus, 128
Guizot, François, 19, 131
Guyton de Morveau, Louis, 196

Haüy, René, 196
Henry IV, 28
Herodotus, 108
Highlanders of Scotland, 150
Hoche, Louis, 161, 196, 207
Holy Alliance, 199
Homer, 17
Horace, 16, 132, 185

India, 131-33, 150, 190
Indians of North America, 150
Innocent III, 128
Ireland, 20, 183-84
Italy, 20, 77, 182

Jacquard, Joseph, 118
Jansenists, 128
Jesuits, xiii, 3, 78, 80, 87
Jews, 12, 34, 38, 65, 93, 133
Joan of Arc, xxi, 191, 207
Jura, 170

La Fontaine, Jean de, 140
Lagrange, Joseph, 140, 195-96
Lamartine, Alphonse Marie de, 5, 111
Lamennais, Félicité de, 5
Laplace, Pierre de, 195-96
Latin America, 63
Lebanon, 150
Leclerc, Charles, 17
Le Havre, 172
Limousin, 29
Lollards, 46-47
London Stock Exchange, 93
Louis XI, 27
Louis XIV, 27, 29, 96, 191, 197
Louvet, Jean Baptiste, 73-74

Louvet, Lodoïska, 74
Louvois, Marquis de, 96
Louvre, 183, 204
Luther, Martin, xx, 192
Lyons, 173

Machiavelli, Niccolò, 8
Machinism, 42-43, 95-97
Mahabharata, 131
Marceau, François, 207
Marx, Karl, xxvii
Mazarin, Cardinal, 28-29
Michelet, Athenaïs (née Mialaret), xxiii
Michelet, Pauline (née Rousseau), xvii, xix, xxi, 122
Middle Ages, xxii, 34, 176; life in, 126, 149, 151, 160, 180, 207; thought of, 95-96, 124-28, 131-36, 178, 198
Milton, John, 192
Monge, Gaspard, 196
Montesquieu, Baron de, 190
Morvan, 172

Napoleon I, 12, 35, 151, 161, 191, 196, 199, 207
Napoleonic Empire, 76, 89
Neufchâtel, 188
Newton, Isaac, 140
Niebuhr, Barthold Georg, 121
Nîmes, 30
Normandy, 170-71
Notre Dame, 183, 204

Paine, Thomas, 191
Palissy, Bernard, 118
Papinianus, Aemilius, 190
Passy, Hippolyte, 36
Perdiguier, Agricol, 52
Picardy, 172
Pitt, William (the Younger), 50
Place de la Concorde, 204

Plato, 159, 180
Poinsot, Paul, 122, 160
Poitou, 29
Poland, 20, 182
Polytechnic School, 196
Poncy, Charles, 60
Poret, Henri, 17
Portsmouth, 172
Préault, Antoine, 122
Proudhon, Pierre Joseph, 87
Puy, 30

Quinet, Edgar, 3, 198

Racine, Jean, 60
Ramayana, 131-32
Raphael, 146
Reign of Terror, 86, 195-96, 198
Rembrandt van Rijn, 146
Renaissance, 95, 128
Restoration, 35, 62, 83, 89
Richard III, 192
Richelieu, Cardinal, 28
Robespierre, Maximilien, 195, 198
Robin Hood, 192
Roman Empire, 96, 126, 132, 165
Romantics, 9
Rome, 185, 190, 193, 200, 207
Rousseau, Jean Jacques, 17, 19, 190
Rubens, Peter Paul, 146
Russia, 20, 77

Sacrifice, 4, 10, 162, 176, 209
Saint Bonaventura, 128
Saint-Hilaire, Geoffroy, 140, 196
Saint Ignatius of Loyola, xx
Saint John's Day, 203-4
Saint-Just, Louis de, 198
Saint Louis, 190-91
Saint-Pierre, Abbé de, 27
Saint Teresa of Avila, xx
Saint Thomas, 128

Sand, George, 7, 60
Schelling, Friedrich von, 179
Scotland, 106, 178
Sfondrati, Niccolò (Gregory XIV), 128
Shakespeare, William, 192
Sibyl, 135
Siegfried, 192
Socialists, xxvi
Sophocles, 17, 180
Sue, Eugène, 7
Sutherland, Duchess of, 26
Switzerland, 87, 188

Theocritus, 17
Thierry, Augustin, 19
Titian, 146
Tuileries, 183, 204

Upper Rhine, 26

Vatard (usurer), 12
Vico, Giovanni, xv, xviii, 121
Villemain, Abel, 17
Villermé, Louis, 51-52
Virgil, 16, 59-60, 132, 135, 138, 160
Volney, Constantin de, 197
Voltaire, 190

Wales, 178
Weavers, 46-47, 173
Wolf, Friedrich, 121
Women, 5, 49-50, 56-57, 73, 76, 114, 165-67

Young, Arthur, 27